The Hundred Years War

Each volume in this series is designed to make available to students important new work on key historical problems and periods that they encounter in their courses. Every volume is devoted to a central topic or theme, and the most important aspects of this are dealt with by specially commissioned essays from specialists in the period. The editorial Introduction reviews the problem or period as a whole, and each essay provides a balanced assessment of the particular aspect, pointing out the areas of development and controversy and indicating where conclusions can be drawn or where further work is necessary. An annotated bibliography serves as an up-to-date guide to further reading.

PROBLEMS IN FOCUS SERIES

Britain after the Glorious Revolution 1689–1714
edited by Geoffrey Holmes

Britain Pre-eminent: Studies of British world influence in the nineteenth century
edited by C. J. Bartlett

Popular Movements c. 1830–50   edited by J. T. Ward

The Republic and the Civil War in Spain
edited by Raymond Carr

Financing Development in Latin America
edited by Keith Griffin

The Hundred Years War   edited by Kenneth Fowler

FORTHCOMING TITLES:

Conservative Leadership 1830–1940
edited by Donald Southgate

Aspects of Victorian Liberalism   edited by Leyland Lyons

The Interregnum: The quest for settlement 1646–1660
edited by Gerald Aylmer

Urban Studies   edited by A. M. Everitt

Industrial Revolutions   edited by R. M. Hartwell

Sweden's Age of Greatness 1632–1718
edited by Michael Roberts

The Reign of James VI and I   edited by A. G. R. Smith

The Origins of the Civil War   edited by Conrad Russell

The Hundred Years War

EDITED BY
KENNETH FOWLER

Macmillan
St Martin's Press

First published 1971 by
THE MACMILLAN PRESS LTD
London and Basingstoke
Associated companies in New York Toronto
Dublin Melbourne Johannesburg and Madras

Library of Congress catalog card no. 71–156288

SBN 333 10011 5 (hard cover)

Printed in Great Britain by
RICHARD CLAY (THE CHAUCER PRESS) LTD
Bungay, Suffolk

Contents

Preface

ANY collection of essays on a theme as wide as 'The Hundred Years War' is bound to be selective, and there are some obvious omissions from this volume. Separate attention could well have been given to numerous important problems which are only dealt with summarily in the following pages; equally, a more chronological and 'regional' approach might have been adopted, dealing with the main phases of the war: in Scotland, the Low Countries, Brittany, Gascony, the Iberian Peninsula, Normandy, and so on. However, for a volume of this kind, a topical approach seemed more appropriate, dealing with those aspects of the war which are currently interesting historians or which have hitherto been neglected. Some attempt has been made to review the subject as a whole in the Introduction, and the first two essays provide a chronological framework to those which follow. All quotations from contemporary sources and from foreign languages have been translated into English, although the originals of many of them appear in the notes to the essays concerned. All books cited in the volume were published in London, unless stated otherwise.

The editor would like to thank the contributors for their co-operation in the preparation of the book, which made his task a relatively light and enjoyable one; to his wife thanks are due for the translation of the sixth essay in the collection.

K. F.

Edinburgh
July 1970

List of Abbreviations

Arch. comm.	Archives communales, France
Arch. dép.	Archives départementales, France
Arch. nat.	Archives nationales, Paris
BEC	*Bibliothèque de l'École des Chartes*
Bibl. nat.	Bibliothèque nationale, Paris
BIHR	*Bulletin of the Institute of Historical Research*
BM	British Museum
CCR	*Calendar of Close Rolls*
CPR	*Calendar of Patent Rolls*
DNB	*Dictionary of National Biography*
EcHR	*Economic History Review*
EETS	Early English Texts Society
EHR	*English Historical Review*
Foedera	*Foedera, Conventiones, Litterae, etc., or Rymer's Foedera*, original edition, 20 vols, 1704–35; Record Commission edition, ed. A. Clarke, J. Bayley, F. Holbrooke and J. W. Clarke, 4 vols in 7 parts, 1816–69
PPC	*Proceedings and Ordinances of the Privy Council of England*, ed. N. H. Nicolas, 7 vols, Record Commission, 1834–7
PRO	Public Record Office, London
Rot. Parl.	*Rotuli Parliamentorum ut et Petitiones et Placita in Parliamento, 1278–1503*, 6 vols, 1783; index, 1832
TRHS	*Transactions of the Royal Historical Society*

Introduction:
War and Change in Late
Medieval France and England

KENNETH FOWLER

I

THE title of this book, though now familiar to students of history, calls
for some explanation. The expression 'The Hundred Years War'
appears to have been first coined in France at the beginning of the
nineteenth century, and from the time of the Franco-Prussian War it
gained widespread currency on either side of the Channel.[1] Some historians have found the idea misleading, either because they see the
Anglo-French hostilities between 1337 and 1453 (the traditional limits
of the war) as no more than the continuation of a much larger conflict
which had its roots in the Norman conquest of England and the
Angevin inheritance of Aquitaine, and which continued beyond 1453;
or, alternatively, because they regard the wars begun by Edward III in
the fourteenth century and by Henry V in the fifteenth century as two
distinct episodes. But while the concept does not lack critics, it is not
simply the invention of historians, seeking a convenient periodisation
of the past. Contemporaries who themselves witnessed the hostilities
were aware that they formed part of a long and distinctive struggle, a
struggle which, at least to some, appeared to have begun in 1337, to
have continued into the fifteenth century, and to owe its duration to the
claim of English kings to the throne of France.[2]

While it seems now to be generally agreed that the origins of the war,
which form the subject of a subsequent essay,[3] are to be sought in the
earlier history of the English and French monarchies, the war aims of
the protagonists are still open to discussion.[4] In this connection, one
significant difference between the period extending from 1337 to 1492
and the years which preceded and succeeded these two terminal dates
should perhaps be noted at the outset: that, except for nine years of
incompletely ratified peace between 1360 and 1369, it was a period
which saw a continuous state of war or truce between England and

France.[5] It is therefore logical to speak of one war, rather than of a series of wars, for, unlike preceding or succeeding conflicts between the two countries, which though frequent were relatively short in duration and were always concluded by a peace treaty, the hostilities begun in 1337 were not terminated by a formal peace until the conclusion of the treaty of Étaples on 3 November 1492.

However, it would be pedantic in the extreme to extend the traditional limits of the Hundred Years War by a further thirty-nine years, and there is much to be said for sticking to the generally accepted terminal dates. For although no peace treaty followed the French conquest of Aquitaine in 1453, although English armies intervened in France in 1474, 1488 and 1492, although Calais continued to be held by the English Crown until 1558 and kings of England did not abandon the title of 'King of France' until the treaty of Amiens in 1802, nevertheless, as things turned out, the fall of Bordeaux to the French in 1453 marked an important turning-point. Between that date and 1477 the real threat to the French monarchy did not come from England, which was in the throes of civil war, but from Burgundy, and none of the subsequent English incursions into France proved militarily significant. Moreover, between 1475 and 1492 English kings, while they did not renounce their claim to either the French throne or to the old English territories in France, came to accept their 'adversary of France' as the effective ruler of the French kingdom and, from the time of Richard III, even accorded him the title 'King of France' in their correspondence with him.

II

Much recent work has both deepened and broadened the traditional concept. Historians have long been urging that war cannot be studied as a closed reality, that it must be linked with all man's activities, and that military history must overflow into other fields of study. As Professor Piero Pieri observed in a paper delivered to the École des Hautes Études in 1962:

> Any history neatly divided into chapters, successively devoted to political events, to agriculture, to industrial progress, to commerce, even to military history, is no longer acceptable today. It is rather the interconnection between these phenomena which permit one to grasp in depth and elucidate the powerful process of history. This having been said (and it is a statement of the obvious), I think that it is never

possible to consider war on its own, as an activity closed in on itself, but on the contrary one must, in order to study it, link it up with other human activities. Briefly, it has to be placed in context among the entire mass of actions and chain reactions. Everything is involved: politics, economy, society, evolution of civilisation, technical progress, and so on. . . . To be of any validity military history has to overflow into other spheres of history.[6]

It is in this spirit that historians have been tackling many of the problems connected with the Hundred Years War. Not only has the Anglo-French conflict been given its larger European canvas, but our understanding of it has been deepened through its treatment in the wider context of economic and social history. We now know a good deal more than we used to about the military and diplomatic entanglements in the Iberian Peninsula, about the military and naval organisation of the period, and about the motives and the obligations of the men who served in the war. Attention has also been given to the financing of the war, to its impact on the economy, and to the contemporary Law of Arms, which sought to regulate the behaviour of soldiers in public and private warfare and within the general framework of which the war was fought. These and other inquiries have aroused considerable interest in the civilian population, both as participants in and victims of the war, and have thrown new light on the political and social developments of the period. In this essay, an attempt will be made to tie together some of these different strands: first, to examine some of the main issues in the Anglo-French hostilities of the fourteenth and fifteenth centuries; second, to consider some of the ways in which the war modified the economic, social and political institutions of the two countries, and, third, to briefly examine the attitudes and reactions of contemporaries to the convulsions and changes that the war brought about.

III

The Issues at Stake
The issues in the Anglo-French dispute were, of course, multiple and changing, but they may be broadly classified as political, economic and strategic. To begin with, the political issues: During the course of the second half of the thirteenth century a cross-Channel feudal empire was breaking up under the stresses arising from the attempts of the Capetian kings to centralise their political authority at a time when similar

developments in England were having the effect of transferring the continental dominions from the king's personal and private sphere of interest and subordinating them to English political institutions as the property of the Crown. While Edward I sought to govern Gascony from Westminster and to hear the petitions of her subjects in the English Parliament, Philip the Fair was intent on making the duchy part of metropolitan France. Further sources of conflict were added to those created by these tensions with the conclusion of a Franco-Scottish alliance in 1295 (which was renewed at Corbeil in 1326), the extinction of the Capetian line in 1328, and the subsequent claim of the kings of England to the throne of France arising, first, from Edward III's close relationship to the last Capetian king and, second, after 1420, through the treaty of Troyes and Henry V's marriage to Charles VI's daughter, Catherine. Thus a war which arose out of a feudal issue developed into something more than a feudal dispute and could not be concluded through the incompatability of the claims of either side. Various schemes for a compromise solution were put forward, but always came to grief owing to the inability of the French to surrender their sovereignty over territories in France and the refusal of the English to give up their dynastic pretensions in return for anything less than lands in full sovereignty. The different nuances of these political issues are brought out in the next two essays.[7]

The economic and strategic issues have been less well covered, but were none the less important. The former were largely concerned with three staple medieval commodities: wine, wool and salt. At the outset of the war, the economic importance of the king of England's French possessions lay in the customs on wine levied in Bordeaux which, before the war began, equalled and in some years – 1307–8 for instance – surpassed the ordinary revenues of the English Crown. The conditions for raising the money were ideal and smuggling could easily be checked, since the wine ships had to pass up the Gironde estuary from Bordeaux, where the cargoes were collected, taxed and shipped. No less important, the entire revenues derived from the wine trade, like those secured from the wool trade with Flanders, were sufficiently large and regular to secure credit advances from Italian bankers.[8] Moreover, the wine trade was not simply a one-way trade, it was a reciprocal one; during the fourteenth century the Bordelais gave up trying to meet its need for wheat locally and came to rely on England for supplies of grain, salted fish, wool and, later, cloth.

The strategic issues were multiple and, as one would expect over such a long period of political and technological change, they were not constant. They were in part a consequence of the economic ones. It was essential to keep the wool supply open to Flanders and to prevent the Flemish ports from falling into enemy hands, either by securing the neutrality of or an alliance with the count or the communities of Flanders.[9] To keep the wine trade open with Gascony, the salt trade with the Bay of Bourgneuf in the marches of Brittany and Poitou and, as the fourteenth century wore on, to secure alternative supplies of salt and maintain the increasing if diversified trade with Portugal, the king of England relied upon the friendship or at least the neutrality of the duke of Brittany. For the sea route to the south was then necessarily a coastal one, involving piloting – for a payment – by the Breton authorities and stops off at the southern Breton ports.[10] So that, if in many ways the Gironde estuary was the Suez of the fourteenth century, the rocky coast of Finistère was the Gibraltar. Considerations such as these do much to account for Edward III's prohibition on the export of wool to Flanders in 1336, his blockade of the Flemish ports between 1336 and 1338, and his military intervention in the Low Countries in the latter year.[11] They also explain his intervention in Brittany and his occupation of the southern Breton ports between 1341 and 1362, the English control of Brest and most of Finistère from the latter date to 1397, of Castle Cornet and Mont Orgueil in the Channel Islands, of Cherbourg from 1378 to 1394 and Les Sables d'Olonne on the Vendée coast during the same period.[12] Moreover, they were at least one good reason for the English intervention in the Iberian Peninsula between 1367 and 1387, which as Professor Russell has fully demonstrated was intended to put an end to the Franco-Castilian (Trastamaran) alliance that threatened, first, English communications with Gascony and then, second, as the Castilian galleys secured bases in the Normandy ports in the 1370s, the security of England herself.[13] For more than a decade the English coast was subject to Franco-Castilian attacks, and the menace which they still constituted at the beginning of the fifteenth century is demonstrated by a chronicle of the deeds of the captain of a squadron of Castilian galleys, Don Pedro Niño, written by his standard-bearer, and by a projected Franco-Castilian intervention in Wales in 1404.[14] These raids do much to explain the importance to England of Cherbourg and Brest in the fourteenth century, and they were at least one good reason for Henry V's conquest of Normandy and his attempt to colonise Harfleur, Cherbourg and Caen on the Calais pattern. This question will be examined in a subsequent essay.[15]

The importance of the defence of England as a major issue in the war must not be overlooked.[16] It is too often assumed that Edward III was responsible for the outbreak of the war through his intervention in Scotland and the Low Countries in the 1330s. The fact that, from its inception, the war was fought in France and elsewhere on the Continent, rarely in England, has had a strange effect upon our historical perspective. But it has recently been convincingly demonstrated that Edward had real cause for alarm in 1335-6, that plans were then afoot for the disembarkation of French troops in Scotland and for the invasion of southern England.[17] In 1336 the long-prepared, supposed Crusading fleet, was moved from the Mediterranean to the Channel ports. Small wonder that Edward set up a kind of home guard – the *garde de la mer* – bought the alliance of the princes of the Low Countries at so high a price, made use of his control of the wool supply to Flanders to get in first and, luckily for England, smash the great French fleet assembled at Sluys before it was too late.[18]

The sophistication of military strategy during this period, and the elaborate and complex organisation that lay behind it are well illustrated by such fragments as remain of the minutes of the English Council,[19] and by the papers of the marshal of France, Mile de Noyers, at Dijon.[20] The latter include not only schedules of the number of troops needed to man the frontier garrisons in northern and southern France in 1339, with details of how they were to be financed and of the extent to which their numbers could be reduced in the event of the conclusion of a truce; they also include proposals from the then admiral of France, Nicolas Behuchet, for the assembly of a fleet of Genoese and Provençal galleys in the Seine estuary near Rouen, and for various means of destroying the English merchant fleet and of enforcing a naval blockade. These included suggestions for the destruction of the following shipping: all merchant vessels arriving to take on cargoes of salt in the Bay of Bourgneuf in July and August; the naval escort due to convoy the wine ships from Bordeaux in the autumn, after the *vendage*; an estimated 6000 small fishing-boats from England, Hainault and Flanders, said to be due to assemble off Great Yarmouth at the end of September; ships carrying cargoes of wool to be collected by Italian merchantmen in the Channel Islands. All of these schemes – extravagant as some of them may seem – were carefully costed, and estimates were made – however wild – of the probable loss that they would incur to the English Exchequer. There can be little doubt that they formed the preliminaries to the assembly of the invasion fleet at Sluys in the following

year, that they were to have been combined with a French intervention
in Scotland, and that they were part of an integrated strategy based on
Philip VI's *ordonnance* for the invasion and conquest of England, issued
on 23 March 1339, subsequently discovered by Edward III's troops
during the sack of Caen in 1346 – a marvellous boost to his war propaganda – and a copy of which may be seen today in the Archives nationales
in Paris.[21]

Between 1340 and 1369 the invasion threat was reduced, though never
entirely eliminated, by the naval victory at Sluys, the recovery of the
Channel Islands in 1345, the acquisition of Calais in 1347, which provided a bridgehead for subsequent English *chevauchées* into France, by
the establishment of English garrisons in Flanders, Brittany and
Normandy and, after 1360, by the peace of Brétigny.[22] But in the 1370s
the south coast of England again came under attack, in 1385–6 another
great French fleet was assembled at Sluys for the invasion of southern
England, and on this occasion the then admiral of France, Jean de
Vienne, actually led an expeditionary force to Scotland. Professor
Perroy long ago dismissed this armada as 'intended more to reopen
normal trading relations with Flanders', where a wool blockade was
again being enforced, 'than to lead to an actual conquest of England'.[23]
A very different picture emerges from the accounts of the two treasurers-
of-wars responsible for financing the expedition. They tell the story of
the immense preparation and organisation that went into the assembly
of an expeditionary force of at least 50,000–60,000 men – as large, if not
larger, than the Crécy and Agincourt armies – even though two-thirds
of them were non-combatants.[24] Too many men, maintained for too
long a period of time and at too great expense, it would seem, to end a
mere wool blockade.

But where is all of this in the chronicles? Where indeed. We must not
be blinded to the political, economic and strategic considerations of the
war by the *Chronicles* of Jean Froissart and his chivalrous contemporaries and successors, still less by the limited horizons of their cloistered
colleagues. Nor should we forget that the audience for whom Froissart
and his fellows were writing wanted the harsh realities and the bloodier
side of the events they had lived through dressed up in tales of romance
and of noble deeds of arms. Froissart mirrored the ideals of his age, the
deeds of valour and of heroism that the chivalrous class aspired to, the
way men liked to think of themselves and of the part which they had
played in affairs, rather more than what was at stake, with which he was
not particularly concerned.[25] Thus pride of place in his account of the

naval battle off Winchelsea in 1350 is given to King Edward, standing in the prow of his ship, *La Salle du Roi*, 'wearing a black velvet jerkin and a black beaverskin cap which greatly suited him'. 'On that day', Froissart continues, 'I was told by some who were with him, he was in a gayer mood than he had ever been seen before. He told his minstrels to strike up a dance tune which Sir John Chandos, who was there beside him, had recently brought back from Germany. And out of sheer high spirits he made Sir John sing with the minstrels, to his own vast amusement.'[20] A much nicer story for the old soldier to hear by his baronial fireside than that the Castilian fleet had molested English ships convoying wine from Gascony and had threatened communications with Bordeaux, which was why the battle was fought.[27]

It should now be clear that the Hundred Years War was not just fought for fun, for chivalrous young men to partake of noble deeds of arms, to gain fat ransoms or to get away from the boredom of it all at home. Certainly, many men went to France in the hope of finding all of these things; but others did not want to go, recruitment was often difficult and desertion not infrequent. There can no longer be any doubt about the profit motive and the social advancement that the war offered as an incentive to service in France; the extent to which Henry V's conquest of Normandy was spurred on by such considerations has recently been amply demonstrated.[28] If ransoms and booty were what most soldiers sought in the fourteenth century, an even wider prospect was opened to military men and non-combatants alike in the fifteenth: French lands, offices and titles. This was conquest and settlement with a vengeance. But it has too often been assumed that these were the only issues at stake, and that the self-interest of the ordinary soldier, and even of the aristocracy, dictated royal policy. We must be careful to distinguish between the motives of the men in the field and those of the men in Paris and in Westminster. For the latter, meeting in the royal councils where military and diplomatic policy were worked out, were more or less aware of the wider political, economic and strategic issues involved.[29] Governments did not fail to make peace because they did not want to. They repeatedly tried, but failed to find a way out; hence the long years of truce, truce that can only be described as an interval between major campaigns rather than as a cessation of hostilities.[30] Men hoped and expected to make a profit out of the war; it is another matter to conclude that that is why it was fought.[31]

IV

The Economic and Social Repercussions of the War

In any examination of the impact of the war on the economic and social institutions of England and France during the fourteenth and fifteenth centuries certain general considerations should be borne in mind. First, the duration of the war – that it lasted for more than a hundred years. Second, this was a period of 'crisis', of plague, famine and economic disequilibrium, throughout the greater part of Europe, so that it is extremely difficult to single out the effects of warfare in the general configuration of circumstances. Thus the Anglo-French dispute inflamed, aggravated and became inextricably interwoven with political and social conflicts which sprang from different sources of tension. Take, for instance, the decline in seigniorial incomes which appears everywhere to have forced the nobility to seek out royal appointments, to secure control of royal revenues and – at the lower level – to turn to warfare and brigandage.[32] This was a vicious circle in which the war and war taxation worsened the situation which had caused them. Over such a long period of time the nature of warfare was itself modified by political, economic, technological and other factors, just as the war wrought changes in all of these fields. The interaction worked in all directions.

The war affected the social institutions of England and France in three principal ways: through the redistribution of wealth, the devastation of the countryside and taxation.

(i) *The Redistribution of Wealth.* In a controversial but nevertheless influential work entitled *Military Organization and Society,*[33] Stanislav Andrzejewski developed a theory of the Military Participation Ratio, in which he argued that the greater participation of lower-status groups involved in any war effort, the stronger the levelling tendency. Andrzejewski was covering the whole range of human history. Does the evidence for the Hundred Years War bear his theory out?

There can be little doubt that the role of the contract armies and the English archers in the war, the employ of armourers, fletchers and other non-combatants in the whole business, the profit and loss and the redistribution of wealth, both individual and national, which the war entailed, to say nothing of the higher pay, the prospects of advancement and the new horizons which were opened up to many were bound to have their repercussions on the English domestic scene. But we need to know more, for instance, of the impact of the war and of war taxation

on the series of revolts that hit England, Flanders and southern France
in 1379–82 and of the frustrations and the aims that lay behind them.[34]
How many men were there like Robert Salle of Norfolk, in 1335 a
bondman of the village in that county whose name he bore, who got
himself recruited by the commissioners of array for service in Brittany
in the 1340s and did sufficiently well for himself in the army to be made
captain of the strategically vital fortress of Marck in the Pas-de-Calais
thirty years later, by which time he had been knighted?[35] By the time
he made his will in 1380 he had made a substantial fortune for himself,
mostly invested in land, and in the following year, as captain of Norwich,
he was brought from his horse and cut up, piece by piece, by peasants
who remembered his background but had not been so lucky. Let
Froissart tell his story:

> The captain of that town was a knight called Sir Robert Salle.
> He was not of gentle birth, but in appearance, reputation and fact
> he was a brave and experienced fighting man. King Edward had
> knighted him for his sterling worth and physically he was the best-
> built and strongest man in all England. Litster (who led the rebels
> outside Norwich) and his followers thought that they would take this
> knight with them and make him their commander, in order that they
> should become more feared and more popular. They sent a message
> asking him to come out and speak with them, or else they would
> storm the city and burn it. The knight considered that it would be
> better to comply than risk such a disaster, so he took his horse and
> rode alone out of the town to where they were waiting. They treated
> him with all respect and asked him to get off his horse to talk with
> them. He did so, which was an act of folly. As soon as he was on the
> ground, they surrounded him and began pleading with him frankly
> but gently: 'Robert, you are a knight and you have a great reputation
> round here as a brave and worthy man. Of course you are one, but we
> know very well that you are not a gentleman, but the son of a com-
> mon mason, of the same sort as us. Come with us and you shall be our
> master and we will make you so great a lord that the fourth part of
> England will be under your rule.'[36]

Here surely lies the crux of the matter. In a paper delivered to the
Royal Historical Society in 1957 the late K. B. McFarlane told the un-
forgettable story of 'The Investment of Sir John Fastolf's Profits of
War'.[37] The effect was electrifying, and many historians were persuaded

that every Englishman who went to war in France made a fortune for himself, and made the deduction that that was why he went, forgetting about those others, and they were by no means few, who spent sometimes agonising periods of their lives in French prisons, who had to sell up their estates in England to buy back their freedom, or who died in captivity through failure or inability to raise the sums in question. The higher they climbed up the military ladder, the greater the risk of loss as well as the chance of gain; for against the thirds of all the winnings of war that a captain was entitled to from his men must be set the increased price placed upon his person by his enemies. Significantly, it is Professor Postan who has reminded us of the need for a quantitative approach in his paper on 'The Costs of the Hundred Years' War'.[38] Were Knowles and Calveley in the fourteenth century, and Fastolf, Molyneux and Winter in the fifteenth among the few who hit the military jackpot and got out of the game before they risked the chance of losing their winnings? There is a strong possibility that they were – though many others clearly made more modest fortunes – and that it is the redistribution of wealth arising from profit *and loss* that is significant, especially in an England in which demographic, economic and legal changes were allowing manumitted peasants and lucky gents to accumulate leases and buy up property from those whose fortunes were declining.

The gain and loss to the country as a whole is a different matter, and Postan's argument that 'in real terms England's net balance of loss and gain in the Hundred Years War was bound to be in the red' is very persuasive; even in financial or bullionist terms he is surely right to conclude that disbursements of treasure were far in excess of receipts?[39] It is rather more difficult to dismiss 'the circular tour of wealth in wartime England' as 'at best a makeweight, not the mainspring of social change'. Surely that tour by which 'wealth wrung from the agricultural interest by war taxation was eventually brought back into the countryside by merchants, soldiers and officials investing in land' was the most fundamental factor of all, since the little that came back for the amount that was laid out was altering the social complex of late medieval England. As McFarlane put it, 'whatever did return, returned elsewhere from whence it came'. If the war was a makeweight, was it not the weight that tipped the scales?[40]

Without doubt, a similar process was at work in France, which had her profiteers as well as men who lost their fortunes during the course of the war – families like that of Perrote in Normandy who built up,

between 1380 and 1460, a considerable inheritance of landed property
at the expense of the victims of the hostilities, mostly from money made
in trade;[41] and more than one fourteenth-century critic of the social
scene in France waxed strong about the military and financial officers
who were making their pile from the war and the machinery of military
finance and taxation which it had brought into being.[42] Before turning
to them, let us look at the more general question which has interested
French historians, of what part the war played in the economic and social
difficulties of the period, for the obvious reason that it was largely
fought on their soil.

(ii) *The Devastation of the Countryside.* The first, and the most
obvious factor, is that the war was destructive of both lives and property;
this subject, and the plight of the non-combatant in the war, has
aroused considerable interest in recent years and will be examined in
depth in subsequent essays.[43] The great *chevauchées* of the fourteenth
century were designed to destroy the enemy's resources by devastating
the countryside, burning the defenceless villages, small townships and
the suburbs of walled towns. As the war proceeded, the static garrison
warfare hardened into fairly well-defined frontier zones – in Brittany in
the 1350s, Guyenne from the 1380s and Anjou and Maine from the
1420s – where the troops maintained themselves by levying protection
money from the countryside surrounding the fortresses which they
controlled.[44] For long periods central control was weak, sufficient
funds were not forthcoming to pay the troops, both English and French,
or else they were embezzled by the military and financial officers, and
the situation got out of hand. Economic hardship and private feuds
were added to and inflamed public quarrels, and the country fell prey
to *routiers,* brigands and free companies.

However, the impression of over-all disaster which the documentation conveys does need qualification. To begin with, some sources are,
to say the least, suspect. Too many historians, particularly in the last
century, have swallowed whole the sad tales of hardship to be found in
the literally thousands of royal letters of pardon and grants of exemption from taxation recorded in the French Chancery Registers – grants
which arose from the pleadings of petitioners in whose interest it was to
paint the gloomiest picture possible. And we must guard ourselves
against the invectives of fifteenth-century propagandists like Alain
Chartier and Juvenal des Ursins. Although the war was certainly a
killer, it killed much fewer than famine and plague. The armies of the
period were relatively small and the depredations of the soldiers were

less murderous than contagious disease. Moreover, the destruction was not spread equally throughout the land; it was limited in time as well as in place. The great campaigns were few in number, they affected limited and changing geographical areas, and they were interspersed by long periods of truce. Yet when all this has been said, the overwhelming impression remains – from reliable local records and the documentation of the truces – that within the areas directly affected by the war there was appalling misery, and that plague, famine and depopulation were often set in motion by it.[45]

Nor is this simply an impression. During recent years a considerable number of regional studies and monographs on individual estates have confirmed the close correlations between demographic swings and military campaigns.[46] Although the destruction of crops was transitory, rents fell; to replace livestock, buildings, farm equipment and other stock required capital resources which the victims, both lords and peasants, all too often did not possess.[47] In some areas the situation was aggravated by panic, army requisitioning, the stockpiling of wheat in anticipation of an emergency or by profiteers, and by frequent prohibitions on its export from one region to another.[48] Since many places depended upon a distant source of supply, this often had dire effects; thus, for instance, the granaries of Le Puy were sometimes full while people in Languedoc were starving, and interference with the convoys of wheat shipped from England led to famine in Gascony. In areas where military activity was at its greatest, the burden of local taxation to meet the requirements of defence was added to the growing demands of royal taxation to put armies into the field. The most notable consequence in the affected regions can be summed up in one word – emigration; emigration to the security of walled towns, to neighbouring and even to distant provinces.

These movements of population are becoming increasingly easy to document, though they remain difficult to quantify. For the fourteenth century they have been traced in the names of families, streets and suburbs of towns. In Velay, people moved across the river Loire, from west to east.[49] Bordeaux took in immigrants from both Languedoc and Languedoïl, above all from Poitou, Saintonge, Limousin, Périgord and Quercy.[50] In Toulouse they came from towns and villages on the frontiers of Guyenne and Languedoc, and there are other more or less well-documented examples.[51] However, the documentation for the fifteenth century is much fuller. In a pioneer, if intensely patriotic work, Léon Puiseux long ago demonstrated, from the evidence of safe-con-

ducts enrolled on the Norman Rolls, the extent of emigration from
Normandy during the English occupation of that province.[52] So alarmed
were the English authorities that they attempted to restrict, then to
prevent the emigrants from leaving, and finally to entice them to return
– as had the negotiators of the truces in Guyenne in the 1380s, by remis-
sions of rent and tax concessions.[53] Some of the refugees moved as far
afield as Flanders and the Île-de-France, but most of them made for
neutral Brittany; a large number settled in Rennes, where they have
been traced in letters of naturalisation issued by the duke.[54] On the
opposite side of the kingdom, in southern Champagne, the same process
was at work. In his well-documented study of that region, M. Fossier
has noted that the movement was from west to east, that it reached its
peak during the military activity of 1410–30 and 1445–50, that most
people fled to Burgundy, and that when Philip the Good's lands were
brought into the theatre of military operations by the *Écorcheurs* the
emigration shifted to Lorraine.[55]

As yet, the total effects of these movements of population are by no
means clear, though some of their immediate consequences are obvious.
For the provinces deserted they meant a further reduction in the labour
force, and hence of seigniorial and royal revenues, thus aggravating still
further the economic recession of these regions. The emigrants from
Normandy and Champagne were mostly peasants, and Fossier has
observed that they were from the most active age group (between
twenty and thirty), thus leaving old people behind and preventing
population recovery by depriving the region of its next generation.[56] To
the countries of adoption the opposite of all these things was the case,
and immigration could contribute towards their relative prosperity.
Writing of the year 1465, Philippe de Commynes comments in his
Mémoires that the subjects of Philip the Good were rich 'because of the
long years of peace which they had enjoyed', and because the duke
'imposed few *tailles* upon his subjects'.[57] Neutral Brittany also prospered – Rennes, for instance, from the cloth industry which the immigrants set up there,[58] and other towns must have benefited from
immigration and prospered, if only relatively and for limited periods.

To conclude. The war was resulting in some major shifts in population in fourteenth- and fifteenth-century France, and was accelerating
the movement from the country to the towns. Is it going too far to detect
a possible breakdown in provincial prejudices and loyalties from these
trends, and with it the emergence of a greater sense of national identity?
We shall be returning to this question later.[59]

V

The Political Repercussions of the War

The war inevitably challenged the participants' political as well as their social institutions. Nowhere was this more evident than in late medieval France, a kingdom which had reached the height of prosperity, political harmony and international prestige in the mid thirteenth century, under St Louis. In subsequent generations men were to look back, like Thomas Basin in the later fifteenth century, and see it as her golden age. Even Edward III, in much of his propaganda put out for consumption in the French provinces, promised to put the clock back 'and to re-establish the good laws and customs that were in force in the time of his progenitor St Louis'; and to some extent, like Bedford after him, he endeavoured to give his propaganda concrete form.[60]

The political structure of mid-thirteenth-century France was the product of historical circumstance, a feudal kingdom in which the interests of king and aristocracy were for the most part in equilibrium. It was in many ways a federation of duchies and counties in which 'federal' (i.e. royal) and 'state' (i.e. ducal or comital) spheres of influence were more or less in balance, if nowhere clearly defined.[61] Even among the lesser nobility seigniorial rights and jurisdiction on the one hand were not, on the whole, in conflict with royal and princely interests on the other. But already before the end of the thirteenth century the balance was breaking up. The practical implications of new notions of sovereignty, entailing as they did the development of the appelate jurisdiction of the Parlement of Paris and the extension to the entire kingdom of royal legislation, including rights to extraordinary taxation, were leading to conflict, not only with the king of England in his capacity as duke of Aquitaine, but also with other French peers who felt their interests threatened.[62] The conflict with England under Edward I, the provincial revolts of the second decade of the fourteenth century, the disputed succession of the next and, finally, the beginning of the Hundred Years War in 1337, held up the development of French government and society along lines which would have reinforced royal rights. The crunch came with the English invasions of the forties and fifties of the fourteenth century, for France then lacked a sense of 'nationhood' and a 'national' system of defence. Her still virtually independent dukes and counts were at loggerheads with the Valois dynasty; some of them shared Edward III's grievances and others swallowed whole his propaganda. The years which followed the defeat of John II's army at Poitiers in 1356 were years of unparalleled crisis in medieval France: the years of the Parisian Revolution, the Jacquerie, the formation of the free companies, the threat from England and from Charles of Navarre, in short, the complete breakdown of central authority.

How were the men responsible for the destiny of France to see their way out? From as early as 1351 attempts had been made to create a royal army composed of coherent companies whose captains were to hold commissions from the Crown, and an hierarchy of military command – of constable, marshals, lieutenants and captains – had been created and defined which cut across feudal and provincial loyalties.[63] The years between 1356 and 1369 saw an inevitable reorganisation in all of those spheres in which the old governmental and social structures had failed; for these were the years which saw a major extension of extraordinary taxation, of direct taxes (the *taille*) and indirect taxes (*aides*, *gabelle*, customs), of which the first were assessed by new officials, the *élus*, in new and ever-increasing financial districts, the *élections*, or else they were voted in or imposed upon the provinces which still had Estates for the delegates to divide and raise the sums as they saw fit.[64] It was a period which saw the recruitment of the first standing field army, a body of 6000 (in reality more around 3000) professional soldiers financed by the *élus*, in permanent being, and holding their commissions from the Crown.[65] But there was much else besides: the impress of royal rights into the confines of privilege and immunity, the conversion into royal *establissemens* – the nationalisation if you will – of strategically important seigniorial castles which lay outside the *apanages* and great fiefs, and the systematic destruction of others which could not be defended or were not worth the effort.[66]

These changes, and many more besides, reached their apogee during the reign of Charles V (1364–80). It was a period in which, with hindsight, we can say the 'absolute monarchy' was not born, but was first established. It was a period when a wise king, surrounded by able councillors, recognised – often reluctantly – the need for change. More like Edward IV in fifteenth-century England than like his grandson, Charles VII, he sought sound and impartial service from wherever he could get it, not to the exclusion of the aristocracy (as witness the service which he secured from his brothers, especially Louis I of Anjou), but bringing in new men from the lesser nobility or wherever else he found them: councillors like the clerk Raoul de Presles, the knight-administrator Philippe de Mézières, the chancellors Jean and Guillaume de

Dormans, the *prévôt* of Paris Hugues Aubriot, and Bureau de la Rivière. Moreover, these were the years which saw military and naval command placed in capable, if relatively speaking humble hands, not only of Bertrand du Guesclin as constable (1370–80), Arnoul d'Audrehem (1351–68), the elder Boucicaut (1356–68) and Moutain de Blainville (1368–91) as marshals, and Jean de Vienne as admiral (1373–96), but also among the lieutenants and captains-general of the reign.[67]

The tragedy for France was that Charles V died young, and that the changes which had been brought about had been made too quickly – certainly they were too much to have accomplished in twenty years. During the reign of his son, public morality rapidly declined, and with the dissipation of central authority the dangers inherent in French government and society were revealed. They were commented upon at length by that great French soldier, publicist and statesman, Philippe de Mézières (1327–1405), in his *Songe du Vieil Pelerin*, which was written for the instruction of Charles VI and completed in 1389.

Although bitterly aware of the sufferings of the French people from the devastation of war, Mézières was nevertheless much more critical of the machinery of arbitrary taxation that he had seen grow up within his own lifetime, and of the abuses of the rapidly expanding bureaucracy of military and civil officials which the war and war taxation had brought in their train.

> The ancient way of government of this kingdom has [he writes] been badly interrupted and neglected. You can see the effects of this. Because of the taxes and the widespread devastation resulting from feeble defence, your people begin to complain and to say that they have been more harassed than free men should be. From such oppression are born treason and rebellion. Your royal councillors and great officers, on the other hand, complain that your subjects are not fulfilling their obligations. Thus there is no longer union between yourself and your people and this, in turn, has helped towards defeat in war.[68]

The taxes, he says – and it was almost a century before Bishop Thomas Basin wrote on that subject (*c*. 1475) – had 'brought a free people to slavery'; they were dissipated through royal gifts and embezzlement by royal officers, 'and their yield has been in part lost through the poverty of your subjects who have been forced to abandon their country'. There was no end to the evils they engendered. The army leaders returned false musters, they 'lived extravagantly on funds which should have been spent on the war', they bought up land and 'spend two or three months in Paris or on their estates, looking after their private interests. . . . They give food to the well-fed and drink to the drunken, while fighting men go hungry.' Nor were the military men alone to blame; he severely castigates the finance officers for corruption and, on more than one occasion, returns to the people who 'without number are leaving their homes to avoid the harshness of the tax collectors'.

There are many contradictions in Mézières's reactions. While he approved of a professional standing army and was aware of the need for permanent garrisons in the frontier districts – even during times of truce – he at the same time advocated the abolition of the machinery of extraordinary taxation which had largely been brought into being to support them. But it is impossible to do justice to his observations in the context of this essay. Mézières was examining France's new body politic while it was still in embryo, and what he found profoundly disturbed him. There are few other works which penetrate so deeply into her historic dilemma.

The backlash came during Charles VI's minority and madness; for it was then that the great feudatories were quick to seize their opportunities to exploit to their own advantage the monster that had been born. The irony of Charles VII's achievement was that, in almost every sphere of governmental reform (finance, the army) he was merely picking up where Charles V had left off, or else elaborating his grandfather's work and ideas. In some senses Edward IV and Richard II provide a parallel in England, although in their case historians are apt to praise Edward for achieving what they condemn Richard for trying to accomplish.

However, the position in England was very different from that in France. For, apart from the burning of her southern ports and endemic warfare on the frontier with Scotland – albeit important – she did not, as things turned out, see the enemy permanently established on her soil. Her political and social institutions were challenged in quite a different way by the overwhelming demands for war finance and the debates over war policy which those demands entailed. Here lies the essential clue to the growing powers of Parliament, and particularly of the Commons, in the fourteenth century. The need for money created by war and diplomacy, the need, quite often, to get it quickly, and the concessions which that entailed; all these, and the debates over them, helped to create a form of government which, in the fifteenth century, both Sir John Fortescue and Philippe de Commynes were able to recognise as essentially different from that of France, although both of these writers looked to the past and their views were somewhat dated.[69] What is important about the knights and burgesses of fourteenth- and early fifteenth-century England assembled in the Painted Chamber or the Chapter House at Westminster is not the powers they gained – though they, however transient, are not to be scoffed at – but the pretensions which they voiced and the notions of political authority implicit in them. On either side of the Channel political theorists as well as propagandists had come to recognise that the manner in which decisions were made and implemented in the two countries was essentially different.

It was not until the late 1430s that English political institutions were severely challenged; for unlike France, where Charles VII's military and financial reforms were to make themselves felt in the 1440s, her governmental machinery was then quite out of date. Lacking an adequate system of credit and taxation, the parliamentary hand that had fed her in the years of victory was an encumbrance and all too often unyielding. The armies that had brought victory in the past had done so in part because, unlike those of France, they had not been over-professionalised. For all the opportunities the contract armies had given to humble men, as will be seen in a subsequent essay the high command of the army had rested with the aristocracy, and while the system of recruitment was relatively new, it operated in the same social milieu.[70] The English forces in France, though financed by the Crown, drew heavily upon the loyalty and the resources of the nobility. The commissioners of array who recruited the forces were often the leading retainers of the contracting captains, engaging men who held land from these military leaders or had a long tradition of service with their families, and the paymasters of the troops were as often as not drawn from the treasurers and wardrobers of the noble household staffs in England. It was very different from the royal officials at work in France: the *baillis* and *sénéchaux* who recruited the French forces, or the treasurers-of-wars and their clerks, responsible ultimately to the Chambre des Comptes in Paris, who paid them; and the extensive powers of the constable and marshals of France and their deputies had no parallels in England.[71] The English successes under Edward III, Henry V and the duke of Bedford owed much to long periods of harmony and common purpose among the English aristocracy, just as the failures under Richard II and Henry VI arose in large part from rivalry and discord between them. The standing field armies of Charles V and Charles VII were in some senses an insurance against that risk. England had neither needed, wanted nor could afford them, and it is a commonplace that Edward IV's great lesson from his bankrupted predecessor was to be paid to keep out of France, a lesson which was not lost on Henry VII.

VI

The Emotional and Psychological Repercussions of the War: The Attitudes and Reactions of Contemporaries

What impact did the war have on the civilian population of France and England? How did Frenchmen react to the depredations of the enemy, to murder, rapine, burning, looting and other horrors and suffering which they witnessed? What impressions did an English soldier bring back from France, of victory, boredom, suffering or defeat? How did the English at home react to the news of all of these things, and what impact did the invasion scares of the 1330s, 1370s and 1380s have upon her government and populace? The collective psychology of any period and the subtle shifts and changes in it all too often elude us, and doubtless they require deeper and more sophisticated treatment than that which they have up till now received.

Very little seems to stir in the chivalrous literature of the times, like the *Chronicles* of Jean Froissart and Enguerrand de Monstrelet, the Chandos Herald's *Life of the Black Prince*, or the *Livre des faicts* of Marshal Boucicaut, with their sense of international knightly solidarity. These works, like those of Geoffrey Chaucer, were produced for the royal and princely courts, and they owed much to the *esprit de corps* of knightly society, which was brought together by tournaments, chivalric orders and devices, crusades to Prussia, as well as in court circles. In this sense the war may be said to have been producing a literature of its own, and Froissart was its greatest single product.[72] But at another level, and appealing to a different social milieu, we may discern the voice of protest, in chronicles and poems, treatises and sermons, government records and other works of literature. Some of these writings are expressive of growing national feeling, of xenophobia; others simply reflect the anguish of the times, and still others are works of social and moral criticism.[73] Some appealed to the emotions, others to the intellect, and some – but by no means all – were propaganda. A bellicose national consciousness is already evident in the songs of Lawrence Minot, which were composed between 1333 and 1352, and for a very different public than that for which the Chandos Herald was writing. His heroes are drawn from a different stratum of society: a Master Archer, John of Doncaster, and ship-master from Rye, John Baddyng. They combine extreme patriotism with a contempt for all foreigners. Across the Channel similar sentiments, directed at the English, are scattered throughout the 1500 or so poems of Eustache Deschamps (c. 1346–c. 1406), who was writing in the last decades of the century.[74] Over forty years ago Georges Ascoli demonstrated, from the French literature of the times, the unfortunate image of the English which was emerging in France during the course of the war, and more recently M. Bossuat and Dr Lewis, in examining some of the more subtle aspects of fifteenth-century war propaganda in both France and England, have shown how the confrontation of the two countries in what was becoming increasingly a 'national' war forced men to think in terms of 'French' or 'English'.[75]

Without doubt the emotional propagandists 'fanned the flames of patriotism and xenophobia' and harnessed them to their cause; but much other literature was a genuine and spontaneous reaction to the miseries of the times and came from those who suffered most: people like Jean de Venette, a man of peasant origins who saw the village whose name he bore, near Compiègne, burnt to the ground in 1359, and even of Eustache Deschamps, whose birthplace of Vertus-en-Champagne suffered a similar fate in 1380.[76] Even Alain and Jean Chartier, and Robert Blondel – who figured among the propagandists – were, it should be observed, refugees from Normandy.[77]

Such uprooting and other traumatic experiences led not only to hatred of the English, but also to social and moral protest. For Venette, as for the author of La Complainte sur la bataille de Poitiers, the nobility were not fulfilling their role as defenders of the realm: the chivalrous class ransomed one another, they did not suffer the horrors of war.[78] Honoré Bonet wrote:

'God well knows that the soldiers of today take from their prisoners great and excessive payments and ransoms without pity or mercy, and this especially from the poor labourers who cultivate lands and vineyards, and, under God, give sustenance to all by their toil. And my heart is full of grief to see and hear of the great martyrdom that they inflict without pity or mercy on the poor labourers and others, who are incapable of ill in word or thought; who toil for men of all estates; from whom Pope, kings, and all the lords in the world receive, under God, what they eat and drink and what they wear.'[79]

Not that the peasantry stood back idly. On more than one occasion they took the defence of their localities into their own hands, and they went further, not simply in the Jacquerie, of which Venette strongly disapproved, but also in massacring native as well as English troops, and even the knightly prisoners of French noblemen. The author of *La Complainte* thought that this was as it should be: prisoners should be killed, not ransomed, and one French chronicler of humble background, reflecting upon the killing of 'English' troops who surrendered the fortress of Le Homme in Normandy in 1366, commented that 'if the same had been done in the past the wars would not have endured as long as they have'.[80] As the war did drag on, seemingly interminably, during the next century even great captains like Sir John Fastolf and Jean du Bueil could advocate draconic measures to bring it to a conclusion.[81] A new *raison d'état* was making short shrift of the old chivalrous notions.

But pity, and human tenderness, could still cut across the growing national antagonism, and churchmen not only preached against the war and the manner in which it was being conducted; the Church took positive and practical steps to bring it to an end and to alleviate the suffering.[82] In one of his poems Jean Régnier has left a telling account of how he was moved by the sight of an unfortunate English prisoner who, surrounded by Frenchmen whose language he could not understand, called out, uncomprehended, in English, for help.[83] And a baffled English soldier had this to say about the plight of some of the refugees who, as Henry V's forces advanced through Normandy, fled to Rouen, only to find themselves expelled by the authorities and caught between the city walls and the English lines:

There one could see a piteous spectacle – one could see wandering here and there children of two or three years of age begging for bread, for their parents were dead. These wretched people had only the sodden soil under them, and they lay there crying for food – some starving to death, some unable to open their eyes and no longer breathing, others cowering on their knees as thin as twigs. A woman was there clutching her dead child to her breast to warm it, and a child was sucking the breast of its dead mother. There one could easily count ten or twelve dead to one alive, who had died so quietly without call or cry as though they had died in their sleep.

John Page wrote this story without fable or falsehood in rough and not in polished rhyme (because he had no time to do this). However, when this war is ended, and if he is alive and has the inclination, he will put this right. May He that died for us upon a tree bring His blessing to those who have heard this reading; for charity's sake let us say, 'Amen'.[84]

This is certainly not propaganda; it is the voice of pity and a commentary upon the tragedy of war as witnessed by an ordinary English soldier who, while he did not question the justice of Henry V's conquest of Normandy, had a distinct sympathy with its victims and found that his religiosity aroused within him serious moral scruples. Or are we to be so cynical as to suppose that, in the Middle Ages, men were so used to suffering that they did not have such sentiments, and that all the teachings of the Church, the sermons and the devotional literature of an an intensely religious age, had not left their mark? Those enjoying lands, offices and pensions down on the Normandy frontier doubtless could contain their twinges; but for many soldiers like Page, who saw only hardship and suffering and failed to make a profit, the war must often have seemed pointless.

During the Hundred Years War, as at other times, all men did not think or feel alike about the events they lived through, nor were they moved by the same motives and ambitions. Later medieval France and England had their Rupert Brookes as well as their Wilfred Owens, and the sentiments of the Bascot de Mauléon, as recorded by Froissart, are echoed in Yeats's 'Irish Airman'.[85] Nor were people obsessed by the war, as much of the foregoing might appear to suggest. For although it lasted for over a hundred years it was in no sense 'total' war, and even a casual reading of the Paston Letters would suggest that it was as remote from the consciousness of English shire society in the fifteenth century as the Napoleonic Wars and nineteenth-century India are in the novels of Jane Austen. The following essays have been written in the hope that they may illumine some of its manifold aspects.

NOTES TO INTRODUCTION

1. For a fuller discussion of the concept, see the Introductions to K. A. Fowler, *The Age of Plantagenet and Valois* (1967), and P. Contamine, *La guerre de Cent ans* (Paris, 1968).

2. Ibid.

3. See pp. 28–50 below, 'The Origins of the War'.

4. See pp. 51–74 below, 'The War Aims of the Protagonists and the Negotiations for Peace'.

5. See pp. 184–215 below, 'Truces'.

6. P. Pieri, 'Sur les dimensions de l'Histoire militaire', *Annales*, xviii (1963), 625.

7. The remainder of this essay represents, not a mature statement of conclusions, but an airing of ideas, substantially as they were presented at the Anglo-American Conference of Historians in London on 11 July 1969.

8. For a convenient discussion of the importance of the wine trade, see 'Bordeaux sous les rois d'Angleterre', ed. Y. Renouard in *Histoire de Bordeaux*, ed. C. Higounet, (Bordeaux, 1965), iii, 53–68, 233–66; G. P. Cuttino, 'Historical Revision: The Causes of the Hundred Years War', *Speculum*, xxxi (1956), 468–9, and *Le Livre d'Agenais* (1956), pp. xiii–xiv. For the loans secured by Edward II on the revenues of Aquitaine, see T. F. Tout, *The Place of Edward II in English History* (Manchester, 1914), pp. 216–21.

9. See K. A. Fowler, *The King's Lieutenant: Henry of Grosmont, First Duke of Lancaster* (1969), pp. 16, 34, 75–83, 93, 95–102.

10. Ibid., p. 16.

11. Ibid., p. 34.

12. For the occupation of these places, see K. A. Fowler, 'Les finances et la discipline dans les armées anglaises en France au XIVᵉ siècle', in *Actes du Colloque International de Cocherel, Les Cahiers Vernonnais*, iv (1964), 56–74.

13. P. E. Russell, *The English Intervention in Spain and Portugal in the time of Edward III and Richard II* (Oxford, 1955), pp. 5–6, 227–47.

14. Gutierre Díez de Games, *El Victorial; Crónica de Don Pero Niño*, ed. Juan de Mata Carriazo (*Colección de crónicas españolas*, i, Madrid, 1940). This has been translated into French as *Le Victorial; Chronique de Don Pedro Niño, Comte de Buelna*, by Le Comte Albert de Circourt et Le Comte de Puymaigre (Paris, 1867); an English translation of the relevant section is to be found in *The Unconquered Knight: A Chronicle of the Deeds of Don Pero Niño*, trans. J. Evans (1928). For the projected Franco-Castilian intervention in Wales, see Arch. nat., K 1482, fo. 22; published in L. Suarez Fernandez, *Navegación y comercio en el golfo de Vizcaya* (Madrid, 1959), pp. 164–5, Appendix xv.

15. See p. 112 below, and the same author's remarks in his article 'The Keeping of the Seas During the Hundred Years War: 1422–1440' *History*, xlix (1964), 284: '. . . control of Normandy gave the coastal shires of England almost thirty years of security . . . if the French Channel coast was held then the Channel itself became only the second line of defence. . . . Once the sea became the battle area again the southern shores of England were in danger.'

16. See pp. 76–8, 170–1 below.

17. J. Campbell, 'England, Scotland and the Hundred Years War in the Fourteenth Century', in *Europe in the Late Middle Ages*, ed. J. R. Hale, J. R. L. Highfield and B. Smalley (1965), pp. 188–91. See p. 96 below.

18. K. A. Fowler, *The Age of Plantagenet and Valois*, p. 55.

19. e.g. documents among the files of Chancery Miscellanea in the Public Record Office (C.47/2/26, 29, 31, 33, 48, etc.).

20. Arch. dép., Côte-d'Or, B 11715 and 11875; published by M. Jusselin, 'Comment la France se préparait à la guerre de Cent ans', *BEC* lxxiii (1912), 209–36, especially documents iv and vi–vii; cf. M. Jassemin, 'Les papiers de Mile de Noyers', *Bulletin philologique et historique du Comité des travaux historiques et scientifiques, année 1918* (Paris, 1920), pp. 192–7, document vii.

21. Arch. nat., J 210, no. 4; cf. Adae Murimuth, *Continuatio Chronicarum*, and Robertus de Avesbury, *De Gestis Mirabilibus Regis Edwardi Tertii*, ed. E. M. Thompson (Rolls Series, 1889), pp. 205–12, 257–63, 363–7.

22. See pp. 97–101 below.

23. E. Perroy, 'Franco–English Relations, 1350–1400', *History*, xxi (1936–7), 153.

24. L. Mirot, 'Une tentative d'invasion en Angleterre, 1385–6', *Revue des*

Études Historiques, lxxxi (1915), 249–87, 417–66; cf. P. Contamine, *Azincourt* (Paris, 1964), pp. 158–9.

25. See p. 122 below.

26. *Froissart: Chronicles*, ed. and trans. G. Brereton (Penguin Classics, 1968), p. 115.

27. Avesbury, op. cit., p. 412; *Chronicon Galfridi Le Baker de Swynebroke*, ed. E. M. Thompson (Oxford, 1889), p. 109; Fowler, *The King's Lieutenant*, pp. 86, 91–2; however, see pp. 100–1 below.

28. C. T. Allmand, 'The Lancastrian Land Settlement in Normandy, 1417–50', in *EcHR* 2nd ser., xxi (1968), 461–79.

29. See pp. 123–5 below.

30. See pp. 184–215 below, 'Truces'.

31. The remarks of Dr Allmand are apposite: '. . . to suggest Henry's probable motives for re-opening the war is one thing; to claim that these motives were necessarily shared by those accompanying him on his expeditions is quite another': C. T. Allmand, *Henry V* (Historical Association Pamphlet, General Series, no. 68, 1968), p. 17.

32. See pp. 149–52, 155–6 below.

33. S. Andrzejewski, *Military Organization and Society* (1st ed., 1954), pp. 33–8.

34. On the latter, see P. Wolff, 'Les luttes sociales dans les villes du Midi français, XIIIᵉ–XVᵉ siècles', *Annales*, ii (1947). The 1356–8 crisis in France is examined below, pp. 152–5.

35. He was given custody of Marck on 26 October 1373 (T. Carte, *Catalogue des rolles gascons, normans et françois* (2 vols, London and Paris, 1743, ii, 111), and again on 22 June 1377 (*Foedera*, iv, 2; the indenture of custody is PRO, E.101/68/7, no. 155; cf. *CPR 1377–1381*, p. 201). He appears as a bondman in Kirkhall Court Rolls for 1335, and his will, preserved in Norwich Consistory Court, was made at Oxnethe on 8 September 1380 and proved on 3 July 1381.

36. *Froissart: Chronicles*, pp. 222–3.

37. K. B. McFarlane, 'The Investment of Sir John Fastolf's Profits of War', *TRHS* 5th ser., vii (1957), 91–116.

38. M. M. Postan, 'The Costs of the Hundred Years' War', *Past and Present*, 27 (1964), 34–53.

39. The present writer's calculations of the direct cost to the Exchequer of financing military expeditions and maintaining garrisons and military installations in France, while they cannot be dealt with here, lead him strongly to doubt that the treasure coming back from ransoms, booty, offices and lands could in any way be equal (see, however, Fowler, 'Les finances . . .', loc. cit.); but, of course, whereas the former have left behind a reasonably full documentation, the latter are impossible to calculate. Professor Postan's tally of indemnities (*rachâts*) received for the evacuation of occupied castles and towns is rather more mystifying. How can it ever be completed? Only the cost to the Exchequer can.

40. The whole question is examined below, pp. 130–2, although no definitive conclusion can yet be drawn.

41. See, however, p. 151 below.

42. e.g. 'La complainte sur la bataille de Poitiers', ed. C. de Robillard de Beaurepaire in *BEC* xii (1851), 257 ff.; Philippe de Mézières, *Le Songe du Vieil Pelerin* (2 vols, Cambridge, 1969), i, 412–15, 422–3, 457–62, 520–4; cf. the many complaints against the finance officers in *Oeuvres Complètes de Eustache Deschamps*, ed. Le Marquis de Queux de Saint-Hilaire and Gaston Raynaud (11 vols, Société des anciens textes français, Paris, 1878–1903), x, 35, 59 and *passim*.

43. See pp. 163–83 below, 'The War and the Non-Combatant', and pp. 86–90.

44. K. A. Fowler, 'Les finances . . .', pp. 61–79; *The Age of Plantagenet and Valois*, pp. 165 ff. See pp. 204–9 below.

45. The reliability of the source material is examined below, pp. 173–4.

46. Notably R. Boutruche, *La crise d'une société; seigneurs et paysans du Bordelais pendant la guerre de Cent ans* (Paris, 1947); G. Fourquin, *Les campagnes de la région parisienne à la fin du moyen âge* (Paris, 1964); R. Fossier, 'Remarques sur les mouvements de population en Champagne méridionale au XVe siècle', *BEC* cxxii (1964), 177–215; cf. L. Genicot, 'Crisis: From the Middle Ages to Modern Times', in *The Cambridge Economic History of Europe*, i (2nd ed., Cambridge, 1966), ch. viii and bibliography, p. 843.

47. See pp. 149–51 below.

48. E.-R. Labande, 'L'administration du duc d'Anjou en Languedoc aux prises avec le problème du blé (1365–1380)', *Annales du Midi*, lxii (1950), 1–14; M.-J. Larenaudie, 'Les famines en Languedoc aux XIVe et XVe siècles', ibid., lxiv (1952), 27–39.

49. J. Monicat, *Les grandes compagnies en Velay, 1358–1392* (2nd ed., Paris, 1928), pp. 161 ff.

50. Boutruche, op. cit., pp. 188–90 and *passim* (cf. index, p. 585, 'immigration'); 'Bordeaux sous les rois d'Angleterre', cit. supra. pp. 433–4; C. Higounet, 'Mouvements de population dans le Midi de la France du XIe au XVe siècle', *Annales*, viii (1953), 20–4.

51. e.g. B. Guenée, *Tribunaux et gens de justice dans le bailliage de Senlis à la fin du moyen âge, vers 1380–vers 1550* (Paris, 1963), pp. 40 ff. and table 1.

52. L. Puiseux, *L'émigration normande et la colonisation anglaise en Normandie au XVe siècle* (Caen and Paris, 1866).

53. Fowler, 'Les finances . . .', p. 79; see p. 206 below.

54. Puiseux, op. cit., p. 39.

55. Fossier, op. cit., pp. 186–9.

56. Ibid., pp. 190–8.

57. Philippe de Commynes, *Mémoires*, ed. J. Calmette (3 vols, Les Classiques de l'histoire de France au moyen âge, Paris, 1924–5), i, 13.

58. Puiseux, op. cit., p. 39.

59. See pp. 20–1 below.

60. See J. Le Patourel, 'Edward III and the Kingdom of France', *History*, xliii (1958), 180 ff. Bedford's work is the subject of a number of articles by B. J. H. Rowe and R. A. Newhall in *EHR* xxxvi (1921), xlvi (1931), xlvii (1932), l (1935), and in *Essays Presented to H. E. Salter* (Oxford, 1934); cf. E. Carleton Williams, *My Lord of Bedford* (1963), ch. xi. A different view is to be found in R. Jouet, *La résistance à l'occupation anglaise en Basse-Normandie, 1418–1450* (Caen, 1969).

61. For a recent discussion of the relation between 'national' and 'provincial' loyalties and interests in medieval France, see B. Guenée, 'L'histoire de l'État à la fin du moyen âge vue par les historiens français depuis cent ans', *Revue historique*, ccxxxii (1964), 331–60; 'État et nation en France au moyen âge', ibid., ccxxxvii (1967), 17–30; 'Espace et État dans la France du bas moyen âge', *Annales*, xxiii (1968), 744–58; J. R. Strayer, 'Normandy and Languedoc', *Speculum*, xliv (1969), 1–12.

62. See pp. 32–5 below, and the same author's article on 'Edward III and the Kingdom of France', loc. cit.

63. For these changes, see Fowler, *The Age of Plantagenet and Valois*, ch. 3.

64. For a convenient discussion of these developments, see D. Hay, *Europe in the Fourteenth and Fifteenth Centuries* (1966), pp. 100–5. The crisis of 1356–8 and the origins of the *élus* are dealt with below, pp. 152–5.

65. Fowler, *The Age of Plantagenet and Valois*, pp. 134–7.

66. P. C. Timbal, *La guerre de Cent ans vue à travers les registres du parlement, 1337–1369* (Paris, 1961), ch. 3, especially pp. 144–9, 184–200; see Fowler, *The Age of Plantagenet and Valois*, p. 176.

67. Fowler, *The Age of Plantagenet and Valois*, pp. 126–30.

68. Philippe de Mézières, op. cit., ii, 76, 386–7, and i, 412–15, and ii, 65–8, 79–84, for what follows.

69. Sir John Fortescue, *The Governance of England*, ed C. Plummer (Oxford, 1885), cap. iv; Commynes, op. cit., ii, 8–9. See the observations of D. Hay, op. cit., pp. 83–5.

70. See pp. 78–80, 126–9 below.

71. K. A. Fowler, *The Age of Plantagenet and Valois*, ch. 3; *The King's Lieutenant*, pp. 183–6, 222.

72. Chivalric ideals and sentiments are discussed below, pp. 129–30.

73. See pp. 174–8 below.

74. *Oeuvres Complètes*, cit. supra.

75. G. Ascoli, *La Grande-Bretagne devant l'opinion française* (Paris, 1927), pp. 1–22; A. Bossuat, 'La littérature de propagande au XVᵉ siècle: le mémoire de Jean de Rinel, sécretaire du roi d'Angleterre, contre le duc de Bourgogne (1435)', *Cahiers d'histoire*, i (Grenoble, 1956), 131–46; P. Lewis, 'War Propaganda and Historiography in Fifteenth-Century France and England', *TRHS* 5th ser., xv (1965), 1–21.

76. *The Chronicle of Jean de Venette*, ed. R. A. Newhall (New York, 1953), pp. 93–4; *Oeuvres Complètes de Eustache Deschamps*, cit. supra, v, 6.

77. Puiseux, op. cit., ch. ix, pp. 40–7.

78. *The Chronicle of Jean de Venette*, cit. supra, p. 6; *La Complainte . . .*, loc. cit. However, it should be noted that, unlike the author of *La Complainte*, François de Monte-Belluna blamed all sections of society for the defeat of Poitiers, and not simply the nobility; internal discord had invited the disaster: ' *Le Tragicum argumentum de miserabili statu regni Franciae* de François de Monte-Belluna, 1357', ed. A. Vernet, in *Annuaire-Bulletin de la Société de l'Histoire de France* (1964), pp. 120–2.

79. *The Tree of Battles of Honoré Bonet*, trans. and ed. G. W. Coopland (Liverpool, 1949), p. 5.

80. *Chronique des Quatre Premiers Valois*, ed. S. Luce (Société de l'histoire de France, Paris, 1862), pp. 169–70.

81. See 'Sir John Fastolf's Report upon the Management of the War in France upon the Conclusion of the Treaty of Arras, 1435', in *Letters and Papers Illustrative of the Wars of the English in France*, ed. J. Stevenson (2 vols, Rolls Series, 1861–4), ii, 575–85; *Le Jouvencel par Jean de Bueil*, ed. C. Favre and L. Lecestre (2 vols, Société de l'histoire de France, Paris, 1887–9), ii, 20–1.

82. See pp. 175–80, 185 ff below.

83. Ascoli, op. cit., p. 18.

84. H. F. Hutchison, *Henry V* (1967), Appendix, pp. 246, 250. The original English poem on the siege has been published several times, notably by J. Gairdner in *The Historical Collections of a Citizen of London in the Fifteenth Century* (Camden Society, 1876), pp. x–xvi, 1–46.

85. Rupert Brooke, 'The Soldier', in *The Oxford Book of English Verse, 1250–1918*, ed. Sir Arthur Quiller-Couch, no. 960; Wilfrid Owen, 'Anthem for Doomed Youth' and W. B. Yeats, 'An Irish Airman Foresees His Death', in *The Faber Book of Modern Verse*, ed. M. Roberts, pp. 70, 179; *Froissart: Chronicles*, pp. 280–94.

1. The Origins of the War

JOHN LE PATOUREL

THE series of conflicts between the kings of France and of England that historians have agreed to call the 'Hundred Years War' was of such importance in the history of the two countries that a good deal has naturally been written on the causes of so prodigious a conflict. Dr Templeman[1] in England, Professor Wolff[2] in France and Professor Cuttino in the United States[3] have each, in recent years, published papers which survey the literature on the origins of the war and make it unnecessary to attempt any such survey here. All three, and other recent writers also,[4] are broadly in agreement that the root cause of the trouble lay in the position of King Edward III, sovereign[5] in his kingdom of England, a vassal of the king of France in his duchy of Aquitaine.[6] There are different nuances in their interpretations, as one would expect; Professor Wolff in particular addresses himself specifically to the problem presented by the fact that a relationship which appeared natural and reasonable in the time of St Louis and King Henry III proved impossible in the time of King Edward III and King Philip VI, a matter which certainly needs to be explained. Historians also seem to be mostly agreed that Edward III's claim to the throne of France was secondary, and was, indeed, little more than a tactical device for pursuing other aims. But there are really two quite distinct questions in this old problem of the origins of the Hundred Years War: What were the origins of the war that started in 1337? and, why was that war a 'Hundred Years' war? These two questions should be tackled separately.

I

By an order dated 24 May 1337, King Philip VI commanded his seneschal of Périgord and his bailli of Amiens, respectively, to take the duchy of Aquitaine and the county of Ponthieu into his hand.[7] The order stated that there had been long and serious discussion in the Council before the decision to do this had been reached; and while it implied that there were several reasons for the decision, the only reason stated explicitly was that the 'king of England, duke of Aquitaine, peer of France, count of Ponthieu' (i.e. King Edward III), who was the liegeman of the king of France by reason of the duchy, peerage

and county, had received and given aid to Robert of Artois, who was the
'capital enemy' of the king of France and who had been banished from
the kingdom 'for many crimes'. To harbour such a man was contrary
to Edward's obligations as a liege vassal by universal feudal custom;
and it entailed the penalty of 'commise', that is, the confiscation of his
fiefs. Since the sanction, in this case, involved taking possession of
territories like Aquitaine and Ponthieu, and such action would certainly be resisted, it meant war; and as French troops immediately over-
ran Ponthieu, attacked (and for a while occupied) the Channel Islands
and invaded Edward's lands in Aquitaine in execution of the king's
order, these operations do indeed mark the beginning of the Hundred
Years War. It is true that both sides had been fearing an outbreak for
some time; that tension between them had been rising to the point
where an explosion seemed very likely and that each side had been
making preparations that could be considered provocative by the other;
it is even possible that Edward III might have invaded France at some
point even if Gascony had not been attacked; nevertheless the spark
which did in fact light the fuse was the action of the king of France when
he put into execution the sentence of confiscation. This was a feudal
procedure, initiated for feudal reasons; it was based upon the feudal
relationship between the two kings that existed because Edward III
held his duchy of Aquitaine and his county of Ponthieu as a liege vassal
of the king of France and as a peer of France.

In the form which it took in 1337, this feudal relationship had been
created by the treaty of Paris of 1259.[8] That treaty had been intended
to bring to an end the state of war that had existed more or less con-
tinuously since the accession of King Philip Augustus in 1180, and, in a
positive sense, to create conditions of peace and justice for the future.
As such treaties go, it was not unsuccessful. It did in fact keep the peace
for thirty-five years and established a relationship which at least two
successive kings of England and three successive kings of France
thought was workable. By this treaty King Louis IX gave to King
Henry III the rights which he had, as king of France, in the three
dioceses of Limoges, Cahors and Périgueux, together with similar
rights in the Agenais, southern Quercy (i.e. the part of the diocese of
Cahors then held by the king's brother Alphonse de Poitiers) and the
part of Saintonge to the south of the river Charente if certain conditions
were fulfilled in the future. He also recognised King Henry's right to
those parts of the kingdom of France of which he was at that moment
in effective possession, that is, some fragments of the duchy of Aqui-

taine and certain off-shore islands (in practice, Oléron and the Channel Islands). In return, King Henry abandoned his rights in Normandy, in Anjou, Maine and Touraine and in Poitou,[9] and agreed to hold not only what he had acquired by the treaty, but what he had possessed in the kingdom of France at the time when the treaty was being negotiated, by liege homage and as a peer of France.

Whatever the relationship between the two kings had been before the wars which this treaty brought to an end (a matter which will be discussed later), their relationship from this point onward was quite clearly defined. King Henry had been given an opportunity to reconstruct the ancient duchy of Aquitaine for himself, and to hold securely the Channel Islands and Oléron which, if small in extent, were of very great importance to his communications with Bordeaux, now quite clearly the capital and economic centre of his duchy of Aquitaine. But these lands were specifically declared, in the treaty, to be part of the kingdom of France, and they could therefore only be held by King Henry and his successors under the overriding sovereignty, as it was then understood, of the king of France. This applied to the Channel Islands and to the county of Ponthieu (when King Edward I acquired it in 1279) as well as to the duchy of Aquitaine. Moreover, the liege homage which the king of England owed for these lands, was the most binding and comprehensive form of homage. Originally, there had been but one kind of homage, and it created an exclusive relationship between a vassal and his lord; but in course of time, as men placed more emphasis on the land for which a vassal did homage than upon the personal relationship which homage created, vassals began to hold land of several lords; and when that happened, naturally, the relationship between vassal and lord could no longer be exclusive. Liege homage had then been devised as a kind of 'priority' homage, the obligations of which took precedence over any other such obligations that the vassal might have; and this was the relationship that King Henry III entered into by the treaty of 1259.[10] The peerage simply reinforced this. Whatever the origins of the peers of France may have been, they were regarded in the thirteenth century as an inner ring of nobles whose relationship to the king was particularly intimate,[11] and the king took advantage of this to bind them more closely to his allegiance and service. Thus, when King Philip IV created a peerage for the duke of Brittany in 1297, he did so to flatter a great noble and to divert him from notions of autonomy; and a similar intention undoubtedly underlay the creation of a peerage for King Henry III, as duke of Aquitaine, in 1259.

King Louis IX was blamed by his contemporaries, and both he and King Henry III have been blamed by historians for accepting the terms of this treaty and for failing to foresee what their consequences were likely to be; but such criticism is quite beside the point. Neither the kings nor their advisers could see into the future any more than we can; the implications of the relationship they had created were in fact only worked out in detail in the following thirty years or so; and it could be said that it was quite a normal way of organising the relationships between kingdoms and principalities at the time. It was the way in which the kings of England had long tried to regulate their relations with the kings of the Scots.

If they did not show themselves at once, however, the implications of the relationship created by the treaty were very important when they did appear. The first was that, by feudal custom, a vassal had to do homage to his lord when he succeeded to the fief and when his lord succeeded to his lordship; and it was also the custom that the vassal should perform this act at his lord's principal residence. In this case the king of France insisted that the king-duke should do his homage in person, because, according to the ideas of the time, the relationship was not fully established until the vassal had done homage and had been received as vassal by his lord. Now, although the kings of England might have no overwhelming objection in principle to doing this homage (his lands in France were of considerable value to him), there were almost always difficulties to be settled about the precise extent of the lands and rights which formed the subject of the homage; it meant a journey to France at times that might not always be convenient to the king-duke; however fine a display he might make on the journey and at the ceremony, there was no getting away from the fact that at the central point of the ritual he appeared as the feudal inferior of a brother king; and this may have been made a little worse by the fact that the king of France, for his part, had established the doctrine that, even when he acquired lands for which homage was due, he personally did homage to no one. It was certainly made worse by the fact that, early in the fourteenth century, there was a series of short reigns in France (Louis X, 1314–16; Philip V, 1316–22; Charles IV, 1322–8), so that one act of homage had hardly been organised and performed before the demand came again.

A vassal owed loyalty and service to his lord. In the strictest interpretation there should be no conflict or interest between lord and vassal. This could have very important implications in the relationship between

the king-duke and the king of France. For example: it had been the
policy of the thirteenth-century kings of France to bring the county of
Flanders more fully into their obedience than it had been in the eleventh
and twelfth centuries, as it was their policy in other parts of the kingdom. The count's resistance led, in the 1290s, to war. Now the king of
England also had a strong interest in Flanders, partly traditional, partly
commercial; and it was not to his advantage that the king of France
should establish a close control of the county. As early as 1292, Edward
I was in secret negotiation with Count Guy; but he could not intervene
openly until he had himself broken with King Philip in 1294, for to do
so would have been as disloyal as Edward III was in his reception of
Robert of Artois in the 1330s.[12] In effect, then, though it might be possible to distinguish in theory between the king of England and the duke
of Aquitaine, in practice the fact that the king of England was a vassal
of the king of France for his duchy of Aquitaine gave to the king of
France a very large control over what we should now call 'English
foreign policy' in western Europe, wherever, indeed, the king of France
had any interest. When King Louis IX was defending the concessions
he had made to Henry III in 1259, he said: 'It seems to me that I have
made good use of what I have given him, for he was not my man and
now he has entered into my homage.'[13] It is not impossible that Louis
had such implications of 'loyalty' in mind at the time; whether he did
or not, the territories and the promises of territory that he gave to Henry
were a very sound political investment indeed.

A vassal also owed service to his lord and, at this level of the feudal
hierarchy, service meant military service. The king of France, that is to
say, could not only threaten to confiscate the duchy of Aquitaine and the
county of Ponthieu if the king-duke supported his enemies, he could
demand military service from him against them; and the king of France
did in fact make such demands upon Edward I.[14] This clearly could put
severe limitations upon the freedom of action of a ruler like King
Edward I, who had a great many interests on the Continent in addition
to those within the kingdom of France.

The most troublesome implication of the vassalage of the king of
England in his capacity as duke of Aquitaine lay, however, in the
developing ideas of royal sovereignty in France. Partly through the revived study of Roman law, partly by making more effective the powers
which a feudal structure gave to a suzerain, as the king of France
grew materially stronger during the course of the thirteenth century the idea grew, and was lovingly tended by his lawyers, that the

king was 'emperor in his kingdom'. This made the king not only independent of any other lay power, but made him the source of legislation
applicable to the whole of his kingdom, even within the great counties
and duchies, and made his court the ultimate court of appeal for all who
were in feudal relationship with him, together with their vassals and
sub-tenants; and it implied that the great counts and dukes should hold
their counties and duchies on conditions prescribed by the king and his
court, so that the government of those duchies and counties should be
ancillary to the royal administration, should concern itself, in fact, only
with those affairs which the royal administration was not yet prepared
to take over. Towards the end of the thirteenth century, and more in the
fourteenth, the king extended his legislation to Gascony;[15] and all that
the king-duke could do, in the last resort, was to legislate in the same
sense and argue that his courts in the duchy were applying his own laws
rather than those of the king of France, or come to some arrangement
by negotiation. The question of appeals[16] was more explosive because, if
the claims of the French lawyers were pressed, they could bring the
administration of the duchy to a standstill and discredit the ducal courts
there. When an appeal was made, the appellant was at once put under
the protection of the king of France, whose men could enter the duchy
to make that protection effective. If, for example, a man who had been
entrusted with the collection of some part of the ducal revenues failed
to render his account when it was due, and, having been brought before
the ducal courts, made an appeal, this meant that, even if he lost the
appeal in the end there would be considerable delay before he could be
brought to book and the ducal finances would suffer; but if he succeeded in his appeal, a most difficult situation would arise.[17] The
difficulties were there even if the French king's officers acted reasonably
and moderately; but they did not always do so. From time to time the
king-duke obtained, as a personal concession, that what were coming
to be regarded as the rights of the king of France in this respect would
not be pressed in Aquitaine; but such concessions did not remain
effective for very long. The king of England, therefore, though he was
as sovereign in his kingdom as the king of France was in his, could not
be sovereign in his French lands; and this was more than a matter of
legal theory, it might make the difference between being able to govern
his duchy and to realise the full value which it might have for him and
not being able to do so.

There were other causes of difficulty. When, for example, King
Louis IX ceded to King Henry III, by the treaty of 1259, 'what he

held' in the three dioceses of Limoges, Cahors and Périgueux, he
meant that and no more. It soon became apparent that he had possessed
very little there, and that many of the great seigneurs were 'privileged',
that is, they had been given the privilege that their allegiance could not
be transferred to another lord against their will. 'What the king held'
in the three dioceses, other than his sovereignty of which he did not
divest himself in 1259, was no more than a complex and varying bundle
of rights and jurisdictions, often barely effective, a fruitful source of
disputes and appeals – to such an extent that it has been said that the
appellate jurisdiction of the king's court, the Parlement of Paris, was
developed very largely on the appeals from the three dioceses in the
years after 1259.[18] In the sense that ducal and royal rights and jurisdictions were often inextricably entangled, similar difficulties obtained
over most of the lands held by Edward I in France. The king-duke
would have a piece of land here, rights of jurisdiction there, the right to
take or levy a custom somewhere else; in many places his jurisdiction
was simply one point in a hierarchy of courts at the head of which was
the king's court, the Parlement of Paris. No one, in the fourteenth
century, could have put a board by a roadside, with the inscription
on one side 'You are entering the territory of the king-duke', and on the
other 'You are entering the territory of the king of France', for both
might have rights over the same territory. The duchy of Aquitaine was
not bounded by anything remotely like a modern frontier.

However, the full force of all these problems was not revealed until
near the end of the thirteenth century. As far as can be seen, Edward I
honestly tried to make the system work, unpromising as it may seem to
us, for it did no violence to the ideas of the time; and since it had been
established, there was much to be gained by taking the advantages
which it offered. It was only as those who advised the kings of France
developed the idea of his sovereignty and applied it more confidently
and aggressively that the situation deteriorated. In 1293, King Philip IV
claimed jurisdiction over certain acts of violence committed at sea and
on the coasts of the Bay of Biscay, and summoned Edward I, as duke of
Aquitaine, to attend his court and to answer for the conduct of his men,
as any lord might require of his vassal. Edward sent his brother, Edmund
of Lancaster, to negotiate; but King Philip, by what seems very like
sharp practice, confiscated and took possession of Gascony. This led to
the war of 1294.[19] It was concluded by the peace of 1303 which, so far
as territory was concerned, restored the *status quo ante* completely.
There are many things which are hard to understand in this war; but

what was perhaps more important for the future than the fighting or the diplomatic manœuvres were the arguments which the English lawyers developed in the course of the protracted negotiations between the truce of 1297 and the peace; for they then produced a theory of English sovereignty in Aquitaine to counter the sovereignty which the French lawyers attributed to their king throughout his kingdom.[20] Henceforward it was, in a sense, one sovereignty against another in Aquitaine, and the king of England made less effort to accommodate himself to the relationship created by the treaty of 1259.

There was a second war between the years 1324 and 1327,[21] arising out of local resistance to the building of a French bastide at Saint-Sardos in the Agenais, when again Gascony and Ponthieu were in French hands for a while; but on this occasion only a part of the duchy was restored at the peace. The treaty was made only a few months after the accession of Edward III, when Isabella and Mortimer, who were then in control of England, had to liquidate all foreign commitments as quickly as they could. If personal feelings counted for anything, Edward might well have felt that a considerable part of his Aquitainian inheritance had been given up when he was powerless to prevent it; but the 'War of Saint-Sardos', as it is called, raised no new question of principle.

There were several attempts, between the years 1303 and 1337, to settle the problems to which this feudal relationship between the two kings gave rise by talking rather than fighting.[22] There was a meeting known as the 'Process of Montreuil' in 1306;[23] another, known as the 'Process of Périgueux' beginning in 1311,[24] and a 'Process of Agen' from 1332 to 1334.[25] In these meetings, naturally, each side put its claims at their highest; and for this reason alone these meetings probably did more harm than good (as in a modern international conference when positions are taken up more for their propaganda value than as serious points for negotiation), quite apart from the fact that these processes failed to produce any very useful result. For there was a fundamental misunderstanding. The English, as they approached these 'processes', envisaged a conference between equals; but the French always fell back on the sovereignty which their king claimed over all his kingdom and its adjacent waters, and tended to make the occasion more and more like an action in his court (a 'process') in which he was judge. This clearly made negotiation impossible.

Since the conditions under which the king-duke held his lands in France put so many restrictions not only upon his government of those lands but also upon his interests elsewhere, and since, in the complexities and intermingling of jurisdiction and administration both kings could so easily become involved in the miscalculations and even the sheer violence of those acting in their name, it is easy to see how a sailors' row, giving rise to a dispute over jurisdiction, could lead to the war of 1294, and how the refusal of Edward's seneschal of Aquitaine to attend the court of the French seneschal of Périgord to answer for the violent action of a lord of Montpezat could lead to the war of 1324, particularly in an atmosphere of tension when the king of France clearly thought Edward II was trying to avoid the homage he had been summoned to do; and again, how Edward III's 'disloyalty' in harbouring Robert of Artois, also in an atmosphere of tension when there were other causes of dispute (in Scotland and in Flanders), could lead to the war of 1337. But after the first war the whole of Ponthieu and Aquitaine, and after the second the whole of Ponthieu and at least part of Aquitaine, had been restored to the king-duke. The hold which the king of France had over him through his position as duke of Aquitaine, peer of France and count of Ponthieu was then of greater value than the absorption of Gascony into the royal demesne or its transfer to a French noble with no interests outside the kingdom could have been; and the king-duke, on his side, quite apart from the consideration that his honour demanded that he should defend his heritage, possessed in Aquitaine an asset of enormous value to him – a steady and reliable revenue from the wine customs levied in Bordeux which,[26] since they could easily be assigned to pay off the loans which any active king desperately needed from time to time,[27] were worth far more to him even than the figures for their annual yield might suggest. Thus the 'feudal theory', 'the problem of Gascony' can explain why there was a war in 1337, but it does not explain why that war was different from the two earlier wars, why in fact it was a 'Hundred Years War'.

II

Even on the surface of things the war of 1337 looks as though it involved more than the feudal issue. In the wars of 1294 and 1324, even though Edward I did launch a belated campaign in Flanders during the year 1297, the fighting was essentially for the defence or the recovery of Gascony. In 1337 and in the years that followed, there was certainly fighting in Gascony as local forces in the allegiance of the king-duke strove, in the end successfully, to hold the invading French armies at bay, but many of the important campaigns, and all those in which King

Edward III was personally involved, took place in the north, far from Gascony, and apparently with other objectives. This at once suggests that other issues were in question beside Gascony. Of these issues, some go even deeper than the ramifications of the feudal relationship between the king-duke and the king of France; others were, in a sense, accidental.

The deeper issues involve the whole political development of the kingdom of France on the one hand and of the dominions of the rulers who were, among other things, kings of England, on the other. The Hundred Years War was not a conflict between two nations, France and England. National autonomy, though it was achieved to some extent in the two countries as the result of the war, certainly did not exist at the beginning of it; though one might say that the kings of France and England were brought into conflict as they groped their way towards some notion of national autonomy.

The treaty of 1259 had deprived the king-duke of more than it might appear to have done at first sight. King Henry had renounced all the rights which he had or had ever had in Normandy, in Anjou, Maine and Touraine, and in Poitou. Because he was not in possession of these lands at the time when the treaty was being negotiated, and had not been in possession of them (other than parts of Poitou) for over fifty years, historians have tended to treat his renunciation as a concession of relatively little importance; but the legal (as distinct from the military) basis on which King Louis could demand this renunciation was still the sentence of confiscation pronounced in the court of King Philip Augustus in 1202, and some people had doubted the legality of that sentence in general and, in particular, had doubted whether a punitive sentence directed against King John ought to go on being enforced against his innocent son. Henry III had found some support in Normandy in 1230, when he was making one of his attempts to recover his father's and his grandfather's lands in France;[28] his support among the barons of Poitou had flowed now one way and now the other; he was building up a very promising relationship with Brittany,[29] and even in the years immediately before the treaty a change in personalities and politics in France or in England might still have made it possible for a militarily competent king of England to recover the position that King John had held in 1200. Until 1259 Henry still used, formally, the titles 'Duke of Normandy and Aquitaine, Count of Anjou'. Thus the rights which he renounced in 1259 were not unsubstantial; and as we look further into them they appear quite fundamental, for Henry's ancestors in the male line had been dukes of Normandy, counts of Anjou and even dukes of Aquitaine before they had been kings of England, and their continental inheritance was quite as important to them, perhaps more important, than their insular kingdom.

Those who say that the Hundred Years War really began in 1066 are right in the sense that it was the Norman conquest of England, ultimately, which created the conditions which the treaty of 1259 was intended to bring up to date but which, in fact, largely survived it. Both the battle of Hastings and the less famous campaigns of Henry fitz-Empress in 1153 brought French noblemen to the throne of England; but they did a great deal more than that. Though William the Conqueror might endeavour to rule England as an English king and Henry set about to restore the 'customs of his grandfather' in the country, both conquests not only brought about great changes there but also created a political relationship between England and parts of France. It is this relationship that must be analysed, and its development studied, if the Hundred Years War is to be understood.

William the Conqueror did not cease to be duke of Normandy after he had made himself king of England; and neither he nor his sons intended that England and Normandy should ever be separated. To them, England and Normandy, together with all the rights and superiorities which a king of England could exercise beyond his kingdom and a duke of Normandy beyond his duchy, constituted an indivisible inheritance,[30] as the kingdom of France had come to be for the kings of France. This in itself was a long step towards political integration. It is true that England and Normandy were separated by the Channel, though the sea could be as much of a highway as a barrier, and that they were separated not only by differences of language but also by differences in custom and tradition; but even these differences need not have proved more of a hindrance to political union in the long run than the differences of language and custom that were to be found within the kingdom of England itself; while unity was vastly strengthened by the fact that the higher ranks of the baronage, and not only they, characteristically possessed lands and interests on both sides of the Channel to the extent that one could not speak of a Norman baronage and an English baronage, but only of one single Normano-English baronial society. Except in so far as the provinces of Rouen, Canterbury and York were separate units of ecclesiastical government, the same was true of the higher ranks of the clergy. The union of England and Normandy was thus far more than a temporary union in the person of the ruler, as is shown, almost paradoxically, by the manner in which

Stephen of Blois obtained the kingdom and the duchy;[31] and there were beginnings, though only the beginnings, of institutions to cope with the problems of government which this union created.

When Henry fitzEmpress made himself King Henry II of England, he was already count of Anjou (and descended directly, in the male line, from the counts of Anjou), duke of Normandy and, since his marriage to Eleanor, duchess of Aquitaine in her own right, was beginning to style himself 'duke of the Aquitainians'.[32] Later he found the means to take over the government of Brittany, to establish his suzerainty over Scotland, over the still-independent princes of Wales, over the great county of Toulouse and other lands; and as a result of baronial enter-prise in Ireland, he extended his rule over the colonists there and his suzerainty over the still-independent Irish kings, as over the Welsh princes. But the construction of this vast feudal empire was not accom-panied by any fresh immigration from France into England, or at least none of any importance; though the relationship between Normandy and England created by the Norman king-dukes was revived and main-tained. Such unity as Henry's empire came to achieve was brought about by other means.

The problem of governing this huge assemblage of territories stemmed from the fact that Henry claimed to be count of Anjou by hereditary right, and to be king of England and duke of Normandy also by hereditary right even though this right had had to be realised by force. He was thus bound to rule England as a Normano-English king, Normandy as a duke of Normandy, Anjou, with Touraine and Maine, in accordance with the customs and practices built up by his Angevin ancestors; while the circumstances of his acquisition of the duchy of Aquitaine meant that he could not do otherwise than act in a similar manner there. All demanded, to a greater or less degree, personal rule; but Henry could not be everywhere at once. Some means had to be found to overcome this difficulty if Henry was to continue to hold, and perhaps to extend, the accumulation of lands and authority he had acquired; and honour as well as the logic of the situation required that he should do this, since it seems to be a characteristic of such empires that they begin to disintegrate as soon as they cease to expand.

The constitutional history of the Angevin 'empire' has yet to be written, and historians have not, perhaps, recognised that there was any such thing; yet the Hundred Years War results from the converging and ultimately clashing development of the government of this empire, or what was left of it by 1337, and the development of royal government in the kingdom of France. It was more than the feudal relationship between king and king-duke; it was the overlapping and ultimately the conflict of two growing structures of government.

On the Angevin or Plantagenet side the scheme of government, which was to be the chief means of holding the various elements of the 'empire' together, grew out of the older traditions of each country included within it. To some extent, the king-duke could hold his lands together by itineration, visiting each of them whenever he was needed there and trying not to leave any one country too long without his presence. The king-dukes of England and Normandy had done the same; but something more was needed. To the businesslike minds of these kings, the accounts of their finances in England or Normandy could not wait for their next visit to the country; nor could a great many judicial matters; and there were other affairs which could be dealt with adequately by delegated authority and so prevented from piling up and defeating the king when he did come. During the course of the twelfth century a system of administration which met these difficulties and which went some way towards providing the empire with a unitary government, was gradually evolved.

The king-duke-count and his household, which included the organisation of the king's own finances (the Chamber) and the secretariat of his government (the Chancery) formed the common centre of government for all his lands, moving constantly from one to another and capable of issuing orders for any one of them from any point on the itinerary; and wherever the king might be, attended by his servants and courtiers and the magnates of the land in which he found himself, with others who had business there, he held his court, accessible to suitors from all parts. In those lands over which he exercised no more than suzerainty, Scotland and large parts of the periphery of the duchy of Aquitaine for example, the native ruler carried on his government with little interference in his internal affairs; but in those lands where the king was himself the 'native' ruler by inheritance or conquest, some form of continuous administration was needed. In these there was gradually evolved a responsible official, called a justiciar in England and in Ireland, a justiciar or seneschal in Normandy, a seneschal in Brittany, in Anjou and in Aquitaine (sometimes there were separate seneschals for Gascony and for Poitou and even for other parts of Aquitaine), and this official acted as head of the administration when the king-duke-count was present in the country and as something like a viceroy when he was elsewhere. This official directed a body of justices in England and

Normandy and the auditors who examined the accounts of the sheriffs in England and of the *vicomtes*, *prévôts* and *baillis* in Normandy. The two groups overlapped considerably, and made up what was called the 'Exchequer' in England, in Normandy and in Ireland. In Anjou, Aquitaine and Brittany the seneschals do not seem to have possessed so highly organised an administration to help them; but they did have a number of deputies, clerks and castellans under their orders, and a local organisation for the collection and administration of the duke-count's revenues and to keep the peace, with at least the beginnings of a judicial organisation. Local administration, the shires in England, the *bailliages*, *vicomtés*, *prévôtés* and other units in the continental lands, though they might be influenced by the fact that the government of the king-duke-count was concerned with many lands, largely retained their traditional forms and functions; and, indeed, the most important feature of the whole structure was that the administration of each land grew naturally out of the institutions that were beginning to form when its king, duke or count was that and nothing more. The process in the twelfth century was one of bringing them together and making them function in the service of one king-duke-count, not of imposing a common pattern.

In so far as this government had developed towards a logical system by the end of the century, it had a considerable unifying effect, tending more and more to make the Angevin empire an integrated political unit. The only ambiguous factor was the succession. Henry II's designation of his son Henry as king of England and duke of Normandy, Richard as duke of Aquitaine, Geoffrey as duke of Brittany and John as lord of Ireland, if this was indeed his plan for the succession, seems to imply partition, however he might try to insist that the younger brothers should do homage to the elder; though as it turned out all his lands descended substantially intact first to Richard and then to John.

The disasters of the early thirteenth century, when the king of France conquered Normandy and ultimately Poitou, and when Brittany and Anjou-Maine-Touraine went over to him, though they altered the whole territorial balance of the Plantagenet lands so that the centre of interest and the normal residence of the king-duke were now in England rather than in his continental lands, influenced but did not determine the constitutional development of the lands that remained to him. The fact that he still had important interests on the Continent, lands to be recovered and lands to be defended, as well as interests in Wales, Scotland and Ireland to be safeguarded and if possible extended, put enormous pressure upon England to provide the men and the money for enterprises beyond the kingdom. This pressure does much to explain the changes in military organisation and the development of Parliament during the thirteenth century, though these developments grew naturally out of English institutions and traditions. On the other side of the Channel, the fact that the king-duke could no longer visit the distant duchy of Aquitaine so frequently as he had done[33] meant that the hitherto somewhat rudimentary administration there would have to be vastly developed so that it could function effectively with the king-duke normally absent rather than frequently, if intermittently, present. Though there were some beginnings under Henry III, this was substantially the work of Edward I. The seneschal was relieved of his financial responsibilities by the creation of new offices, those of the constable of Bordeaux and the controller; some of his judicial responsibilities were taken off him by the appointment of judges at different levels; at the end of the century an officer with the title of lieutenant (i.e. lieutenant of the king-duke) was appointed to take over abnormal military responsibilities and some of the king-duke's appellate jurisdiction; and the seneschal was provided with an official council and with under-seneschals in various parts of the duchy. On their much smaller scale, similar developments took place in the Channel Islands. Finally, any doubt there may have been about the unity of the succession was cleared up in 1254 when Gascony, the Channel Islands and Ireland were formally declared to be annexed to the Crown of England, so that whoever in future was the lawful king of England was, by that fact alone, the lawful duke of Aquitaine and lord of Ireland and of the Channel Islands, at least in English law.

Though the superficial effect of these developments might seem to be to make each unit of the Plantagenet lands better able to stand on its own if need be, the more profound effect was to provide the necessary conditions for linking them in an integral political union. Thus even in the fourteenth century, his continental lands and his continental interests were as fully a part of the king-duke's dominions and responsibilities as his kingdom of England, not distant dependencies expendable in times of difficulty. Moreover, and this was perhaps even more important, King Edward I and his successors continued, in the government of their dominions as a whole, the tradition of Henry II's time. The considerable developments in the administration of Aquitaine and the Channel Islands did not follow an English model; they were, essentially, the developments that could have been brought about by a 'French' duke of Aquitaine or duke of Normandy if he had been that and nothing else;

they were entirely, that is to say, in the native tradition – and they were so notwithstanding the fact that something like a higher civil service was growing up whose members could serve in any of the king-duke's dominions, as the biographies of some leading officers clearly show.[34] This growing integration of the Plantagenet lands through political and administrative development, and the fact that the king-duke was not only a French prince by descent but was governing his French lands as a French prince of the time would have done, make it reasonable to suggest that when the English lawyers in 1297 and the following years claimed that Gascony was not a part of the kingdom of France according to the French idea of the kingdom, they were not simply making a slick answer to the French lawyers' assertion that their king was 'emperor in his kingdom'; there was a great deal of patient and inventive political construction behind their arguments. Other French dukes would soon be saying much the same thing about their duchies.[35]

However, on the French side, the king's claim to sovereignty over all his kingdom was equally the expression of at least two centuries of political construction and consolidation. At the time of the Norman Conquest, the great dukes and counts, such as the dukes of Normandy or the counts of Anjou, were the king's vassals certainly, but only in a personal sense, and the relationship influenced their actions very little. The dukes of Normandy did homage, when they did do it, 'on the march', that is on the frontier, implying an element of equality between duke and king. But the Capetian kings, having achieved the stability of their dynasty and the indivisibility of their inheritance so that their small achievements (as they were at first) could be cumulated from one generation to another, were gradually able to intensify this relationship until it became one of the chief principles on which their growing authority in their kingdom was built. This can well be seen in the history of the homages which the Norman and Angevin rulers did as dukes of Normandy. First it came to be specified that the homage was indeed for Normandy, i.e. Normandy was a fief held of the king by homage and fealty (this first appears in 1120); then, by the middle of the twelfth century, the homage is described as 'liege'.[36] Finally, when King John settled with King Philip Augustus, at Le Goulet in January 1200, the terms on which he should succeed to the lands of his brother and his father, it was made quite clear in the treaty that they were to be held as fiefs of the king of France in the fullest sense of the term.[37] The terms of the treaty of Paris of 1259 were, therefore, only the next step in a process of definition which had been going on since the beginning of the twelfth century or before, and in which the relationship created by homage was being intensified in the interest of the king of France and of the integration of his kingdom.

There were, naturally, other elements in this process whereby the king of France was bringing the whole of his kingdom more and more under his authority – the influence of Roman law, and the development, as elsewhere, of the actual machinery of administration. What the 'English' regarded as 'French' interference in Gascony was often the normal pressure of zealous officials and competent administrators carrying out their duties as they understood them; but it was the more galling to the king-duke's officers there precisely because they were willing and had the means to do all that the French officials were claiming to do. The difficulties in Aquitaine, therefore, were more than a conflict of two largely theoretical sovereignties occasionally applied; it was also the clash of the two state-building enterprises operating in the same territory. The 'Angevin empire' and the 'Norman empire' had been formed under the conditions of the eleventh and twelfth centuries, when the king of France was weak and his nobles could build principalities that included lands both within and beyond the kingdom. Those days were passing; but as they passed both the kingdom of France and the 'feudal empire' of the Plantagenets were developing with the times into ever-more complex and sophisticated political structures; and in the geographical regions and in the spheres of government where they overlapped it could not be supposed that such structures, patiently built up over the centuries, would be abandoned after a battle won or lost. And it may perhaps further be suggested that the political edifice which the Plantagenet king-dukes were constructing was as valid for its day as the Capetians' kingdom; and no one could then have said whether the future lay with the one or the other.

This is perhaps the chief reason why the war of 1337 developed into something more than a feudal dispute. It was also a large part of the force behind Edward III's claim to the throne of France.[38] There was nothing preposterous about this claim; one could almost say that it was to be expected sooner or later, for the kings of England were of French origin, they had retained very important interests in France and, as dukes of Aquitaine and peers of France, they were a part of the fabric of government in France. Edward III's mother was a French princess and the royal families of England and France had long been closely related. If there were at any time any serious doubt about the succession to the throne of France, it was in the highest degree likely that a claimant would be found in the royal family of England; and Edward in 1328 could rightly say that he was the nearest living relative of King Charles IV. In the crisis of that year his claim was rejected not entirely by law and reason, but very largely on the practical consideration that he was then a boy of fifteen and under the control of the hated Isabella and her lover Mortimer; Philip of Valois was in almost every way a more suitable candidate and he was on the spot. But Edward's claim was reasonable in itself and it always had some support in France; if he really believed in it, as he could well have done, it was his duty to prosecute it.

Even his claim had quite a long history to it. The idea that the king of England might have a claim to the kingdom of France or part of it first appeared explicitly in 1317; but it had been in a sense implicit in the claim to sovereignty in Aquitaine, for if that claim was not conceded, as it would not be, the only way to realise it would be to seize the kingdom itself. The suggestion that Edward should take the title was made in 1328, and the claim was formally made in that year. Though he was in no position to press it then, echoes of it sound in English official documents for the next two or three years. Edward actually assumed the French title in letters patent that were prepared in 1337, though probably never used; and when he took the title formally in January 1340, this can only have been as the result of long and careful deliberation. The claim had not been made lightly and it would not be abandoned lightly.

Behind the immediate issues of the 1330s, then, behind all the conflicts of jurisdiction and the administrative tangles in Gascony at that time and the failure to find any solution for them, there lay two political structures, both growing in complexity and effectiveness, both developing in part over the same ground, and both seeing in the war issues at stake that were vital to them. But, however deep-seated the cause of conflict, it could not have lasted so long if the two sides had not been fairly evenly matched, taking all things into consideration. At first the English armies were perhaps the better organised and the French were certainly unprepared for the tactics they employed. Once they had found success and all that went with it in booty and ransoms, many an Englishman looked upon France as a land where fortunes could easily and quickly be made; while many Gascons and Bretons and other 'Frenchmen' who gave their allegiance to Edward also found in the war a way to riches. In so far as Edward III, in his capacity as duke of Aquitaine, was resisting royal centralisation, he was leading a movement

which others were prepared to join, the duke of Brittany, the cities of
Flanders, even the duke of Burgundy; and Edward, by campaigns
designed to win local acknowledgement of his right to the throne of
France and by offering himself as an alternative king to all who were
discontented with Valois rule, looked at one point as though he might
almost win the kingdom of France by instalments.[39] In one sense the
Hundred Years War could be described as a civil war in France, in
which the two principles of royal centralisation and princely independence were disputed. But in the end, the reserves of men and wealth in
France and the sheer size of the country were too much for Edward and
his successors; though the combination of a good cause (in their own
eyes) and the memory of early successes, quite apart from the deep
traditions that this chapter has attempted to analyse, would not allow
them to give up; while the French, for their part, either could not find
the means to throw them out completely, or, very much more likely,
took a long time to see that that was the only solution to their problem;
for they also stood to benefit from the fact that the king of England was
also the duke of Aquitaine – if only he would play their game.

The war of 1337 began in a way very similar to those of 1294 and
1324 and for very similar reasons. But the earlier wars were incidents
in a feudal relationship when the confiscation of the fief was intended
more to bring a disobedient vassal to heel than to deprive him permanently of his lands and so to break the relationship for ever. The
argument over sovereignty, however, and the political developments
centred on the kings of France and the king-dukes of the Plantagenet
dominions were brought to a head by Edward III's claim to the throne
of France; and a feudal dispute was converted into a long conflict in
which the old feudal overlapping and interlocking gave way to the auto-
nomous and self-contained national kingdoms of France and England;
and the Frenchmen and Englishmen began to hate one another as
Englishmen and Frenchmen – perhaps not a very great advance after all.

BIBLIOGRAPHICAL NOTE

Standard accounts of the Hundred Years War and its origins will be found in
E. Perroy, *The Hundred Years War* (English trans. W. B. Wells, 1951) – though
the circumstances in which this book was written should be noted – in M.
McKisack, *The Fourteenth Century* (*The Oxford History of England*, iv, Oxford,
1959), and most recently, with new ideas and a full bibliography, in K. Fowler,
The Age of Plantagenet and Valois (1967). M. Gavrilovitch, *Étude sur le traité de
Paris de 1259* (Bibliothèque de l'École des Hautes Études, fasc. 125, Paris, 1899)
is fundamental. There are more detailed studies of the beginning of the war in
E. Déprez, *Les préliminaires de la guerre de Cent ans: La Papauté, la France et
l'Angleterre, 1328–1342* (Paris, 1902) and in H. S. Lucas, *The Low Countries
and the Hundred Years War, 1326–1347* (Ann Arbor, 1929); but the most significant of recent work on the general political conditions (though to us they may
well seem more legal than political) which led to the war is contained in a
number of articles by P. Chaplais, most of which are cited in the notes. To these
should be added his collection of documents on *The War of Saint-Sardos,
1323–1325* (Camden Third Series, lxxxvii, 1954). Some economic and social
conditions are brought out in R. Boutruche, *La crise d'une société: seigneurs et
paysans du Bordelais pendant la guerre de Cent ans* (Paris, 1947) and in Y.
Renouard (ed.), 'Bordeaux sous les rois d'Angleterre' in *Histoire de Bordeaux*,
ed. C. Higounet, iii (Bordeaux, 1965); while the structure of politics in France
itself, of considerable relevance if the first phase of the Hundred Years War is
regarded as having some of the characteristics of a French civil war, has been
made much clearer by R. Cazelles, *La Société politique et la crise de la royauté
sous Philippe de Valois* (Paris, 1958) and P. S. Lewis, *Later Medieval France, the
Polity* (1968).

The fundamental collection of official documents is contained in *Rymer's
Foedera*, Record Commission edition, ed. A. Clarke, J. Bayley, F. Holbrooke
and J. W. Clarke (1816–69); supplemented on the English side by the *Calendars
of Patent Rolls, Close Rolls*, etc. published by H.M. Stationery Office and, more
particularly, by the *Treaty Rolls* (vol. i, *1234–1325*, 1955) when later volumes
of this and connected series are published; and on the French side by *Comptes
Royaux*, ed. R. Fawtier and F. Maillard [*Recueil des historiens de France, Documents financiers*, iii, *1285–1314* (Paris, 1953–6), iv, *1314–1328* (Paris, 1961)] and
Registres du trésor des chartes, ed. R. Fawtier (*Archives nationales, Inventaires et
Documents*, Paris, 1958, 1966) as these two publications progress. A useful
indication of the scope of the registers of the Parlement is given by P.-C. Timbal,
La guerre de Cent ans vue à travers les registres du parlement, 1337–1369 (Paris,
1961). The two most important French chronicles on the origins and the early
phases of the war are those of Jean le Bel and Jean Froissart. The standard
edition of the first is *Chroniques de Jean le Bel*, ed. J. Viard and E. Déprez
(Société de l'histoire de France, Paris, 1904–5) and of the second, *Chroniques de
Jean Froissart*, ed. S. Luce, G. Raynaud, L. and A. Mirot (14 vols, Société de
l'histoire de France, Paris, 1869–1966), but there are a number of useful documents and tables published in an earlier edition of Froissart – *Oeuvres de
Froissart*, ed. Kervyn de Lettenhove: *Chroniques* (Brussels, 1867–77) especially
in vol. xviii. There are a number of translations of his chronicle into English.
Although *The Chronicle of Jean de Venette* (ed. R. A. Newhall, New York, 1953)
does not begin until 1340, it should be read as corrective to the aristocratic
attitudes of Jean le Bel and Froissart and for the editor's valuable bibliography

(note in particular the articles of J. Viard). Perhaps the most relevant English chronicles are the *Continuatio Chronicarum* of Adae Murimuth and *De Gestis Mirabilibus Regis Edwardi Tertii* by Robertus de Avesbury. These are edited together in one volume by E. M. Thompson (Rolls Series, 1889).

NOTES

1. G. Templeman, 'Edward III and the Beginnings of the Hundred Years War', *TRHS* 5th ser., ii (1952), 69–88.
2. Ph. Wolff, 'Un Problème d'origines: La Guerre de Cent Ans', in *Éventail de l'histoire vivante: Hommage à Lucien Febvre*, ii (1953), 141–8.
3. G. P. Cuttino, 'Historical Revision: the Causes of the Hundred Years War', *Speculum*, xxxi (1956), 463–77.
4. e.g. E. Perroy, *The Hundred Years War*, p. 69; M. McKisack, *The Fourteenth Century*, ch. iv. There is a full bibliography in K. Fowler, *The Age of Plantagenet and Valois*, pp. 204 ff.
5. The terms 'sovereign' and 'sovereignty' are used here in their medieval sense. For medieval theories of sovereignty, see W. Ullmann, 'The Development of the Medieval Idea of Sovereignty', in *EHR* lxiv (1949), 1–33; and for their application in this particular case, P. Chaplais, 'La Souveraineté du roi de France et le pouvoir législatif en Guyenne au début du XIVe siècle', *Le Moyen Age*, lxix (1963), 449–69.
6. The terms 'Aquitaine', 'Guyenne' and 'Gascony' have often given rise to confusion. The king-duke's title was *Dux Aquitanie*, as it had been since Henry fitzEmpress (Henry II) married Eleanor of Aquitaine and subsequently made himself king of England. The duchy, which he then held in right of his wife, had been formed about a century before by the union of an earlier 'duchy of Aquitaine', centred on Poitou, with the duchy of the Gascons. When King John and King Henry III had lost Poitou in the thirteenth century, and with it most of the earlier duchy of Aquitaine, it was perhaps natural to speak of what remained as 'Gascony', even officially (e.g. 'Rotuli Vasconie' for the rolls of letters relating to the king-duke's interests in south-west France); and this continued even when Henry II's duchy of Aquitaine had been reconstructed to some extent in accordance with the provision of the treaty of Paris of 1259. In this paper some attempt has been made to use the term 'Gascony' when it seemed geographically appropriate and 'Aquitaine' when referring to the duchy as a political unit whatever its effective geographical limits at the time; though it is difficult to make the distinction consistently. 'Guyenne' is simply a variant French form of 'Aquitaine'.
7. *Oeuvres de Froissart*, ed. Kervyn de Lettenhove, xviii, 33–7.
8. On the treaty and the conditions that it created see M. Gavrilovitch, *Étude sur le traité de Paris de 1259* (Paris, 1899), and P. Chaplais, 'The Making of the Treaty of Paris (1259) and the Royal Style', *EHR* lxvii (1952), 235–53. Chaplais has also studied the practical working out of these conditions in 'Le Duché-pairie de Guyenne', *Annales du Midi*, lxix (1957), 5–38, and ibid., lxx (1958), 135–60.
9. In this context 'Poitou' means primarily the historic county of Poitou; but as the title 'count of Poitou' remained as an alternative to 'duke of Aquitaine' almost to this date, it probably implied also 'all non-Gascon Aquitaine'.
10. On liege homage, e.g. F. L. Ganshof, *Feudalism* (trans. Grierson, 1952), pp. 93–5.

11. The origin of the peers is one of the mysteries of French history (M. Sautel-Boulet, 'Le role juridictional de la Cour des Pairs au xiiie et xive siècles', in *Recueil de Travaux offert à M. Clovis Brunel* (Paris, 1955), ii, 507–20). Unless the grant of the peerage to Henry III in 1259 be regarded as the revival of an earlier peerage held by the dukes of Aquitaine, the policy behind it seems to be an approach to that of the fourteenth century, on which see R. Cazelles, *La Société politique et le crise de la royauté sous Philippe de Valois* (Paris, 1958), pp. 379–82, and C. T. Wood, *The French Apanages and the Capetian Monarchy, 1224–1238* (Cambridge, Mass., 1966), pp. 33–5.

12. On Edward's relations with Flanders, H. Pirenne, *Histoire de Belgique*, i (5th ed., Brussels, 1929), 376–409; F. M. Powicke, *The Thirteenth Century*, pp. 622–3, 648, 659, 664–5, 667–9, etc.; P. Chaplais, 'Le Duché-pairie . . .', loc. cit., p. 28; and for Edward's similar embarrassments in the Spanish kingdoms, ibid., pp. 18–23.

13. 'Et me semble que ce que je li doing emploie-je bien, pour ce que il n'estoit pas mes hom, si en entre en mon hommaige.' *Histoire de Saint Louis par Jean, Sire de Joinville*, ed. Natalis de Wailly (Société de l'histoire de France, Paris, 1868), p. 245.

14. e.g. Chaplais, 'Le Duché-pairie . . .', loc. cit., pp. 19–20, 21–2.

15. P. Chaplais, 'La Souveraineté du roi de France . . .', loc. cit., pp. 449–69.

16. Gavrilovitch, op. cit., pp. 84–94; P. Chaplais, 'Gascon Appeals to England, 1259–1453' (London Ph.D. thesis, 1950).

17. e.g. an entry in the account of Adam Limber, constable of Bordeaux, for year 1322–3 (PRO, Pipe Roll, 12 Edward III, rot. 58); 'He [the constable] renders account of £1600 5s 3½d of new bordelais from the issues of the péage of Saint-Macaire which Amanieu d'Albret held of the king's grant for life, and which had been taken into the king's hand because Amanieu, refusing to render his account, had appealed to the Court of France. . . .' In this case the roll had been taken into the king-duke's hand; but it might not always be easy to do this.

18. Gavrilovitch, op. cit., pp. 68–71; cf. *EHR* lxxix (1964), 789–92.

19. e.g. R. Fawtier, *L'Europe occidentale de 1270 à 1328 (Histoire générale: Histoire du Moyen Age*, ed. G. Glotz, vi, 1, Paris, 1940), pp. 314–25; P. Chaplais, 'Le Duché-pairie . . .', loc. cit., pp. 26–38.

20. P. Chaplais, 'English Arguments concerning the Feudal Status of Aquitaine in the Fourteenth Century', *BIHR* xxi (1948), 203–13.

21. P. Chaplais, 'Le Duché-pairie . . .', loc. cit., pp. 154–7.

22. P. Chaplais, 'Règlement des conflits internationaux franco-anglais au xive siècle (1293–1377)', *Le Moyen Age*, lvii (1951), 269–302.

23. G. P. Cuttino, *English Diplomatic Administration* (Oxford, 1940), ch. iii.

24. Gavrilovitch, op. cit., pp. 96–101, 124–44.

25. G. P. Cuttino, 'The Process of Agen', *Speculum*, xix (1944), 161–78.

26. For an estimate of the value of the revenues of the duchy at the beginning of the fourteenth century, G. P. Cuttino, *Le Livre d'Agenais* (1956), pp. xiii–xiv.

27. For Edward II's assignments of the revenues of Aquitaine to meet his debts, T. F. Tout, *The Place of Edward II in English History* (2nd ed., 1936), pp. 194–9; and Edward I's similar use of the revenues of Ponthieu, Hilda Johnstone, 'The County of Ponthieu, 1279–1307', in *EHR* xxix (1914), 448–9.

28. F. M. Powicke, *The Loss of Normandy* (Manchester, 1961), pp. 268–71; cf. the same writer's *King Henry III and the Lord Edward* (Oxford, 1947), i, 179–81.

29. Relations between the king of England and the duke of Brittany during the thirteenth century are summarised in *The Complete Peerage*, ed. G. E. Cokayne, new ed. V. Gibbs, x (1945), 800–14 (art. 'Richmond'): cf. S. Painter,

The Scourge of the Clergy, Peter of Dreux, Duke of Brittany (1937).

30. The writer hopes to argue this point in detail in a forthcoming article. Meanwhile, some of the points concerning the Norman colonisation of England and its consequences are suggested in Le Patourel, 'The Norman Colonization of Britain', in *I Normanni e la loro espansione in Europa nell'alto medio evo* (Spoleto, Centro Italiano di Studi sull'alto medioevo, 1969), pp. 409–38.

31. e.g. Ordericus Vitalis, *Historia Ecclesiastica*, ed. A. Le Prevost and L. Delisle (Société de l'histoire de France, Paris, 1838–55), v, 54–6.

32. For much of what follows, see Le Patourel, 'The Plantagenet Dominions', *History*, 1 (1965), 289–308, and 'The King and the Princes in Fourteenth-Century France', in *Europe in the Late Middle Ages*, ed. J. R. Hale, J. R. L. Highfield and B. Smalley (1965), and the evidence cited in these two articles.

33. It was one thing to cross the Channel from Southampton or Portsmouth to Barfleur, raise an army if necessary in Normandy and Anjou, and progress thus to Aquitaine; it was quite another thing to fit out a naval expedition on a comparable scale in England and to go to Bordeaux by sea.

34. Men like Henry Turberville (*DNB*, s.v. 'Turberville, Henry de') and Nicholas de Meules (references in Le Patourel, *Medieval Administration of the Channel Islands*, 1937, p. 122) in the thirteenth century, Otto de Grandison (C. L. Kingsford, 'Sir Otho de Grandison' in *TRHS* 3rd ser., iii, 125–95) and John Hevering (C. Bémont, *Rôles Gascons*, iii, 1906, lii–lxi) at the turn of the century, or Oliver Ingham (*The Complete Peerage*, ed. G. E. Cokayne, new ed. V. Gibbs, vii, 58–60) and Adam Limber (T. F. Tout, op. cit., p. 351 and H. G. Richardson and G. O. Sayles, *Administration of Ireland*, 1963, p. 94) in the fourteenth century.

35. e.g. Brittany (B.-A. Pocquet du Haut-Jussé, *Les Papes et les ducs de Bretagne*, Paris, 1928, i, 420), Normandy (E. G. Léonard, *Histoire de Normandie*, Paris, 1944, p. 69).

36. J. F. Lemarignier, *Recherches sur l'hommage en marche et les frontières féodales* (Lille, 1945), pp. 73–113.

37. 'Praeterea nobis dedit Rex Angliae viginti millia marcarum sterlingorum . . . propter rechatum nostrum. . . . Item Rex Angliae, sicut rectus heres, tenebit de nobis omnia feoda sicut pater ejus & frater ejus Rex Ricardus ea tenuerunt a nobis, & sicut feoda debent . . .', *Foedera*, i, 84; cf. Powicke, *Loss of Normandy*, pp. 134–8.

38. On Edward's claim, Le Patourel, 'Edward III and the Kingdom of France', *History*, xliii (1958), 173–89.

39. Le Patourel, ibid., and 'The Treaty of Brétigny' in *TRHS* 5th ser., x (1960), esp. p. 25.

2. The War Aims of the Protagonists and the Negotiations for Peace

JOHN PALMER

THE war aims of the two sides during the protracted series of conflicts known collectively as the Hundred Years War have been the subject of long and often heated debates, debates from which no general consensus has so far emerged. No interpretation of the fundamental issues of the war has yet commanded anything like universal agreement, and the particular ambitions of individual kings remain to a large extent either obscure or controversial. Was Edward III (1327–77) aiming for the French Crown, or was he merely defending his position in Aquitaine? Were the Valois kings of France intent on expropriating their neighbour, or were they merely protecting themselves from his unwarranted aggression? Did the aims of Henry V (1413–22) or Charles VII (1422–61) differ substantially from those of their predecessors? Was there any real continuity of objective on either side during the several phases of the war? In short, was the war a feudal,[1] dynastic, national, economic or merely predatory struggle, or was it a stable or fluctuating combination of some or all of these elements? To each and every one of these questions widely divergent answers have been returned, all of them based upon the materials provided by the peace negotiations.

In a certain sense – and in a sense very pertinent to these negotiations – the war was both a dynastic and a feudal struggle from the moment that Edward III assumed the title 'king of France' down to the final expulsion of the English armies from Aquitaine in 1453. Throughout this period it was to the advantage of France to represent the war as a feudal conflict, and to that of England to proclaim it a dynastic dispute. The reasons are clear enough. If the war was 'essentially a feudal quarrel between a Gascon vassal and his French overlord', then the Valois had right on their side and could quite properly chastise their rebellious vassal, even to the extent of confiscating his fief. If, on the other hand, the French Crown was at issue, then the war waged by the

Plantagenets was not a whit less just than that fought by their opponents and they could 'reasonably' – a word much favoured by the English Chancery in this context – lay claim to territories far in excess of their ancestral lands, as compensation for their magnaminity in offering to relinquish their claim to the throne. Each side, of course, rejected the formulation of the other; and though their immediate aims and their actual expectations may at times have fallen well short of their theoretical pretensions, neither ceased to proclaim these last to be their ultimate objectives.

There is no reason to believe that either side would have refrained from putting its claims into effect had circumstances permitted them to do so. Henry V made a calculated bid for the French throne in the autumn of 1419, and Edward III probably set himself the same objective in 1359, if with less assurance. For their part, the French kings were clearly determined to seize and hold Aquitaine. Only the prospect of an expensive war had kept them out of the duchy before 1337, and this deterrent lost all its force when Edward lay claim to the French throne. The war actually began when Philip VI (1328–50) confiscated Aquitaine in May 1337, and his subsequent conduct shows that he intended to retain it if possible. During peace negotiations held in the autumn of 1339 he refused to accept any settlement which left Edward with 'a single foot' of land in France,ª and this condition was repeated by his ambassadors at Avignon in 1344. On the latter occasion the papal mediators took him sufficiently seriously to propose that Edward should surrender the duchy in return for compensation elsewhere. When these negotiations had broken down, Philip publicly announced his intention of disinheriting his vassal by conferring his duchy on his own eldest son (11 September 1345).

Philip's successors shared his ambitions, though their hopes of realising them were rarely as well founded as his own had been. Charles V (1364–80) confiscated the duchy yet again in 1369, and in 1375 papal mediators were once more sufficiently impressed to propose that Edward withdraw voluntarily. At the end of 1399 Charles VI (1380–1422) tried to subvert the duchy, despite the existence of a truce, and two years later, following the precedent set by Philip VI, he created his eldest son, Louis, duke of Guyenne, a title Louis retained until his death in 1415. Thereafter, the military situation made the expulsion of the English a remote possibility for several decades, but when the tide had turned once again in their favour, the Valois showed no inclination to spare Aquitaine. After its final fall in 1453 there was never any prospect of its return to England by a negotiated settlement. Charles VII was thus the first of his dynasty to rule as sole king of France, but he was certainly not the first to entertain that ambition.

Since neither side managed to achieve the necessary political and military ascendency to enforce its own interpretation of what the war was about before 1453, negotiations were necessarily concerned to find a middle way between their extreme pretensions. Up to a point, compromise was always possible. After the early years of the war the French were prepared to offer fairly generous territorial concessions – more generous than is usually recognised – while their opponents repeatedly expressed their readiness to accept much less than the whole kingdom in return for a firm peace. But neither would consent to surrender sovereignty over the territories in question. The Plantagenets held out for a dynastic compromise: they insisted that their French territories should be detached from the kingdom of France and held 'from God alone'. As their ambassadors were prone to define it, they wanted to rule these lands 'as neighbour' to Valois France. For their part, the French would only accept a feudal compromise by which the ceded territories would remain within the kingdom of France, held in homage – the outward sign of the recognition of sovereignty – from the French Crown. The problem of sovereignty was the problem of the whole war in microcosm, and almost every peace conference came to grief over this issue.

Recognising its crucial importance, both sides were fertile in proposals to evade or resolve it. The most-favoured solution was what was quaintly but aptly described in 1439 as a 'half-peace'. This combined territorial concessions by one party with a long truce, an arrangement designed to circumvent the problem of sovereignty by deferring a solution for a number of years, or even decades. In 1439, for instance, mediators suggested a half-peace on the basis of territorial concessions to France and a truce of between fifteen and thirty years, a suggestion which elaborated a proposal made by the French themselves four years previously, when they had offered to postpone the question of sovereignty for seven years in return for immediate territorial concessions. The logical culmination of these proposals was the surrender of Maine by Henry VI (1422–61) in 1446, this being the price he had to pay for the truce of Tours (1444) and its subsequent extensions until 1450. However, a half-peace did not necessarily have to benefit France. On the eve of the Agincourt campaign, when peace negotiations had reached their customary state of deadlock on the issue of sovereignty, Henry V agreed to accept the territorial offers made by his opponents provided they were accompanied by a fifty-year truce, during which time the issue of sovereignty would remain in suspense. Three years later he made a similar offer, though his price had risen in the interval. But perhaps the most striking example of an advantageous half-peace can be found in the treaty of Brétigny; for whatever the intentions of its authors, the final effect of this treaty was to combine substantial territorial concessions to England with a truce of indefinite duration, an arrangement entirely beneficial to Edward III, who surrendered nothing in return for the territories he received. Finally, the device of a long truce deserves to be mentioned in this context. Like a half-peace, it was designed to evade the problem of sovereignty by deferring a solution beyond the lifetime of all concerned. The only difference between the two was that the twenty-six-year truce concluded in 1396, and the forty-year truce proposed in 1376, were both projected on the basis of the territorial *status quo*.

The frequency with which these devices were advocated – in 1356, 1360, 1376, 1396, 1415, 1418, 1435, 1439 and 1444 – highlights the virtual impossibility of arriving at a compromise over the issue of sovereignty. Even the apparently simple task of deferring a decision raised difficulties which almost defied resolution. Whenever a long truce or half-peace was proposed, the French always insisted that since it would permit their rivals to exercise a *de facto* sovereignty in the territories under their control, the English should make a comparable concession by ceasing to use the title 'king of France' for the duration of the agreement. To this demand the English ambassadors invariably retorted that to cease to use the title would be tantamount to acknowledging its illegitimacy, an acknowledgement which would be too dearly purchased by the mere exercise of a *de facto* sovereignty for a limited period. In other words, the attempt to defer a solution gave rise to almost exactly those difficulties which had made an immediate solution impossible. By a circuitous route, the two sides thus tended to arrive back at their original point of departure, the issue of sovereignty; and only in very special circumstances could the customary state of deadlock then be avoided.

Another favoured proposal – made in 1344, 1375, 1384, 1390-4 and 1435 – was to separate England and Aquitaine by conferring the duchy on an English prince, either for a number of years or in perpetuity. As a temporary expedient, this proposal had too many obvious disadvantages to appeal to the Plantagenets. Though it would – it was hoped – reconcile them to French sovereignty by relieving them of the humiliation of doing homage to their rival, this relief would only be short-lived and would be purchased at the expense of encumbering the duchy with French sovereignty for the future. At first sight the alternative of permanent alienation was even more disadvantageous. It would entail the total loss of the duchy to the English Crown and, in all probability, its assimilation to France in due course. Furthermore, the 'constitution' of Aquitaine stipulated that it was not to be separated from England except as a temporary fief for the heir to the throne,[3] and any attempt to infringe this constitution was certain to provoke Gascon opposition. Serious though they were, however, these disadvantages were balanced, if not outweighed by the potential advantages of a settlement of this nature. First and foremost, it was the only feasible diplomatic solution to the war. To the French, of course, it was highly acceptable; and to the English it represented the only solution that would enable them to withdraw from France without suffering public humiliation. Though the duchy would be lost to the Crown, it would remain in the hands of an English prince; and although his dynasty would in course of time almost certainly be assimilated by Valois France, this was too remote a prospect to make the proposal immediately unacceptable. In other respects it even appeared favourable to England; for the French were prepared to make generous territorial concessions in Aquitaine, and even to compromise their sovereignty over the duchy in return for its separation from England. These considerations persuaded Richard II (1377–99) to agree to a final peace on this basis; but unfortunately for all concerned, the treaty he negotiated with France was wrecked by the Gascons, who revolted in 1394 in defence of their 'liberty' of remaining attached to the English Crown.

Yet a third device for circumventing the obstacle of sovereignty was proposed by papal mediators in 1344 and 1375. Since Philip would not relinquish his sovereignty and Edward refused to alienate the duchy to one of his children, the mediators suggested that Edward should surrender Aquitaine to Philip in return for compensation elsewhere. Superficially, this appeared both a logical and an attractive proposal. The acquisition of – for instance – Scotland in return for the duchy might appear a good bargain. But this appearance was illusory, as the English ambassadors were quick to point out in 1344. For all the schemes of compensation proposed by the mediators involved their king in the surrender of both his dynastic and his feudal rights in return for concessions which it was not in Philip's power to make. What right had Philip to dispose of Scotland, imperial territory, or military and ecclesiastical benefices in England? The only way in which he could properly compensate his rival was with territory *in* France; and in this case, the problem of sovereignty remained to be solved. Once again the two sides had found their way back to their original point of departure, and deadlock ensued.

Ultimately, therefore, the feudal and dynastic pretensions of the two sides could not be reconciled and all attempts at compromise proved fruitless. But the very futility of the negotiations is significant of the nature of the war; and above and beyond this, they cast a revealing light upon the particular ambitions of individual rulers.

Until a few years ago there was general agreement among scholars as to the aims of Edward III. It was held that his ambitions fell considerably short of those of Henry V, that his main objective was to consolidate his position in Aquitaine, and that his assumption of the title 'king of France' was merely a tactical device designed to facilitate this end. However, this view has recently been vigorously challenged, and it has been argued that Edward took his claim to the throne seriously, pursued it as a feasible political objective, and was only induced to relinquish it – if, indeed, he did relinquish it – by a damaging military reverse. In the main, the evidence upon which this argument rests derives from the period between the French defeat at Poitiers in 1356 and the ratification of the treaty of Brétigny at Calais in October 1360. Before it is examined, a brief glance at the earlier and less successful part of Edward's reign is necessary.

On the death of Charles IV in 1328 Edward was the nearest surviving male heir to the French throne, and a formal claim to succeed was entered on his behalf; but after the more distant but all-male descent of Philip of Valois had been preferred, his claim was quietly dropped for the better part of a decade. By giving homage for Aquitaine in 1329, and by recognising this homage to be liege in 1331, Edward tacitly acknowledged the legitimacy of Philip's succession; and although English lawyers were subsequently to argue that he was under age and under constraint at this time, the fact remains that he made no effort to renew his claim on attaining his majority. Despite growing tension between the two countries after 1333, Edward continued to recognise his rival as king of France and to seek peace on the basis of the restitution of those of his ancestral lands which had been withheld since the war of 1324. Only after Philip's confiscation of Aquitaine on 24 May 1337 did he resurrect his claim, and even then he acted with considerable hesitancy. He actually adopted the style 'king of England and France' on 7 October 1337, but then immediately reverted to his customary titles, contenting himself with impugning the validity of Philip's title. Even in this he was not consistent. His final assumption of the style and insignia of the French Crown in January 1340 was clearly a result of the war, not its cause; and although this does not necessarily prove anything about his intentions after 1340, it should be a warning against taking too rigid a view of his aims.

Having committed himself to a dynastic war, Edward could no longer be content with a feudal peace; but this did not mean that he would accept nothing less than the Crown. Within a few months of assuming the French title, he had already formulated his terms for a 'reasonable' – i.e. a compromise – peace. In August, and again in November 1340 he informed Pope Benedict XII that he would agree to peace in return for an enlarged Aquitaine in full sovereignty.[4] In other words, he would accept a compromise between his inherited feudal rights and his recently asserted dynastic pretensions.

But the French spurned this offer, demanding that Edward renounce his claim to the throne as a preliminary to peace talks. When the two sides met before Clement VI at Avignon in 1344 – the first major conference of the war – this deadlock had still to be broken: the French would only negotiate on the basis of the last feudal settlement, the treaty of 1327, while the English insisted that their dynastic claims be taken into consideration. A breakdown was momentarily averted when the pope introduced the formula of 'compensation' into the talks; but when these resumed it quickly became apparent that the two sides were talking about different things. The English wanted compensation for their claim to the throne, in the form of additional territories held in full sovereignty; the French would only offer compensation for the surrender of Aquitaine, in the form of comparable (or even lesser) territories held in feudal dependence from the French Crown. This feudal-dynastic impasse could not be resolved and the talks broke down.

This deadlock was not to be broken during Philip's lifetime. On the eve of the battle of Crécy he was still seeking peace on the basis of the feudal settlement of 1327. Even the disastrous outcome of that battle and the imminence of the fall of Calais in the summer of 1347 could not induce him to consider anything like a dynastic compromise. He offered to guarantee the restitution of the Agenais if the siege of Calais were raised, but this was as far as he would go. This was, of course, a long way short of anything Edward was prepared to accept, and he brusquely broke off negotiations to concentrate on the capture of Calais.[5]

During the next few years an almost total obscurity descends upon the negotiations, an obscurity which may well conceal a lack of significant activity. When the darkness lifts in the early spring of 1353 Edward had clearly gained the upper hand, and for the first time (so far as we know) his demands were formulated with some precision: Aquitaine 'as entirely as his ancestors had held it', Normandy, Ponthieu, the over-lordship of Flanders, and the territories he held by right of conquest, all in full sovereignty. At a pinch, he expressed himself ready to relin-quish Normandy if the French could be shown to have the better right to it. In return for all this he was, he said, prepared to resign his claim to the French throne.

Formidable though they were, these demands were greatly increased in the following year. By the terms of a provisional treaty concluded at Guines on 6 April 1354, Edward was granted not only Aquitaine (in-cluding Poitou and Limousin), Ponthieu, Calais and Guines, but also Anjou, Touraine and Maine, all once more in full sovereignty. This was considerably more than Edward was able to extract from the French after the defeat and capture of King John at Poitiers, and John's readiness to contemplate such concessions at this date must be con-sidered the most mysterious episode in the entire war.[6]

The treaty of Guines was to have been finalised before the pope at Avignon in the autumn of 1354. Edward appears to have been eager to ratify it. He had already obtained parliamentary consent to conclude peace, and his ambassadors came to Avignon armed with powers to relinquish his title to the French throne. Moreover, although they were instructed to ask for Normandy as well as the territories stipulated in the treaty, they were empowered not only to forgo this additional demand but even to give up Angoumois and Quercy, previously claimed as part of the duchy of Aquitaine. It was not Edward but John who drew back. The treaty had to be scrapped when his ambassadors refused to surrender sovereignty over the territories they had offered to cede.[7]

Up to this point there is clearly little reason to believe that Edward was determined to win the French Crown. Certainly if he had such an ambition, he set about achieving it in a very curious manner. He had repeatedly expressed his readiness to settle for much less; he formally announced this fact to his own subjects on at least two occasions (1346, 1353), and he twice (1353, 1354) authorised his ambassadors to renounce his title in return for adequate compensation.[8] These scarcely seem the acts of a ruler sure of his rights and determined to enforce them. But though his ambitions may have fallen short of the Crown before 1356, the defeat and capture of his rival at Poitiers in that year obviously put him in an incomparably stronger position than any he had previously enjoyed: how did he react?

Between the triumphant return of the Black Prince to Bordeaux in the autumn of 1356 and the ratification of the treaty of Brétigny at Calais on 24 October 1360, no fewer than five separate agreements were concluded. Of the first, sealed at Bordeaux in March 1357, nothing is known. By the second, known as the first treaty of London (8 May 1358), Edward was granted an enlarged duchy of Aquitaine, the counties of Ponthieu and Guines, and the towns of Calais (with its march) and Montreuil, all in full sovereignty, together with the enormous sum of 4 million crowns (£666,666) for the ransom of King John. Aquitaine was generously defined to include, in addition to what Edward already held, Saintonge, Angoumois, Poitou, Limousin, Quercy, Périgord, Bigorre, Tarbes, Gaure and the Agenais: in other words, virtually all France south of the Loire, west of the Massif Central and north of the Pyrenees – something like a third of the kingdom.

The French were apparently willing to implement this treaty; but when they were unable to raise the first instalment of the ransom on time, Edward seized the opportunity afforded by their increased internal difficulties to tear up the treaty and press for an even more generous settlement. By the second treaty of London, concluded with the captive king on 24 March 1359, he was granted all that had been conceded by the treaty of 8 May 1358 *plus* the county of Boulogne, and Anjou, Touraine, Maine and Normandy – the whole of the Angevin empire, something like half of the kingdom – all in full sovereignty. But this was too much for the dauphin and the French Council, who rejected the agreement negotiated by their king with the now famous remark that it was 'ni passable, ni faisable'. Edward retaliated by invading France with the largest army he had so far launched across the Channel, only to be frustrated by the Fabian tactics of the dauphin. Towards the end of an inconclusive campaign the two sides resumed negotiations at Brétigny, near Chartres. There, two years to the day after the conclusion of the first treaty of London, the treaty of Brétigny was sealed (8 May 1360). Its terms were more or less identical with those of the earlier agreement. Aquitaine was enlarged by the addition of Rouergue and the Calais march by the inclusion of Hammes, but these concessions were counterbalanced by the reduction of King John's ransom from 4 million to 3 million crowns (£500,000). One other feature of the treaty was to prove crucial for the future. The clauses providing for John's renunciation of his sovereignty over the ceded territories and for Edward's renunciation of the Angevin empire and the French Crown were made prospective; and when the two kings ratified the treaty at Calais on 24 October, these clauses (11, 12) were taken out of the text – this was the only substantial alteration made at Calais – and embodied in a separate agreement known as the *littere cum clausula c'est assavoir*. The object of this arrangement was to allow time for the territorial clauses of the treaty to be implemented before the renunciations were exchanged. The *littere* provided that the renunciations would be made as soon as the territories had changed hands, and in any case before the end of November 1361. In the interval each party was to retain *but not use* its respective rights: Edward was to cease to call himself 'king of France' and John was to refrain from exercising his sovereignty over the ceded territories. In the event these renunciations were never exchanged, a fact which allowed Charles V (1364–80) to argue that he was entitled to resume the use of his sovereignty. He did so, precipitating the second phase of the war in 1369.

Superficially, these agreements prove that Edward's ambitions fell a long way short of the Crown, since their one common feature was his offer to disclaim it. But, as we have seen, this has been disputed, and it has been pointed out that the only concession demanded of Edward by the first treaty of London was the ransom of King John. Since this treaty did not stipulate that Edward should renounce his claim to the French throne it has been argued that it was not a *peace* treaty (as had previously been assumed), but simply a ransom pact, similar to those he negotiated at about the same time with the duke of Brittany (1356) and the king of Scotland (1357). As for the second treaty of London (24 March 1359), its terms were so extravagant that Edward could not possibly have intended to stop there: 'Did anyone seriously suppose that these territorial provisions could be carried out, or, if they were, that the rump of the kingdom of France could have survived as an independent state?' Finally, the treaty of Brétigny-Calais was a concession extracted from Edward by the disastrous failure of his campaign of 1359–60, and he clearly revealed his dissatisfaction with its terms by refusing to implement the renunciation clauses. Throughout these negotiations his object had been to weaken France by obtaining major territorial concessions without sacrificing any of his own rights: in a sense, this is what he achieved.

There is much in this argument which commands agreement. Once it is conceded – as it must be conceded – that Edward was fighting for more than his inherited rights, then there is clearly no reason to believe that he had set any sort of arbitrary limit to his ambitions. The alacrity with which he tore up the first treaty of London, and his failure to implement the renunciations which would have finalised the treaty of Brétigny both show that he was by no means satisfied with their terms, generous though these have been judged to be; and to this extent he has been underestimated by historians.

But it is a long jump from this to the conclusion that he made a sustained bid for the Crown in the years after the battle of Poitiers. In fact, at the very outset of these negotiations, Edward seems to have been prepared to settle for rather less than he eventually obtained. Though the terms of the provisional treaty concluded between the Black Prince and King John at Bordeaux in March 1357 are unknown, Edward's secret instructions to his son for the conduct of these negotiations have survived.[9] They reveal more clearly than any treaty could do just how limited – and just how opportunistic – his ambitions were at this date. The prince was instructed to initiate *peace* – the word deserves emphasis – talks, 'always remaining adamant on the question of having perpetual liberty with all the lands one can obtain'. If John were prepared to concede sovereignty, the prince could formally agree to peace negotiations; if he refused, then the prince was to press for half-peace: increased territorial concessions coupled with a temporary cession of sovereignty.

These instructions make it difficult to believe that the first treaty of London was intended simply as a ransom pact. Since only a draft of the terms of this treaty has survived, its failure to stipulate Edward's renunciation of the Crown is not necessarily conclusive. Against this omission must be set the fact that throughout the text of the draft Edward is denied the title 'king of France', which is freely accorded to King John and his successors. In view of the fact that the draft was produced by the English Chancery, this usage is incomprehensible unless we assume that Edward's renunciation of the title had in fact been agreed in principle. Moreover, the draft is headed 'The treaty and discussion of *peace*', and King John himself, his son and the pope all referred to the agreement as a peace treaty in their official correspondence.[10] Finally, though the analogy with contemporary ransom treaties with Scotland and Brittany is a tempting one, the fact remains that these agreements were simply financial transactions which, unlike the first treaty of London, did not involve territorial concessions.

Although the second treaty of London marks an enormous advance in Edward's pretensions, these still stopped some way short of the whole kingdom of France. Only when his inflated claims had been rejected by the French Council did he make a public bid for the throne by besieging Rheims and Paris; and when this gamble failed, he was forced back on the terms of his first agreement with King John. With the possible (but brief) exception of the winter months of 1359–60, therefore, Edward's utmost expectation seems to have been – as in 1354 – the old Angevin empire; and frustrated designs in this direction may account for his failure to implement the renunciation clauses of the treaty of Brétigny. But in any case, his failure to do so was quite consistent with his attitude to France throughout his reign. Within the broad limits set by his demand for more than his inherited rights at the one extreme and the French throne at the other, his ambitions were elastic and changed with changing circumstances. To the extent that he was an opportunist, his ultimate ambition was the Crown; but as he himself acknowledged by his repeated offers to renounce it, his chances of winning the throne were too unlikely for this to be considered his serious political objective.

The aims and achievements of the two French kings during this period have been rather obscured by the attention lavished on Edward III, and Philip VI has suffered particularly from this neglect. On the evidence of the peace negotiations, he was the most successful of the Valois kings until the very last years of the war. So far as is known, he never agreed to any substantial concessions, and for most of his reign he felt strong enough to hold out for an English surrender of Aquitaine. Even after the disaster at Crécy he would only offer Edward the restitution of his ancestral possessions, and then only if he raised the siege of Calais. Judged by what he was prepared to concede, he was considerably more successful than his much-praised grandson Charles V.

By contrast, his son John was easily the least successful of his dynasty. He was the only one of the French kings who could be reduced to agreeing to a partition of the kingdom, and about the only thing that can be said in his favour is that he did try to wriggle out of this concession. He eventually refused to ratify the treaty of Guines in 1354; and although he was saved by Edward's ambition rather than by any positive contribution of his own after 1360, he should perhaps be credited with the negative virtue of failing to implement the renunciation clauses of the treaty of Brétigny himself. For under the terms of the agreement made at Calais, renunciation by either party automatically involved renunciation by the other; so John could, had he so wished, have secured

Edward's surrender of his pretensions by disclaiming his own. He at least had the courage to take advantage of Edward's over-confidence. At the risk of losing even more of his kingdom, he was thus able to retain the sovereignty which his son was to exploit so effectively.

During the half-century following the renewal of the war in 1369, peace negotiations were dominated by discussion of the treaty of Brétigny, in much the same way as those prior to 1340 had been dominated by the treaty of Paris (1259). Once again, the issue of sovereignty reduced most of them to futility. If anything, this issue had become more acute than ever; for the skilful way in which Charles V turned the non-fulfilment of the renunciation clauses to his own advantage demonstrated afresh the crucial importance of sovereignty and the comparative insignificance of the territorial clauses of an agreement. The problem came to the fore in the first major conference of the period, held at Bruges between 1375 and 1377. As in 1344, papal mediators suggested that the English should relinquish their French possessions in return for compensation elsewhere and, again as in 1344, the suggestion was rejected out of hand. Next, they proposed that Aquitaine should be alienated to Edward's second surviving son, John of Gaunt, who should surrender his English lands to his father and become, in effect, a French prince and the founder of a new dynasty in Aquitaine. This proposal dominated the ensuing discussions. The French accepted it without reserve, and although he objected to becoming a vassal of Charles V, John of Gaunt did not reject the proposal outright. To get round Gaunt's objections, the mediators then suggested that Charles's sovereignty be subjected to certain limitations or 'modifications', a suggestion which apparently found favour with both sides.

Initially, therefore, a settlement appeared to be possible, but this hope was quickly shattered by two external factors. In the first place, John of Gaunt had an unresolved claim to the Castilian throne, and the French were naturally reluctant to see him established in Aquitaine before he had renounced it. Secondly, Gaunt himself came under a considerable cloud in England at this time. Both his father and his elder brother were dying, and he was suspected of harbouring designs on the throne of his nephew, the future Richard II. Indeed, it was even rumoured that he was using the peace negotiations as a cloak to hide his conspiratorial dealings with – of all men! – Charles V, who was to help seat him on the English throne in return for the surrender of the French possessions of the Crown. In such circumstances it was clearly out of the question to conclude a peace which would involve his own acquisition of Aquitaine at the expense of his nephew's inheritance, since this was certain to provoke a violent reaction from his domestic enemies.

Thereafter, the chances of a settlement receded rapidly. To minimise the problem of sovereignty, the mediators suggested various complicated partitions of the duchy, some parts being allocated to England in full sovereignty, others in temporary sovereignty for the life of Edward III, and others still in subjection to the French Crown. But these schemes failed to satisfy either side and eventually came up against Charles's adamant refusal to compromise his sovereignty in any respect. A proposed forty-year truce fared no better, for unresolved dynastic disputes in Brittany and Castile, and Charles's unwillingness to allow Edward the use of his French title during the truce, made it unacceptable to England. Though it dragged out its life until June 1377, the Bruges conference never looked like being successful after the failure of the mediators' initial proposals.

Given the state of the war, the best hope for the future lay in the separation of England and Aquitaine and the creation of a separate English dynasty in the duchy. But until Richard II had come of age and Gaunt's dynastic claims on Castile had been resolved, no such settlement was likely. There was a short-lived hope that both these conditions would be met in the years 1383-4, and towards the end of 1383 a preliminary peace on the basis of the alienation of Aquitaine to John of Gaunt was actually drawn up. But once again external factors wrecked the agreement. The settlement with Castile failed to materialise, and the concurrent outbreak of a succession war in Flanders put an end to the negotiations.

Finally, Gaunt sold out his claims on Castile in 1388, the war with France was brought to an end in 1389, and in the same year Richard declared himself of age. Thereafter, an agreement was only a matter of time. On 2 March 1390 Richard II publicised the basis of the peace he had in mind by creating his uncle duke of Aquitaine for life; and eventually, on 16 June 1393, preliminary articles of peace were drawn up. By these articles, England was granted Calais and its march in the north, and that part of the duchy of Aquitaine which lay to the south of the river Charente: Saintonge, the Agenais, Périgord, Limousin, Quercy (including Montauban), Angoumois, Rouergue, Tarbes, Bigorre and Gaure, together with the homage of the counts of Foix, Armagnac and Périgord and of the *vicomte* of Limoges. North of the Charente special provision was to be made for the key port of La Rochelle.

It has been understood that the duchy would be finally alienated to

John of Gaunt as soon as circumstances permitted. But when Richard attempted to implement this part of the agreement, the Gascons rebelled (April 1394) in order to maintain their attachment to the English Crown; and when Gaunt's efforts to overawe his reluctant subjects by a display of military force failed to induce them to change their minds, the provisional treaty of 1393 had to be scrapped. With it disappeared the most promising solution to the long-drawn-out Anglo-French conflict which had so far been devised.

After this, the two sides fell back on the unsatisfactory expedients of a ong truce and a marriage alliance. During these negotiations (1394–6), Richard seemed for one moment to have been seduced by the ambitions of his grandfather; for he demanded no less than the reconstitution of the Angevin Empire for the benefit of his children by Isabel of France, his prospective bride. But this demand was very quickly dropped, and by two agreements concluded in Paris on 9 March 1396 Richard settled for a large dowry (£166,666) and a twenty-six-year truce, a truce which should have ended the war until 1424. It did so – officially, at least – until 1415. Yet for most of this period negotiations hung fire, a fact which reveals just how remote the prospect of a negotiated peace had now become.

Apart from the abortive attempt to separate England and Aquitaine, the main interest of the second phase of the war (1369–89) lies in the extent to which Charles V and his son were brought to compromise their original hopes of expelling their opponents altogether. Charles had confiscated the duchy at the beginning of the war, and three years later his ambassadors were still proclaiming that it was forfeit because of the 'manifest rebellion' of Edward III and the Black Prince in opposing the Gascon appeals. By 1377, however, the French king was prepared to offer Edward most of the territories south of the Dordogne, together with a string of castles on the right bank of the river. Although Charles reserved his sovereignty, historians have been surprised at the extent of his generosity. However, it has not been observed that only two years later he increased his offer to include Saintonge south of the Charente, Rouergue, Périgord, Montauban and its territory, and – at a pinch – Limousin. A glance at the map will reveal that this almost doubled the offer of 1377, and in subsequent years it was enlarged still further. In 1381 Angoumois was added, and by 1393 Charles VI had agreed to cede La Rochelle, to endorse the English tenure of Calais and Guines, to incorporate Limousin in the duchy, and to recognise the duke's suzerainty over the neighbouring vassals of the French Crown. By this date

the duchy was defined to comprise something like two-thirds of Aquitaine as constituted by the treaty of Brétigny – considerably more than
the territories due to England under the treaty of Paris (1259) or held by
her at the outbreak of the war. Neither Charles V nor Charles VI was
able to take so strong a line as Philip VI, let alone to adopt the haughty
tones of his immediate Capetian ancestors.

Until 1399 the negotiations were dominated by the treaty of Brétigny.
Almost all the conferences took it as their point of departure, and when
articles of peace were agreed upon in 1393 they used the treaty as their
basis and even followed its text verbatim where this was possible.
Negotiations under Henry IV (1399–1413) are extremely obscure, but
they appear to have followed a similar course. When Henry first intervened in the civil war between Burgundians and Armagnacs in 1411,
the price for his assistance to the duke of Burgundy was the restitution
of Aquitaine,[11] and when he allied with the Armagnacs in the following
year, it was stipulated in the treaty of Bourges (18 May 1412) that he
would be restored to the duchy as defined by the treaty of Brétigny.
In neither case, it should be noted, did the rival factions offer to return
these territories with sovereignty.

Until the accession of Henry V (1413–22), therefore, both the French
Crown and the Angevin Empire had faded into the background, but it is
generally recognised that with his advent the war was transformed into
a dynastic struggle. 'Henry', it has been said, 'was not interested in
Aquitaine.' His ambitions were not bounded by the duchy, nor by any
part of France; from the first he was intent on uniting the two kingdoms
under a single dynasty. Since this was what the treaty of Troyes appeared
to give him, it is easy to understand how this belief has arisen; but on
the evidence of the peace negotiations, this is not what he set out to
achieve. Their testimony is unambiguous: until 1416 his ambitions
were limited to the implementation of the treaty of Brétigny, and thereafter they increased only to keep pace with his military conquests. Not
until 10 September 1419 did he make a bid for the French Crown.

According to his biographer, Henry had named the restitution of
Aquitaine as his price for peace within a few months of ascending the
throne. He had certainly set himself this target by the spring of 1414, for
his negotiations for an alliance with the duke of Burgundy at that time
were very largely devoted to the problem of defining the extent of the
duchy. By the autumn it had been agreed that the duchy should have the
boundaries prescribed by the treaty of Brétigny, and also that the duke
of Burgundy should help Henry to 'recover and obtain' – not 'conquer'

– what was rightfully his. But as in 1411, the issue of sovereignty was ducked, presumably because John the Fearless would not make this final concession. The negotiations consequently proved fruitless.

In August 1414, while the Anglo-Burgundian talks were still in progress, Henry's ambassadors were laying his demands before the French Council in Paris. They began with a formal claim to the throne which, after 'a short interval', they reduced to the whole of the Angevin Empire, including sovereignty over Brittany and Flanders, together with the territories between the Somme and Flanders. Having sufficiently impressed their audience, they then 'descended' to their basic conditions: restitution of everything granted by the treaty of Brétigny, including the arrears of King John's ransom, and a dowry of 2 million crowns (£333,333) with the hand of Catherine, daughter of Charles VI. For good measure they threw in a claim to half the county of Provence, a claim dating from the thirteenth century; but they were told that Provence was not the domain of Charles VI, and that their business should be with the duke of Anjou. At this point they refused to budge, insisting that they 'remain and will remain' firm in their demand for the implementation of the treaty of Brétigny. In reply the French, while denying that Henry had any legitimate claim on them, offered him the greater part of Aquitaine south of the Charente: Saintonge south of the river, Angoumois, Périgord, Rouergue, Quercy (excluding Montauban), the Agenais, Bigorre and Tarbes, all in fee and demesne – i.e. not in sovereignty – together with a dowry of 600,000 crowns (£100,000). In view of the generosity of this offer, they expressed the hope that Henry would forgo the arrears of the ransom. In the ensuing discussions the English lowered their price for a marriage to a million crowns and offered to cede Montreuil and Ponthieu in perpetuity to Henry's second son, an arrangement which would in all probability eventually result in their reintegration with France.

When negotiations were resumed in Paris in March 1415 the only substantial development was an increase in the dowry offered by the French, to 800,000 crowns. By this date Henry's military preparations were well advanced. In a dramatic last-minute bid to avoid war, a French embassy was sent to his headquarters in June, authorised to add Limousin and a further 50,000 crowns to their previous offers. Though the territorial gap between the two sides was still considerable, the fundamental problem was once again the issue of sovereignty. To get round this Henry offered to accept the French concessions if they were combined with a fifty-year truce, but the French embassy would not even agree to report this offer back to their government. Their refusal sealed the fate of the negotiations, and on 6 July Henry formally declared war. Despite the enormous sacrifices he had contemplated in passing over his rights to the French Crown, to Normandy, Anjou, Touraine, Maine, Flanders and to the sovereignty of Brittany, the French, he declared, would not even allow him the territories to which he was entitled under the treaty of Brétigny, nor would they specify the manner in which he was to hold the meagre territories they had offered him. It was therefore apparent to all that they were determined to deny him justice, and so to enforce his just claims he had no choice but to go to war.[12]

The French attitude up to this point deserves some comment. Almost unanimously, historians on both sides of the Channel have condemned the 'amazing docility' and 'abject surrender' of the French reaction to Henry's initial demands; but it is difficult to see on what basis such judgements were formed. The Armagnacs had stood firm – and were to continue to do so – on the crucial issue of sovereignty, and their terri-torial offers had not been outstandingly generous: their final proposals would have conceded only fractionally more than Charles V had been prepared to surrender in 1379 and distinctly less than Charles VI would have lost under the agreement of 1393. The dowry they offered with the hand of Catherine was only marginally greater than what Richard II had obtained with her sister Isabel. In view of the virtual state of civil war in France and the obviously aggressive intentions of Henry V, the Armagnacs were commendably firm.

The early stage of the war produced no fundamental change in the attitude of either side. During negotiations held in London in May and June 1416 Henry raised his terms so as to include his one conquest, Harfleur, but otherwise the Agincourt campaign proved sterile. As for the Armagnacs, Agincourt, the naval disaster of 1416, and even the initial stages of the conquest of Normandy failed to shake their nerve. In May 1417 they publicised their determination not to surrender the all-important county of Poitou by conferring it on the new dauphin, Charles; and during a peace conference held at Barneville in November they demanded the surrender of Henry's Norman conquests and offered him in return only part of the duchy of Aquitaine, and that to be held in homage from the French Crown.

By the autumn of 1418 most of Normandy was in Henry's hands and his terms had risen proportionately. At a conference held at Alençon in November he demanded Normandy and the Brétigny territories, either in full sovereignty or under the terms of a half-peace. By this date the Armagnacs had taken a severe beating, not only from Henry but also from the Burgundians, who had not only taken Paris but had got possession of Charles VI. For the first time they were forced to make substantial concessions, but even so they would still offer Henry only what he had actually conquered over and above their original offer of Aquitaine south of the Charente, and they remained adamant in their refusal to relinquish sovereignty over these territories. Once again the negotiations broke down over this crucial issue.

Meanwhile, by acquiring the person of Charles VI, the duke of Burgundy had qualified himself to participate in these negotiations on a more or less equal footing with his rivals. In June 1419 he, Charles and Henry met at Melun, and there agreed on the preliminaries of peace. Henry was to have Normandy and the Brétigny territories, both in full sovereignty. This agreement gave Henry all that he had seriously demanded up to this date; but when the moment came to reduce its terms to writing, the French drew back. First, they demanded that Henry renounce any future rights he might acquire in France, then they raised difficulties once again over the cession of sovereignty, and finally, they refused to ratify the agreement. The conference then broke up in disorder.

A little over a month later the situation in France was completely transformed by the assassination of John the Fearless on 10 September 1419. By this ill-considered act of violence the dauphin threw the Burgundians into Henry's arms. The effect on Henry was electrifying. After Agincourt, he had added one French town to his demands; after the conquest of Normandy, he added Normandy; but after the assassination of the duke of Burgundy, he refused to accept anything less than the whole kingdom. He had made his bid for the throne within a week of John's death. By the new year his conditions had been accepted by the new duke of Burgundy, and on 21 May 1420 they were incorporated in the treaty of Troyes. By this treaty, Charles VI retained his throne for life but the succession was vested in Henry and his successors, to the exclusion of the dauphin. Once united, the two Crowns were to be indivisible, though neither country was to be subject to the other and each was to be governed by its own laws. In the interval Henry was to act as regent, retaining Normandy as a personal appanage. It was stipulated that no one was to treat with the dauphin except with the consent of the other parties and of the Three Estates of the two kingdoms, and Henry promised to do his best to bring the Armagnacs into the obedience of the French Crown. Finally, the treaty was capped by Henry's marriage to Catherine on 2 June.

It has been said that 'whereas the treaty of Brétigny had allayed the feudal quarrel by the creation of an Aquitaine outside French control, the treaty of Troyes settled the dynastic conflict by making Henry V heir to the throne of France'. On paper, this may have been the case, but in practice things were very different. The so-called treaty of Troyes was not in effect a peace treaty between England and France – still less a dynastic settlement between Plantagenet and Valois – but rather an alliance between England and Burgundy. The feudal-dynastic impasse remained unresolved, as Henry himself recognised. On his death-bed he is reliably reported to have instructed his advisers not to consent to peace with the dauphin unless Normandy (and presumably Aquitaine) were ceded to his son in full sovereignty; but even at the very lowest point of his fortunes the dauphin steadfastly refused to consent to a partition of the kingdom.

Henry's dying instructions may be taken as representative of his attitude in general. At the moment when circumstances seemed to favour it, he made his bid for the French throne; but when the continued resistance of the dauphin appeared to put this beyond his reach, he was prepared to modify his ambitions once more to suit changing circumstances in order to extract the utmost possible advantage from them. He was no bigoted idealist, inexorable in his pursuit of 'just rights' to which he was mystically committed. Like Edward III he was a realist and an opportunist of genius. Though their achievements may have been dissimilar, the aims of these two kings were essentially identical.

The deadlock created by the dauphin's refusal to dismember the kingdom, prolonged by military stalemate, was only finally broken by the desertion of the Burgundians, who returned to their French allegiance under the treaty of Arras (21 September 1435), thereby annulling the treaty of Troyes, which played virtually no part in subsequent negotiations. Aware of an impending Burgundian desertion, the English government had resumed negotiations with the French in the early 1430s, and in 1435 a full-scale conference met at Arras. It is usually stated that the talks ended in deadlock over the conflicting claims to the French Crown, but this does not appear to have been the case. For though the English delegation denied any intention of surrendering their master's rights, they eventually implied a readiness to do so on advantageous terms by their final offer: 'the kyng shall content hym withe that he is possessed of in Fraunce at this day, and the partie adverse on that other side to holde stille that he now occupiethe semblably, *eche of hem as voisin* [*neighbour*] *to other*', with such territorial adjustments as might be necessary to rationalise the situation. But once again the French were adamant on the issue of sovereignty and refused to agree to a partition of the kingdom. If Henry would surrender Anjou, Touraine and Maine, give restitution to the disinherited in Normandy and release the duke of Orléans for a 'reasonable' sum, they offered to allow him to hold his remaining lands as fiefs of the French Crown, and even to defer his recognition of sovereignty for seven years. But this was their utmost concession and it was rejected by the English.

Four years later another conference held in Picardy followed a somewhat similar course. The English came prepared to accept the Angevin Empire as their slice of the kingdom, but inevitably the French refused even to discuss a partition. After long and acrimonious discussions the English delegation eventually agreed to refer back to their government the terms of a half-peace proposed by the French as their final offer. In return for a truce of between fifteen and thirty years during which time he was to cease to use his title 'king of France', Henry was offered Normandy (excluding Mont-Saint-Michel), Calais, Guines and what he actually held in Aquitaine, provided that he made restitution to the dispossessed Norman lords and released the duke of Orléans without ransom. Not surprisingly, these terms were rejected by the English government. In their place they offered to accept a final peace in return for the cession of Normandy, Calais and Aquitaine (the latter as constituted by the treaty of Brétigny) in full sovereignty. The French did not even deign to consider this offer.

Thus by 1439 the English were prepared to accept peace on the terms first formulated by Henry V in 1418, and to relinquish Anjou, Touraine and Maine and their claims to the throne in return for a sovereign Normandy and Aquitaine. They maintained these conditions during the last two important conferences of the war, held at Tours in 1444 and in London in 1445. But by this date the French had reduced their offers drastically. Not only did they remain adamant in their refusal to surrender their sovereignty, but now they would not even offer Normandy as a fief. In 1444 they would only contemplate the cession of Guyenne, Quercy, Périgord and Calais; and in 1445 they could only be induced to add Saintonge and Limousin. Charles V had been more generous in 1379 and the Armagnacs had offered more to Henry V even before he went to war. The English were clearly on their last legs. To purchase even a temporary respite they had to agree to the surrender of Maine in 1446.

Characteristically enough, the Hundred Years War was terminated by force, not diplomacy. Even after they had been expelled from France the English could not bring themselves to abandon their pretensions, and subsequent negotiations could never arrive at more than a truce, and that was usually of short duration. Not until 1802 did they finally surrender their claim to the French throne.

At first sight these protracted negotiations present a picture of unrelieved opportunism on both sides. Up to a certain point this is undoubtedly the case. At its most ambitious each side sought to disinherit the other, and this feature was as apparent at the beginning of the war as at its end. At the same time both were prepared to compromise when circumstances dictated, to the extent of making territorial concessions. But on one central issue both remained inflexible. The least the Plantagenets would settle for was a dynastic compromise which gave them a share of the kingdom of France, while the most the Valois would offer was a feudal settlement which preserved its integrity. On this point of principle almost all the negotiations came to grief.

BIBLIOGRAPHICAL NOTE

SOURCES: The major treaties of the war are conveniently gathered in E. Cosneau, *Les grands traités de la Guerre de Cent Ans* (Paris, 1889). In addition, the treaty of Guines is printed by F. Bock, 'Some New Documents Illustrating the Early Years of the Hundred Years' War', *Bulletin of the John Rylands Library*, xv (1931), 34-6; the first treaty of London by R. Delachenal, *Histoire de Charles V* (5 vols, Paris, 1909-31), ii, 402-11; important documents subsidiary to the treaty of Calais in *Foedera*, vi, 219 ff.; and the treaty of 1393 by J. J. N. Palmer, 'Articles for a Final Peace Between England and France', *BIHR* xxxix (1966), 182-5.

Next to the treaties themselves, the journals of the peace conferences provide the most important source materials. That of 1344 is published in Froissart, *Chroniques*, ed. K. de Lettenhove (Brussels, 1867-77) xviii, 235-56;* that of 1375-7 by E. Perroy, 'Anglo-French Negotiations at Bruges, 1374-1377', *Camden Miscellany*, xix (1952);* those of 1377-84 in *Voyage Littéraire de deux Bénédictins*, ed. E. Martène and U. Durand (2 vols, Paris, 1721-4), ii, 307-60; those of 1414 for the Anglo-Burgundian talks by O. Cartellieri, 'Beiträge zur Geschichte der Herzöge von Burgund', *Sitzungsberichte der Heidelberger Akademie der Wissenschaften*, iv, no. 9 (Heidelberg, 1913); that of June-July 1415 in *Recueil de diverses pièces servant à l'histoire de Charles VI*, ed. G. Besse (Paris, 1660), pp. 94-111; that of 1418 in *Foedera*, ix, 632-45; those of 1435 in F. Schneider, *Der Europäische Friedenskongress von Arras* (Griess, 1919), pp· 81–151; that of 1439 in *PPC* v, 334–407;* and those of 1444–5 in J. Stevenson (ed.), *Letters and Papers Illustrative of the Wars of the English in France* (2 vols, Rolls Series, 1861–4), i, 87–159. Finally, miscellaneous memoirs, instructions, notarial instruments, etc. of particular importance can be found in Bock, op. cit., pp. 27–42 (1353–6); *Rot. Parl.*, ii, 251–2 (1353), ibid., iii, 166 (1384), 315–16 (1394); *PPC* i, 19–23 (1390), ibid., ii, 350–8 (1418); *Foedera*, vii, 802–20 (1395–6), ibid., ix, 208–15 (1414–15), 722–7, 779 (1419), 786–91 (1413–19); H. Moranvillé, 'Conférences entre la France et l'Angleterre, 1388–93', *BEC* l (1889), 367–80; P. Bonenfant, *Du meurtre de Montereau au traité de Troyes* (Brussels, 1958), appendices; Schneider, op cit., pp. 151–219 (1435); Stevenson, op. cit., ii, pt. 2, 431–3 (1435); and in E. Martène and U. Durand, *Veterum Scriptorum . . . amplissima collectio*, viii (Paris, 1733), 864–8 (1435).

SECONDARY LITERATURE: There is no good over-all survey. For the negotiations up to 1342, E. Déprez, *Les préliminaires de la Guerre de Cent Ans* (Paris, 1902), is very good and much superior to H. Jenkins, *Papal Efforts for Peace under Benedict XII, 1334–42* (Philadelphia, 1933). In 'La conférence d'Avignon', *Essays to T. F. Tout*, ed. A. G. Little and F. M. Powicke (Manchester, 1925), pp. 301–20, Déprez has also provided a lucid account of the negotiations of 1344. On the mysterious negotiations of 1353–4, Bock, op. cit. provides the essential documentation and Kenneth Fowler, *The King's Lieutenant; Henry of Grosmont, Duke of Lancaster* (1969), the most recent and stimulating discussion. For the various treaties between 1356 and 1360 the superlative work of Delachenal, op. cit., is indispensable, but should be read in conjunction with the challenging essay by J. Le Patourel, 'The Treaty of Brétigny', *TRHS* 5th ser., x (1960), 19–39. E. Perroy's brief and cogent introduction to his volume in the Camden Series (see above) supersedes all earlier work on the negotiations between 1369 and 1377, and my own essay, 'Anglo-French Peace Negotiations, 1390 to 1394', *TRHS* 5th ser., xvi, 81–94, provides new material and a new interpretation for that period. Though still valuable for its documentary appendices, Moranvillé, op. cit., is now superseded. The whole period 1375 to 1399 is reinterpreted in my forthcoming book. The reign of Henry IV is both poorly documented and neglected, but the important negotiations of 1411 to 1413 are well described by F. Lehoux, *Jean de France, duc de Berri*, iii (Paris, 1967). For the negotiations between the assassination of John the Fearless and the conclusion of the treaty of Troyes, P. Bonenfant, op cit., is excellent; but otherwise – astonishingly enough – there is no completely satisfactory analysis of the reign of Henry V. Despite its age, G. du Fresne de Beaucourt, *Histoire de Charles VII* (6 vols, Paris, 1881–91), i, ch. 8, is easily the best of the existing accounts; none of the many English biographies and histories can be trusted. By contrast, J. G. Dickinson, *The Congress of Arras* (Oxford, 1955), provides a model account of the negotiations of 1435, and one which deserves special mention for its careful description of the sources and its detailed exposition of the workings of a medieval peace conference. Finally C. T. Allmand has provided some new material for the negotiations of 1439 in 'The Anglo-French Negotiations, 1439', *BIHR* xl (1967), 1–33, and Du Fresne de Beaucourt, op. cit., iv, a workmanlike account of those of 1444 and 1445.

* = Particularly interesting.

NOTES

1. i.e. concerned with Aquitaine.

2. Froissart, *Oeuvres*, xviii, 93.

3. J. Le Patourel, 'The Plantagenet Dominions', *History*, l (1965), 301–2.

4. *Benôit XII: Lettres closes . . .*, ed. G. Daumet (Paris, 1889), no. 763; E. Déprez, *Préliminaires*, pièce no. 13.

5. Adae Murimuth, *Continuatio Chronicarum*, and Robertus de Avesbury, *De Gestis Mirabilibus Regis Edwardi Tertii*, ed. E. M. Thompson (Rolls Series, 1889), pp. 215, 392–3.

6. The most recent discussion is by K. Fowler, *The King's Lieutenant*, ch. 9, 11.

7. *Chronicon Galfridi Le Baker de Swynbroke*, ed. E. M. Thompson (Oxford, 1889), pp. 123–5.

8. *Rot. Parl.*, ii, 252; *Foedera*, v, 496–8, 779, 795.

9. F. Bock, 'Some New Documents Illustrating the Early Years of the Hundred Years' War', *Bulletin of the John Rylands Library*, xv (1931), 41.

10. R. Delachenal, *Histoire de Charles V* (5 vols, Paris, 1909–31), ii, 62–72 and appendices.

11. F. Lehoux, *Jean de France, duc de Berri* (4 vols, Paris, 1966–8), iii, 242.

12. Arch. nat., J 646/14 (=Museum showcase AE III, 72).

3. The Organisation of War

H. J. HEWITT

THE aim of this essay is to describe the extensive and co-ordinated preparations for landing armies in Flanders or France, and the activities of such armies on the very many days when they were not fighting battles. With leadership, skill in arms, victories and defeats, spoils and ransoms we shall not attempt to deal. It is neither the Romance of War nor the Art of War, but some aspects of the Practice of War that we seek to explain. And the Practice of War involved 'civilians' far more closely than has hitherto been noted.

The neglect of the civilian's involvement in the Hundred Years War is fairly easily explained. War had been considered, to cite the dictionary as a 'contest between states carried on with arms'. It was, therefore, an activity of men who wielded arms, a class whose function was the defence of the realm. Creditable performance in arms brought honour and renown, and led to a literature in which noble conduct in war was among the highest virtues and, therefore, worthy in Froissart's words 'to be enregistered and put in perpetual memory'. The narratives in verse and prose of real or imaginary adventures seldom referred to the subsidiary activities – mere crafts? – which make knightly deeds possible: the provision of arms without which there could be no 'feats of arms', or the provision of ships without which there could be no campaigns beyond the sea, or the sources of food without which – since 'an army marches on its stomach' – there could be no army!

Military historians, basing their studies on the chronicles wrote of the Art of War, pictured the long conflict as the activity of soldiers isolated from the life and work of the nation in England or in France. It is, however, now recognised that an adequate history of any war should include an account of the roles and experiences of the civilians of the warring nations. The field of study is no longer the army-at-war, but the nation-at-war. It should, therefore, cover the work of all who directly or indirectly aid or hinder the nation's effort and the experiences of all whose lives are affected by the war.

If this wider conception of the field of study is applied to the Hundred Years War, it leads to some homely but indispensable aspects of war work, to the discovery of civilian suffering, and to episodes unpictured in the illuminated manuscripts and unmentioned in the chronicles. But it reveals some of the fundamentals of the war.

I

One fundamental was the defence of England. The circumstances of the time made it impossible to conceal preparations for the dispatch of troops to the Continent. The French, therefore, could seek to take counter-measures in their own land, or attack English ports, or plan an invasion of England. The Scots could foresee an opportunity for extensive raiding which the French encouraged them to exploit to the uttermost. Before, therefore, a single English soldier set foot on French soil, the defence of England had to be assured.

From Wales, except during the Glendower period, no danger was to be expected. Cheshire, once the main source of archers for war in the Principality, could provide troops for wars in France; the native Welsh could now be recruited for that purpose. But the northern counties must be ever prepared for attacks by the Scots, and the southern counties ready to repel invasion by the French.

The situation was brought home vividly by a series of French attacks on the southern ports in 1338–40. Harwich was burnt, Southampton plundered and burnt, the Isle of Wight raided and several other places damaged. The distribution and severity of these attacks and the frequent appearances of French fleets off the southern coast revealed the French capacity for menacing, and it might be invading, England. From the Isle of Wight and neighbouring regions and especially from Southampton, the population fled inland. Though prompt measures were taken to rebuild and fortify the town, it was only with great difficulty that the former inhabitants could be induced or compelled to return. Till Henry V's conquest of Normandy, there was a widespread view that the southern counties were never wholly safe from invasion.

That the French would attempt an invasion of England was repeatedly declared by proclamation; it amounted to a kind of news service to the people. Sometimes it was a simple prediction: the French are about to invade England. Sometimes it was more specific: the French intend to land in Kent (or another county). Sometimes it was horrifying: the French are about to attempt a landing; if they succeed, they will perpetrate horrible deeds. The assertions were not wholly groundless, for each side knew a good deal of the other's plans and, indeed, in 1346 an authentic copy of a French scheme for an invasion of England was discovered, brought to London and made known to the nation.

Defence measures, therefore, were taken on a scale and with a thoroughness greater than the nation had hitherto known. On the principle that 'all men must be compelled to repel enemies if they invade the realm', the men of the coastal counties, especially those bordering the Channel, were called on to fulfil their military obligation to defend their localities. The spheres of operations were the 'maritime lands' in their own counties, a strip deemed to extend inland for six leagues from the coast. All men living in these coastal counties were liable for service in this coastal area. Their function was the *garde de la mer*.

Keepers or wardens were appointed for the maritime lands in each county. Their duties were to guard the coast, to be responsible for the beacons and to take whatever action was necessary in their several counties. The sheriff (after due warning) had to parade the posse for their inspection; arrayers had to lead fencible men as the keepers directed; the public were ordered to give the keepers every assistance.

In some instances, the same men acted as keepers for adjoining counties (e.g. Norfolk and Suffolk) and in 1346 a scheme was drawn up under which, at the request of the keepers, men of certain inland counties had to be sent to aid the men of the coastal counties (e.g. the men of Hertford and Middlesex might be sent to Essex). Moreover, as the century advanced, the sheriffs of the coastal counties became associated with, rather than subordinate to, the keepers.

The principles underlying the *Garde de la Mer* had been understood for centuries. Though there were occasional murmurs about the burden of the *Garde*, petitions that it should operate 'at the king's cost', and, of course, efforts to avoid it, the obligation did not violate age-old principles, but its application did impose greater burdens than earlier generations had borne. There arose also the awkward problem of ensuring that men liable for service were actually resident in their counties for, as already mentioned, from the areas in which French attacks had occurred or been predicted, the inhabitants tended to move inland. Time after time proclamations were issued commanding all men holding lands in coastal counties to live on their estates.

When the war was resumed in 1369, the defence system was modified; the keepers of the maritime lands were replaced by the arrayers who were directed to raise men and lead them to the coast or elsewhere within their counties where danger threatened. But warnings about invasion and strict orders for residence in coastal counties continued to be issued. There were stern warnings in 1386, for a large French army and fleet were assembled in Flanders for many weeks with the declared intention of invading England. Additional defence measures were, therefore, taken and there were strong precautions in 1404, 1415 and 1416.

At times, French fleets swept up and down the Channel. Lightning raids could not be prevented but they were few. Winchelsea had been burned in 1360; Rye and Hastings were sacked and Gravesend burned in 1377; the Isle of Wight threatened, Plymouth and other southern ports plundered in 1404. In all, the damage sustained was trifling compared with the damage inflicted in France.

Warnings of Scottish intentions to invade the northern counties were fewer, but there were serious incursions into Cumberland, Northumberland and Durham.

II

Though the chroniclers deal at length with the armies – their leaders, marches and battles – they throw very little light on the methods by which armies were raised, the wages the fighting men received, the ships in which they were taken overseas or the victuals and other stores the ships carried. On these and allied topics much research has been concentrated during the last few decades. Perhaps the most important result has been the clarification of the change which took place in the fourteenth century from obligatory service to contractual service, that is from the compulsory to the voluntary. The change was not introduced as a single stroke of policy, but gradually as circumstances revealed its advantages or even its necessity.

Under the earlier system, when it was necessary to raise an army for service outside the kingdom, commissioners were appointed in each county and directed to 'choose, test and array' a certain number of the best (or it might be the fittest, or strongest or most skilled) men within the county. To these terse instructions there was usually added an order to provide for each man a suit and 'competent arms'. In some instances the arrayers had also to provide horses. It cannot be assumed that they were able to apply uniform standards of selection in their various counties, or that the weapons supplied were uniform in pattern, or that the ratio of men demanded to the population of a county was uniform, though there was evidently a desire to make demands proportional to population.

In practice, the arms supplied were commonly a bow, a sheaf of arrows and some kind of knife or lance. As for the clothing, there is very little evidence of its nature, colour or manufacture except the articles supplied to the Cheshire archers and the lancers of Flintshire. For these groups the material was woollen; the clothing consisted of a short coat and a hat; the colour was green and white with green on the right side, white on the left.

Thus selected, equipped and clothed, the 'civilians' were converted into soldiers and available for service. In some instances they had to be sent to a port immediately. In others, they were to be held in readiness till further instructions were received. There may have been twenty from a small county, forty from another, fifty from a larger county and, though among their number there were probably a few craftsmen, by the time they reached the port, they were likely to fall in with a group recruited specifically for their skill or experience as miners, carpenters or smiths.

Before following them to the coast, mention must be made of a two-fold controversy surrounding the county levies. The principle of obligatory service had been extended from the defence of the locality to the defence of the realm and was now extended to service on the continent of Europe. The legality of this step was warmly disputed. Even if one allowed necessity or loyalty to triumph over principle, there remained the practical question of paying wages for service outside the county. It must suffice here that large numbers of archers were raised by this method for service in France, and that in practice the county provided wages for the men till the day they reached the coast. From that day, even if they waited – as they usually did – a week or sometimes a month for ships, they were 'at the king's wages'.

The distance of the port of embarkation from the county boundary was therefore calculated. The sheriff made his estimate of the number of days needed for the journey – on foot, of course – published a date and place for the assembly of the archers – say Bridgwater, Lichfield or Shaftesbury – held a review, and paid out wages according to his estimate or handed wages to a leader who could pay out as the march proceeded. Many journeys began in summer, but some men had to set out in December or January. Within a year a similar contingent might be required for reinforcements. Men of Cheshire, Derby or Nottingham might walk down to Plymouth (or proceed northward to Carlisle or Newcastle upon Tyne for service in Scotland), but levies from the northern counties normally only served in Scotland. How they fared, where they rested is not known.

The other method of raising armies is now commonly known as the 'indenture system', because contracts of service were drawn up in the form of indentures. In essence it was a system of double contracts: individual lords agreed with the king to supply given numbers of knights, men-at-arms and archers who, on their part, undertook to serve for a certain period at a fixed daily wage. Earls received 6s 8d, bannerets 4s, knights 2s, men-at-arms 1s, mounted archers 6d. The king handed over in advance to the leaders a large part (sometimes a half) of the total sum needed for the payment of the troops for the agreed period, and gradually it became possible to extend the period as circumstances required. As examples of the leaders and their companies, we may cite the earl of Warwick who in 1341 contracted to raise 2 bannerets, 26 knights, 71 men-at-arms, 40 armed men and 100 archers;[1] John de Lisle who went out with the Black Prince in 1355 taking 20 knights, 39 esquires and 40 mounted archers;[2] and Michael de la Pole, who raised in 1418, 3 knights, 56 esquires, 40 men-at-arms and 120 mounted archers.[3] Like the county levies, these men proceeded to the port, and it was at the port that the muster was held – sometimes on the ships – payment dating from the day of the muster and in some instances being made on the ships.

The indenture system proved effective. Under the terms of the contract the king provided ships for the transport of both men and horses, guaranteed compensation for loss of horses lost in his service, and often arranged that he should have a share in the ransoms received for prisoners captured during the forthcoming campaign. In addition to the fixed wages, there was a kind of bonus called a 'regard'. The terms proved very satisfactory. Obligatory service was superseded by voluntary service.

For the great noble bound by family tradition of service, for the lowest outlaw anxious to gain a pardon, for the gay young squire seeking fame or honour, for the ne'er-do-well or the sulky malcontent – for all these, military service offered advantages of companionship, good pay and, particularly in France, opportunities for enrichment by spoils and ransoms.

III

The organisers of the supply of victuals for an army about to be shipped beyond the sea had to accumulate at the port of embarkation enough food and forage to sustain the troops, the horses and hundreds of mariners during the period of waiting at the port, during the voyage, and during the first few days the army spent on foreign soil. The normal problems were increased in the fourteenth century by the fact that never before had such large armies been assembled for service overseas, and never had it been necessary to sustain a large force from English sources for so long a period as that needed for the siege of Calais in 1346–7.

The pattern of operations was broadly as follows: estimates of the total requirements were made, and then estimates of the quantities of this and that commodity various counties might reasonably be expected to supply. The commodities demanded were beef, mutton, pork (usually salted), oats, beans, peas, cheese, fish (commonly dried and for use in Gascony), wheat (usually ground into flour before being shipped) and ale. Transport was, of course, effected mainly by water and eastern England afforded both more foodstuffs and better waterways than western England. Depots for the accumulating stores were planted alongside the rivers and at the ports. Very many containers were needed. Tuns, therefore, cleaned and dried, were in demand.

Agents were sent to the counties to get the quantities of goods laid down. These men, called 'purveyors', were armed with two powers – the right to buy in advance of competing buyers or of the market (pre-emption) and the right, in co-operation with the sheriff, to 'take carriage' (wagons, horses, boats) for the conveyance of the goods acquired to a chosen destination. For carriage by land, some of the vehicles needed might be drawn from monastic granges, though the monks' stocks might be protected. It was necessary also to achieve some measure of co-operation with the admiral in order that river-borne supplies might be transferred at the port to sea-going vessels.

The extensive preparations for King Edward's expedition of 1346 illustrate the operation. Down the tributaries of the Yorkshire Ouse to York, down the valley of the Trent to Hull, from the rivers emptying into the Wash via Boston and King's Lynn, through Norwich to Yarmouth, through Ipswich to Orwell, through Chelmsford to Maldon, the goods were sent, loaded into ships and taken to Portsmouth. From Oxfordshire and Berkshire, the stores were sent via London; from

Kent via Sandwich, while some of the western counties sent their supplies by way of Bristol.[4]

For smaller armies, the resources of fewer counties, of course, sufficed. The needs of the Channel Islands were commonly supplied from Hampshire and the stores of Gascony augmented from several southern counties while, after 1347, the constant and considerable needs of Calais were met partly by purveyance (that is to say the government ensured the supplies), partly by free enterprise.[5]

In view of the circumstances of the period, it is not surprising that occasionally some small part of the stores purveyed proved to be 'surplus to requirements' or unfit for consumption. More serious were the complaints made against the purveyors and in some measure against the system under which they worked. That they did not carry large sums of money with which to make immediate payment – they gave tallies – was part of the common practice of the period, but the delays in payment caused hardship. That they spared the rich and were harsh with the poor, that under the guise of purveyance they bought cheaply and sold for their own advantage, that they demanded 'heaped measure' (as contrasted with 'rased measure') – these and other bitter complaints led to a great outcry and demand for changes in 1362. The purveyors, it must be allowed, were obliged to obtain their various quotas within limited areas and within limited time, and they acted high-handedly. On the other hand, some of them lacked integrity. As for dilatoriness in payment, an example may be cited from the south-western counties where in the summer of 1355 large quantities of victuals were hastily gathered for the army of the Black Prince waiting at Plymouth. They were paid for in the spring of 1357.[6]

For his expedition of 1415, Henry V made important changes in the mode of getting victuals. After a preliminary warning to the people of Hampshire that he desired them to 'bake and brew' in preparation for the arrival of his troops,[7] the king departed from preceding practice by issuing orders for hundreds of live oxen, cows and stirks to be driven from neighbouring counties to depots near Southampton.[8] He tried also to avoid the malpractices of the purveyors; the cattle were to be sold 'as may be with the owners agreed'[9] and if any men felt aggrieved over the matter of purchase and payment, they were to lay their cases before officers of his household. The king promised, on his arrival, he would show them justice.[10]

The first action of the English army after landing in France was the siege and capture of Harfleur. In order to maintain the garrison in this town, and to extend his operations, the shipping of large quantities of corn, bacon, peas, beans and malt was necessary. The work was carried through (as such work was normally done in the preceding century) by granting commissions to merchants to gather specified amounts of this or that commodities in given counties and dispatch them through named ports.[11]

Notwithstanding the copious evidence for the victualling of English armies, research is needed on the arrangements for sharing (or dividing) and cooking the accumulated stores. Indentures of retainer of men serving the king or, say, the duke of Lancaster provided in some instances for wages *with* board, in others for wages *without* board. As for the archers, we know nothing yet of their 'messing arrangements'. But the fact remains that the first and indispensable step towards a victorious campaign in France was the accumulation of supplies of food in England by organising collection and transport even in regions as remote as the dales of Yorkshire.

The Tower of London was the great arsenal for the manufacture and storage of bows and arrows. These arms were also, of course, made in all counties and could be sent to the Tower or a port of embarkation as required. Supplies were accumulated by instructing the sheriffs to obtain certain quantities within their bailiwicks. These they bought – usually at standard prices – at various places and gathered to their chief towns where the bows were packed in canvas and the sheaves of arrows corded (or sometimes placed in tuns) and dispatched to London in hired wagons. Bowstrings also were bought, and from the areas in which iron was worked, such as Salop, Staffordshire and the Weald, iron or steel arrow heads were obtained.[12]

In the earlier part of our period, 'engines' were widely used for attacks on walled towns, but they served also for defence. They might be constructed on the spot (as at Romorantin in 1356), but some were made in England and had to be conveyed to a port and got on board. Long ladders for scaling walls were taken overseas, and from the 1340s onwards orders for quantities of saltpetre, sulphur and charcoal point to the increasing use of gunpowder.

Many carts were taken on the ships and a wide range of miscellaneous goods were indispensable: tools for carpenters, woodcutters, diggers, miners, blacksmiths; horseshoes and nails, forges; tents for the great leaders; arms, armour and clothing for the knights; harness; parchment for the king's secretaries. In the campaign of Edward III, the king and the prince of Wales had physicians, but there is scarcely any reference to medical stores (though Chaucer mentions narcotics, drugs and opium).[13] Henry V, however, took to France a group of 'surgeons' with their 'instruments' and stores.[14]

IV

The assembly of sufficient suitable ships for the transport of an army, its horses and supplies formed one of the most difficult tasks of executive government. Scattered between the Baltic and Bayonne or along English coasts between Berwick and Bristol, unaided by charts and lighthouses, imperfectly equipped both for direction-finding and for navigation, ships ran grave risks from pirates, from their nation's enemies and even at times from their own countrymen, for the sea was no-man's-land; they remained beyond call till they touched port and it was impossible to predict arrival dates. Coasting vessels sailed from port to port, but the wine ships on their annual journeys to Bordeaux were repeatedly directed to assemble at Sandwich, the Isle of Wight or Plymouth and proceed in convoy for their own safety.

Merchant ships were, of course, used for the transport of armies. They might be adapted for combat by having castles built on deck fore and aft, so that from an elevated position archers might achieve a longer range. They had to be adapted for carrying horses. For a typical expedition hundreds of hurdles were made, brought to port and fitted into the ships to make 'stalls'.

A fleet assembled for the transport of troops from an English port to the Continent consisted of ships varying widely in size – from 30 to as much as 300 tons – and drawn from almost all the ports in the country. A hundred vessels and in some instances more than two hundred might be needed. One chronicler[15] even states (and reputable historians[16] have followed him) that Henry V had 1500 ships for the army he led to France in 1415, but the figure should be treated as intended to impress the reader. Judged by modern standards, the crews were very large. In the early part of our period, it is not clear that owners were paid for the use of their vessels, but a practice grew of paying 3s 4d per ton for each quarter-year they were in the king's service.[17]

Once a port of embarkation had been chosen, a broad estimate of the necessary shipping determined, and a date proposed (rather than fixed) for assembly, the admirals took in hand the work of getting the ships and crews. Armed with powers to requisition all vessels of over a given

tonnage, to impress sailors for manning them, and to order masters to
sail their ships to the appointed rendezvous, the two admirals and their
deputies rode from port to port along the stretches of coast in which
they were authorised to act (namely from the mouth of the Thames
towards the north and from the Thames towards the west), seeking
suitable ships. No English vessel of above the required minimum tonnage was exempt. Even a ship laden with cargo destined for a distant
port and calling solely for water was liable to seizure; it had to be
unloaded and sailed to the port of embarkation. Occasionally, a vessel
of a foreign merchant was taken though this was acknowledged to be
irregular.

Many weeks might elapse between the issue of orders to the admirals
and the arrival of ships at, say, Southampton or Plymouth; weeks might
pass while ships and crews lay in harbour waiting for the complement
to be made up; and in some instances troops had to wait for weeks on
land near the port. Seldom, if ever, did an expeditionary force leave
England on the appointed date. Deplorable though such delays might
be, it would be an error to attribute them to administrative incompetence. The convergence of the ships on the port, the adaptation of the
horse boats, the transport of supplies and the marching dates of knights
and men were as well co-ordinated as the circumstances of the period
permitted.

Two factors appear to have governed the choice of a port of embarkation, namely the distance to the port of disembarkation and the need for
a suitable roadstead in which a very large number of miscellaneous
ships could ride in safety and be manœuvred with reasonable speed to
the water's edge for loading and back into mid-stream or mid-harbour.
Little is known of the harbour installations and facilities. A few ports
had quays; some had windlasses; in the mid-fourteenth century,
Sandwich had a dock; new gangways – some of them very wide – were
commonly ordered in the fourteenth century for the expeditions; warehouses are very seldom mentioned though their existence might be
inferred. Lodemen (pilots) were employed fairly often, not only for
entering and leaving harbours but also for long journeys.

London formed the starting-point for only one expedition – that of
Henry of Lancaster in 1355. Orwell (near Harwich) was used for the
departure of troops for Flanders; Sandwich was the port of embarkation of troops moving to Calais; Portsmouth and Southampton were
suitable for landings in Normandy or the mouth of the Seine; Plymouth
was used for expeditions to Brittany and Gascony and for the con-

siderable traffic of the 1360s, when men and arms were being sent to Aquitaine to the prince of Wales. Reinforcements and supplies were sometimes sent from smaller ports, and at intervals troops sailed to Ireland from Milford Haven and from Chester.

In the days preceding departure, the leader was at hand at Port-chester or Plympton or Northbourne by Sandwich. The roads leading to the port were crowded with horse- or ox-drawn wagons bearing victuals, forage, siege material, supplies of many kinds and empty tuns (for drinking-water). Horses were appraised (in order that in the event of their being 'lost in war', compensation might be based on their esti-mated value before they left England). A proclamation (cried locally) announced that knights and men must be in the port by a certain day. Mariners and archers were paid their wages and a review of the troops was held. This was a formal inspection in which two or three knights, appointed for the purpose, reported to the Council concerning the 'sufficiency of the array'.

At last, with supplies on board, tuns filled, horses led up the wide gangways and leaders and men in their appointed ships, the expedi-tionary force sailed away, the destination being undisclosed in 1346, 1415 and 1417. The Black Prince took about eleven days for the voyage from Plymouth to Bordeaux in 1355; Edward III made the journey from Sandwich to Calais in a single day in 1359 (but most of his troops had preceded him); Henry V left Portsmouth on 11 August 1415 and dropped anchor near Harfleur on 14 August; two years later, on a similar journey, he set sail on 30 July and landed just west of the mouth of the Seine on 1 August.

v

After a few days spent in disembarkation and the sorting of men, horses and transport into a column of route, the army was ready to set about its business. This was not to seek and defeat the enemy army, but to bring military pressure on the enemy's country. Moreover, since men and horses had to be fed, victualling was of great importance; and as looting was commonly permitted, that constituted a third regular practice. These three activities were carried on week after week in a period when hastily assembled troops were not fully accustomed to restraint, and when the inhabitants of those towns which preferred siege to surrender expected no mercy should their towns be taken.

Military pressure consisted in inflicting *damnum* (loss), or working havoc by the destruction of the means by which life was maintained – houses, barns, stables, mills, stores, vehicles, boats, and such food and forage as was needed by the victuallers. Fire was the chief agent of destruction. It was widely used and wholly effective, for almost all houses, vehicles, implements and domestic utensils (such as vats and pales) were of wood. It was, of course, difficult to control, and though leaders usually directed that churches and church property were to be spared, they were often engulfed in the general conflagration.

Victualling called for organisation, promptitude and foresight. Wagons had to be taken several miles to right and to left of the line of march, eatables of all kinds requisitioned, cattle driven to a central point, dressed or cooked or boiled.

Looting arose neither from military policy nor from military necessity, but it was gratifying to the troops as well as an incentive in recruiting. The property of the Church was understood to be sacrosanct, but in the exciting episodes following the capture of a town, sacred vessels and altar hangings were often stolen. None of these three activities called for the virtues and skills associated with chivalry.

Constantly needing supplies of food, the invaders seldom spent more than two nights in one place. In many instances at the approach of an English army, the inhabitants fled taking such valuables as they could carry. In other instances, however, towns offered resistance. A few (such as Carcassonne and Périgueux) tried – unsuccessfully – to negotiate immunity from pillage and destruction;[18] a few (Cambrai, Tournai, Rheims)[19] endured sieges and, by the fortune of war, escaped destruction; while in others (Calais,[20] Limoges,[21] Harfleur),[22] the inhabitants suffered very seriously after their town was captured.

The dire conflict of pitched battle was a rare occurrence. The invaders had days of profitable plunder, days of frustration, days of ample food and wine, days of scarcity, and in no campaign did they wholly escape the rigours of war: food ran very short as Edward III approached Crécy and Calais; the Black Prince's army had to swim or ford swollen rivers in November 1355; the king's army marched in appalling weather from Calais to Rheims in November 1359 and spent Christmas in the snow outside that city; the Black Prince led his troops through the bleak pass of the Pyrenees in February 1367; during John of Gaunt's *chevauchée* through central France to Bordeaux in November and December 1373, many men and horses died of cold and starvation; it was a disease-smitten army that marched to Agincourt in 1415.

Far worse was the fate of the French people. Though English

soldiers were at least as well disciplined as any of the period, their routine activities struck at the deepest feelings of their victims; foreign troops insolently seized the whole of their stores of food and wine, carried off their hay and corn, drove their cattle from the fields, entered their houses, ransacked their cupboards and coffers of treasured possessions, sat down to feast and spend the night in their town and the next day set it on fire. From miles away, refugees saw the smoke by day and the red glow in the sky by night. Returning a fortnight later, they could not even locate the sites of their former homes. This was 'the desolation'. Here indeed was housing shortage, increased cost of food, inability to pay rents, landlords' losses, decline of public revenues and general social and economic dislocation.

Though there is so much written evidence of devastation, pillage and burning, it is noteworthy that the illuminators of the chronicles avoided these aspects of the war. Men rich enough to pay such artists desired pictures of more valorous episodes and got them in abundance.

Broadly the military historians also have ignored these non-fighting aspects of the conflict. They have described selected incidents, commented on strategy, tactics and military organisation, and led readers to confuse war with battles. Battles were few and brief. War was the continuous exertion of military pressure – mainly, as we have seen, on the civilian population. It was not for the seizure of food or the looting and destruction of towns that knights had trained themselves in the jousts and archers at the butts. Nor was it by working havoc in a fertile land that men gained fame for chivalry. Nor indeed did they need to 'summon up the blood' and 'lend the eye a terrible aspect' in order to fling burning matter on the thatched roofs of wooden houses. Such things do not fit into the Art of War. Yet they are the outstanding features of the Practice of War, not regrettable by-products but willed and planned operations. They require explanation.

Writing of Edward III's campaign in the Cambrésis in 1339, Colonel A. H. Burne found it 'difficult for us to understand the military object to be achieved by this systematic burning'.[23] Of King Edward's work in 1346, he experienced a 'slight feeling of embarrassment when trying to excuse or explain the burnings in the Normandy campaign',[24] although he allowed that the Black Prince's 'work of destruction' in the campaign of 1355 had a 'clear military object',[25] Sir Charles Oman dismissed that campaign as 'a destructive but rather objectless raid'.[26] Ferdinand Lot regarded it as a 'typical martial undertaking . . . in which pitched battles are avoided and the troops are occupied in pillage, devastation and burning houses and standing crops in order to ruin the enemy'.[27] Here Lot unconsciously mentioned the truth; the operations which he regarded as lying outside his study of the Art of War came to a climax in the 'ruin of the enemy', the very aim of the Practice of War! R. C. Smail summarises more modern views thus:

Historians have not yet fully interpreted the precise purpose and value of these raids. To Oman, as to French scholars, they appear to be entirely aimless and lacking in real military value, contributions to the sum of human misery but failing to apply military means to secure political ends. This verdict has more recently been challenged. The raids have been seen as part of a long-term military plan, designed to provoke the enemy into offering battle and, if he refused, to weaken him materially and to destroy his will to continue the war. They have been seen, too, as part of an ambitious plan for striking at the heart of the enemy's territory from a number of points on his borders . . . (simultaneously as in 1346 and 1356).[28]

An explanation closely related to the evolution of the French State deserves consideration. Though the means used by Edward III were military, his aim was political, namely the establishment of a Plantagenet monarchy in France or at least the recognition of his unqualified sovereignty over a large part of France. He, therefore, needed to weaken the hold of the Valois monarchy on the French people or, more correctly, the Gascons, Bretons, Normans . . . who were gradually coming to regard themselves as members of a French nation, for France was not yet an integrated kingdom. Provincial loyalties remained strong – in some places as strong as national loyalties. Edward, therefore, sought to impress French provincial opinion by demonstrating his might – as he did with impunity – and, by contrast, the feebleness of the French king. Instinctive feeling and expectation was that a ruler who lacked the will or the power to protect his own subjects must forfeit their allegiance. Edward was competing for that allegiance.[29]

The terseness of the chronicles concerning the three recurrent activities of the invaders might leave doubt about the severity of the damage inflicted during a campaign. However, there are more precise sources for an assessment, for apart from the large sums offered by Carcassonne and Périgueux for exemption from destruction, in 1359 the duke of Burgundy actually paid a very large sum in order that his country might be freed from the presence of the English army before it

caused further damage.[30] Another source lies in a report in the Close
Rolls following an incursion by the Scots in 1345. Many inhabitants of
Cumberland had protested that owing to the losses sustained, they were
unable to pay taxes. An official investigation revealed that more than
fifty (named) towns and villages had been 'totally burnt and destroyed'.[31]

A still more precise statement is found in a very long report on relief
work in the region south of Cambrai, where King Edward's troops had
spent a week in the work of devastation in 1339. The report throws a
flood of light on the homelessness, the poverty, the personal sufferings,
and the material damage caused in no less than 174 parishes (all of
which can be identified today). It mentions the names of scores of the
victims and the sums awarded to relieve their immediate needs.[32] Both
here and in Cumberland (above), it is clear that human suffering was
accompanied by very considerable loss of public revenue; it was this
kind of loss that John Wengfeld, the personal assistant of the Black
Prince, emphasised in a statement about the prince's *chevauchée* of
1355.[33]

During the period 1369–96, English invasions of France were on a
smaller scale but they followed the same pattern as those of 1338–59.
In particular, the *chevauchée* of John of Gaunt in 1373, was marked by
pillage and burning. After the battle of Agincourt, however, Henry V
modified the character of the operations. At the beginning of his first
campaign he had issued disciplinary rules for the troops which had been
published only occasionally during the campaigns of his predecessors.
The official aim of his expedition of 1417 was the reconquest of lands
unjustly detained by the French. The people inhabiting these lands he
considered his own subjects. However, it was not for their sake that he
was determined to enforce control in his army, but to make it an efficient
instrument of his policy. The lives of French non-combatants and the
Church's vessels and ornaments were now safer. The wanton destruction of food was stopped. Once a region was gained and peace proclaimed, pillage had to cease. The burning of houses without the king's
explicit orders was forbidden on pain of death.

It would be an error to infer that Henry had changed the Practice of
War. His purpose and that of his successors in France was to occupy
territory rather than to inflict damage on it. Moreover, he did not live
many years, and though the duke of Bedford strove to maintain the
discipline of English armies, the heterogeneous French army (made up
of Scottish, Italian, Bretons and Castilian troops) supported itself by
plundering the people of France.

VI

Intelligence (in the sense of information about the enemy) was, of course, needed, if not for the direction of operations, at least for the timing and point of attack of the expeditions. Concerning the sources and collection of information, there is need for research. For Froissart, the presence of spies was commonplace; he repeatedly states that the intention and preparations of this or that kingdom or province were known outside it. Much information might, however, have been obtained from watchers on the coast, fishermen in the Channel, merchants and masters of ships trading in Sluys and the French ports, from churchmen, diplomats and messengers travelling to and from Avignon, even from pilgrims returning to England. Further, one of the purposes of a fleet assembled in 1359, was 'to bring back to the Council news of the king and his army'. One way or another, 'tidings came', and it is probable that the courteously treated noble prisoners who spent years in England revealed sidelights on their and their neighbours' loyalty to the French throne or on the separatism of the various regions of France.

But we are not concerned solely with secret information reaching the king and Council. It is necessary to consider the information which reached the people as a whole and helped to form the national outlook. The arraying of archers, the passage of troops, the assembly of shipping in the ports, the making of arms, the strengthening of castles, the purveyance and transport of foodstuffs, border warfare in the north, attacks on ports in the south, obligatory residence in the counties bordering the Channel, watches on the coast – all these 'facts' pointed to a state of war. And the Englishman in his homeland gradually developed the attitudes with which, during continental wars, later generations have become familiar: distrust of all foreigners (including alien monks and friars), suspicions about spies and credulity concerning enemy intentions. Later, when the soldiers returned, there was added the gossip of the market-places and the inns. In short, people everywhere had the fruits of local observation mingled with hearsay and prejudice.

A combination of military precaution, administrative policy and enlightened publicity tended in the first part of the war towards an elementary news service which might engage the interest and develop the convictions of the mass of the people. First – as already shown – came the warnings about the invasion: that it was impending, that it would begin in a certain county, and that it would be accompanied by great evils. The news was sent out through the sheriffs and published by 'criers' in seaports, markets, fairs and other public places. If and when invasion occurred, the news would be spread by the well-manned beacons.

More news about the war was sent out for administrative purposes, but it was accompanied – as was common at the period – by explanation of the grounds for action. Mayors and bailiffs of seaports, for example, were directed to prevent the export of horses, or of arms, or of the good English specie; travellers entering or leaving the country were subjected to rigorous search for letters 'prejudicial to the interests of the king'; markets might be closed for a period in given areas; cellars might be searched for hidden stores of wine or arms. Officials explained their actions and the public became aware that such measures were taken in the national interest for the purposes of war.

Parliament was given such news as was available. The Commons were not critical of the aims or conduct of the war. They made large grants for its furtherance, drew attention to grievances (such as the losses of shipowners and the malpractices of purveyors) and expected and often received a statement on the situation at the time of their meeting.[34]

But the clearest examples of communication between ruler and nation lie in letters sent to the sheriffs expressly for publication (i.e. by criers) on the widest scale. It was by this means that English people learned that King Edward had assumed the title 'king of France', that he had won the battle of Crécy, that he had captured Calais and that a peace treaty had been concluded in 1360.[35]

The Church also aided the spread of news, for requests to the bishops to cause the people to invoke divine aid for the success of English arms drew attention to the course of events. The machinery may appear cumbrous: a communication passes from the king to the archbishop; it is forwarded to all the bishops in the province; they turn the message into mandates addressed to the archdeacons and other executive officers, who pass the instructions to the parochial clergy. The instructions are not, of course, uniform throughout a province, but broadly they order 'prayers, processions [litanies] and preaching [sermons]'. Usually, the requests refer to specific expeditionary forces and their leaders. They were sent out in almost every year between 1338 and 1351, and again in 1355, 1356 and 1359. (The Black Prince sent a similar request from Bordeaux in June 1356.)[36] Nor was the king lacking in gratitude; through the same channels, he asked that thanks be offered to God for the victories gained at Sluys (1340), in Gascony (1346) and at Poitiers (1356).

The practice of requesting the Church to offer prayers for the armies may be traced in some of the episcopal registers down to the end of the war,[37] (though in 1439 the special intention was for a peace mission of Cardinal Beaufort). It is doubtful whether there is sufficient evidence for an investigation of the zeal with which the clergy carried out their instructions – Archbishop Chichele[38] referred three times in 1416–18 to their 'growing tepid in their devotions for the success of the king' – but it is probable that in very many places the litanies served to focus worshippers' attention not on war in general but on the nation's latest military effort.

The maintenance of the war depended not only on the military qualities of the leaders and troops in the field, but also on the ability of the 'civilians' at home who organised the defence of the realm, the recruitment of soldiers, the collection of victuals, the production of arms, the assembly of shipping, the transport of the expeditionary (and later, the occupying) forces and even a rudimentary service of news.

By far the greater part of the time of the men serving abroad was used in the seizure of food and in systematic devastation. Both operations had very serious effects.

BIBLIOGRAPHICAL NOTE

E. Perroy, *La guerre de Cent ans* (Paris, 1945; English trans., *The Hundred Years War*, 1951) is a comprehensive survey, useful for the general background.

Concerning the Art of War, the following may be consulted: C. Oman, *A History of the Art of War in the Middle Ages* (1924); F. Lot, *L'art militaire et les armées* (Paris, 1945); A. H. Burne, *The Crecy War* (1955) and *The Agincourt War* (1957). In these works, war is treated as an activity of soldiers only. Lot gets down to the real sizes of armies. Burne's volumes are the studies of a soldier rather than of a historian, and they are not free from errors, although they make lively reading.

A. E. Prince, 'The Indenture System under Edward III', in *Historical Essays in Honour of James Tait*, ed. J. G. Edwards, V. H. Galbraith and E. F. Jacob (Manchester, 1933), forms a guide to one aspect of recruiting, while M. Powicke, *Military Obligation in Medieval England* (Oxford, 1962), though an advanced study of legal aspects, is helpful for the transition to the contractual system of raising armies. R. A. Newhall, *The English Conquest of Normandy, 1416–1424* (New Haven, 1924), throws light on the later period of the war.

Three books go much further than their titles might suggest; while necessarily giving full accounts of battles, they also deal with transport and victuals: H. J. Hewitt, *The Black Prince's Expedition of 1355–57* (Manchester, 1958);

E. F. Jacob, *Henry V and the Invasion of France* (1947); C. Hibbert, *Agincourt* (1964; Pan Books, 1968). H. J. Hewitt, *The Organization of War under Edward III, 1338–1362* (Manchester, 1966), omits battles, deals with shipping, supplies, victuals, etc. and the involvement of 'civilians' in the war.

Froissart's *Chronicles* throw light on several aspects of the war. His figures for the sizes of armies are usually wide of the mark, but his narrative breathes the spirit of the age: the chivalry and challenges to single combat alongside the looting, devastation, sieges and attempts to capture rich nobles for ransoms. The *Chronicles* were translated by Lord Berners in 1521–3 and reprinted by W. P. Ker (6 vols, Tudor translations, 1901–3), and there are single-volume selections such as *The Chronicles of Froissart*, ed. G. C. Macaulay (1924) and *Froissart: Chronicles*, ed. and trans. G. Brereton (Penguin Classics, 1968).

NOTES

1. *CPR 1340–1343*, pp. 264–7.
2. PRO, Pipe Roll E.372/200, m. 7.
3. PRO, E.101/46/24.
4. H. J. Hewitt, *The Organization of War Under Edward III*.
5. S. J. Burley, 'The Victualling of Calais', *BIHR* xxxi (1958), 49–67.
6. Hewitt, op. cit., pp. 168–72.
7. *CCR 1413–1419*, p. 214.
8. Ibid., pp. 217, 218.
9. Ibid., p. 218.
10. Ibid., p. 278.
11. *CPR 1413–1416*, pp. 361, 412; *CPR 1416–1422*, pp. 1, 7, 8, 173.
12. H. J. Hewitt, op. cit., pp. 63–71.
13. *Canterbury Tales* (Everyman edition), pp. 35, 64.
14. *Foedera*, ix, 252 (1415); *CPR 1416–1422*, p. 31 (1416).
15. Thomas Walsingham, *Historia Anglicana* (2 vols, Rolls Series, 1863–4), ii, 307.
16. E. F. Jacob, *The Fifteenth Century* (Oxford, 1961), p. 148.
    Christopher Hibbert: *Agincourt* (1964), p. 27.
17. *Rot. Parl.*, iii, 213, 223; ibid., iv, 79, 104.
18. H. J. Hewitt, *The Black Prince's Expedition of 1355–57*, pp. 59, 60, 89.
19. H. J. Hewitt, *Organization*, pp. 104, 110–11, 119, 130.
20. Ibid., pp. 59, 85, 119. *The Chronicles of Froissart* ed. Macaulay (1924), pp. 107–9, 114–16.
21. H. J. Hewitt: *Organization*, pp. 120–1.
    Froissart ed. Macaulay, pp. 107–9, 114–16.
22. Jacob, op. cit., pp. 150–1.
23. A. H. Burne, *The Crecy War*, p. 45.
24. Ibid., p. 252.
25. Ibid., p. 252.
26. *The Art of War in the Middle Ages*, i, 160.
27. *L'art militaire*, i, 352.
28. *Medieval England*, ed. A. L. Poole (1958), i, 157.
29. J. Le Patourel, 'Edward III and the Kingdom of France', *History xliii* (1958), 188.
30. H. J. Hewitt, *Organization*, p. 131.

31. Ibid., pp. 126–30.
32. Ibid., pp. 124–6.
33. H. J. Hewitt, *Black Prince's Expedition*, p. 73; Robertus de Avesbury, *De Gestis Mirabilibus Regis Edwardi Tertii*, ed. E. M. Thompson (Rolls Series, 1889), p. 443.
34. H. J. Hewitt, *Organization*, pp. 175–7.
35. Ibid., p. 159.
36. *Hereford Episcopal Registers*, John de Trillek, i, 243.
37. *Exeter Episcopal Registers*, John de Grandison, i, 66, 11, 1173; ibid, ii, 120–2; ibid., *Thomas de Brantingham*, i, 186–7, 199, 299, 342, 432; ibid., *Edmund Lacy*, i, 38, 39, 85, 109, 116, 149; ibid., ii, 15, 156, 237, 283, 311, 375.
38. *Registrum Henrici Chichele*, ed. E. F. Jacob (1947), iv, 158–9, 167–8, 176.

4. The War at Sea

C. F. RICHMOND

THE Hundred Years War not only lasted a long time, it also involved principalities and powers other than England and France. It was a conflict as long and as complex as that between these two countries from the late seventeenth to the early nineteenth century and as such is not easily reduced to a patterned order. Important as seapower was in that struggle there is much less difficulty in analysing its use and assessing the consequences of its application than there is during the Hundred Years War. Distance has put us at a disadvantage in this particular matter; evidence there is in abundance for the fitting out of naval forces, but for what they were meant to achieve and for what they did achieve in the context of the over-all war effort we are too frequently forced back on our own devices. Take, for example, the battle of Sluys in 1340.

The opening of the war at sea with France in 1336 increased an already substantial English naval commitment against the Scots. At sea as elsewhere there was no plunge into hostilities, merely a stepping up and broadening of effort. And it was largely defensive at that. The anticipation of a French invasion in the years 1333–5 continued between 1336 and 1340, only with greater justification: in 1336 and 1339 the French had detailed plans for such an enterprise.[1] As alarming were the actual enemy offensives of these years. In the summer of 1336 the French attacked English shipping off the Isle of Wight, in March 1338 they burnt Portsmouth and in October Southampton, in 1339 they raided the south coast from Plymouth to Thanet. In the only notable engagement between English and French ships, off Middelburg in September 1338, the English were beaten and two royal vessels were taken, an indignity heightened by the loss also of the clerk of the king's ships' accounts.[2] To these disasters was added the loss of Guernsey, occupied by the French in the summer of 1338.[3] An English response to this constant pressure was not lacking.

Apart from the measures of coastal defence taken in 1338 and 1339, English squadrons sacked Cadsand in November 1337 and raided Boulogne in the summer of 1339, while patrols were carried out in the North Sea towards Scotland.[4] If the initiative was with the French there was an equal determination on the part of the English to counter their offensives and to take what opportunities there were of moving on to the offensive themselves. In the early summer of 1340 a rare chance of striking hard at French naval power presented itself and it would seem that the English took it.

The French invasion fleet assembled in the Zwyn estuary in June 1340. By that time Edward III had prepared his expedition to Flanders. Undeterred by the news from Sluys he gathered more ships and men and sailed from Orwell on 22 June. He was off the coast of Flanders the next day and, finding the French fleet at anchor in the river, he made a reconnaisance of its strength. If doubts still remain that until this time Edward had not sought an engagement – and his dispatches after the battle are not entirely unambiguous on this point – once contact had been made on 23 June he was clearly ready to attack. Waiting only for the help of the wind and the tide, on the following morning the English bore down on the French, who had chosen to meet the attack where they lay packed closely together. After a long battle which went on into the night the English destroyed or captured the greater part of the French fleet.

It was a great victory. It put an end to French invasion designs and Norman and Picard shipping was hard hit. This was sufficient. In so far as the French had a main fleet it had been beaten and beaten decisively; by speedy mobilisation and prompt action the English had caught and defeated a large enemy force before it had got under way: a classic tactic had succeeded to perfection. Despite the lack of sure evidence as to Edward's intentions when he set out from Orwell on 22 June, there is no reason to suppose that he and the other naval commanders of the Hundred Years War did not appreciate this particular aspect of naval strategy. That there were but few engagements of the like of Sluys during the war was not due to any failure of intelligent application to the nature of seapower on their part, but rather to the fact that naval resources were seldom sufficiently concentrated to enable a decisive attempt to be made against them. And if and when they were, the problems of intelligence, communications and logistics, and the hazards of wind and weather often prevented a timely response or frustrated a response that was made. As in any war, the gap between intention and result was frequently a wide one. Because during the course of the war so many expeditions were prepared or even got to sea, and achieved nothing, this should not lead us to believe that there was incompetence abroad to any more than the usual degree in man's handling of his affairs, nor to exaggerate the wastage of effort involved. The French naval preparations and Edward III's actual expedition of 1355 were indeed sterile, but hardly more so than, for example, the Allied bombing campaign against German U-boat bases in the early part of 1943.[5] For the Second World War, however, we have at our command much fuller information than for the Hundred Years War, and information that allows us to judge which were misguided or fruitless enterprises, who were the men of vision and who were not. For the Hundred Years War we cannot be so sure. Beyond that which stares us in the face – the success of Jean de Vienne and the Franco-Castilian squadrons in the 1370s, the genius of Henry V, the fumbling of the English in the last stages of the war – it is not easy to proceed to judgement on the success or failure of naval activity.

Common opinion would have it that the English victory in June 1340 gave them command of the Channel and made possible the crossing of their invasion force in 1346.[6] It seems inherently improbable that a battle won in 1340 enabled England to send an army across to Normandy six years later, and the events at sea between 1340 and 1346 do not suggest that at one stroke superiority had passed from France to England. In 1342, for instance, the French and their Spanish and Genoese allies caused considerable trouble to English squadrons off the Breton coast and in the summer of that year once again burnt Portsmouth. Nor did the French wait inactively for the coming of the English in 1346. In the spring of that year Norman ships were fitted out for service and Genoese reinforcements were ready at Nice in March: but these galleys were delayed in the Mediterranean and did not reach Rouen until mid-August; the English had disembarked at La Hogue between 12 and 18 July. Thus while it would be true to say that Sluys brought to an end the confident naval activity of the French of the years before 1340 and weakened their resources in the north to the extent that they became more reliant on Genoese and Spanish aid, it did not ensure the successful crossing of the English in 1346. Indeed, Sluys and the landing at La Hogue are in no significant way connected, for the idea that links them – that England won control of the Channel at Sluys – is a wrong one.

The concept of 'command of the sea' is not valid for the Hundred Years War. To attempt to view the events at sea during that war in terms of command being won and lost is to try to impose a pattern on those events which is neither relevant nor one which contemporaries would have recognised. What has been said of the early 1370s is equally true of the greater part of the entire war: 'In this period we are not concerned with control of the seas, but with fluid situations in which the balance of initiative and fighting power shifted from one season to another'.[7] Perhaps a more rewarding way of looking at the continually moving pattern of naval activity is in term of what Captain Roskill has called, albeit in a different context, 'zones of control': '. . . it seems true to say that in the application of a maritime strategy the capacity to establish zones of control where and when they are needed may be fully as important as gaining a general "command at sea"; and that such zones of control are fluid rather than fixed, moving forward as a particular operation progresses. . . .'[8] It would seem that in our period any squadron had a measure of local control for the limited time and limited area of its operations. The seas were free until such time as France or England put ships on them and then for a few weeks, perhaps for a summer, some sort of initiative had been acquired. As intelligence was slow and often inaccurate, and as it took time to get together a naval force, one's enemy was not usually in a position to challenge this initiative, at least in terms of making contact and bringing to action the fleet that he was aware was at sea, perhaps only after it had made a descent on his coasts. And to anticipate was not easy. It is clear, however, that to anticipate, that is to be at sea before one's enemy, was what men considered good strategy; as a royal letter of February 1341 put it: 'If our fleet be prepared and armed in good time according to our commands it will have the start of the enemy fleet and we believe that in this way burnings, massacres, atrocities and other evils will be prevented.'[9] Sound as such thinking was, in the conditions of the time to be constantly prepared was not possible. War was a costly business and what could be achieved at sea was after all little in comparison with what was at stake in the campaigns on land.

The English victory at Sluys, then, has to be seen in its context. All it really achieved was a shift in initiative and confidence: after a lean period England moved on to the offensive. In August 1345 Guernsey was retaken after seven years of enemy occupation. Its recovery demonstrates not only England's growing enterprise; it also made secure the right flank of the landing at La Hogue in the following July. It was perhaps an essential preliminary to that undertaking, far more important than a battle won six years before. Although often attacked thereafter, and indeed Jersey, all but the keep of Gorey castle, was briefly in enemy hands in the summer of 1373, the Channel Islands were never again occupied by the French. The English government, prompt to

relieve Jersey in 1373,[10] tended to be careful of their defence. Of even
greater strategic importance to the English was the capture of Calais in
August 1347 after a siege of almost a year.

The great effort made by Edward at Calais, both by land and sea,
shows how highly he valued the acquisition of that port. The importance
of the English possession of Calais needs to be stressed. For the remainder of the war it gave England a base in northern France. It was a
point of entry for military expeditions – the campaigns of Edward in
1359, John of Gaunt in 1373, Buckingham in 1380, and Gloucester in
1436 all began at Calais. Patrolling of the Straits and naval raids could
also be mounted from there; for example, in 1377, that year of disasters
for England, Hugh Calveley issued out to burn Boulogne. Also the
position of Calais between Normandy and Picardy, on the one hand,
and the Low Countries, on the other, enabled English vessels to strike
from there at French shipping passing between them. For example, in
the autumn of 1385, when the French postponed their plan for the
invasion of England, the large fleet collected at Sluys for that purpose
was dispersed and a number of ships returning to their home ports were
attacked and captured by the English coming out of Calais. The vital
importance of Calais to the English is perhaps best realised if one were
to imagine France in possession of Dover throughout the war and the
advantage this would have given her. The recovery of the Channel
Islands in 1345 and the capture of Calais in 1347, therefore, gave
England increased opportunities of harrying enemy shipping and a
better chance of moving on to the offensive or maintaining an initiative
at sea. There was no further success to add to this decade of English
achievement.

The Franco-Castilian naval agreement of January 1347 did not produce the stipulated Castilian fleet until the first French payment for its
fitting out had been made in July 1349. The fleet proceeded to Sluys to
discharge and take on cargo, for this venture appears also to have been a
commercial one; on its way it had captured some English vessels off
Brittany. The second French payment reached the Castilian commander, Don Carlos de la Cerda, while he and the ships were in
Flanders early in 1350. With this money he manned and munitioned the
fleet for the return to Castile. French preparations at Harfleur for concerted action seem to have come to nought.[11] Knowing on this occasion
of the waters through which his opponents would have to pass, and
given time to make ready by the Castilians' long stay in Flanders,
Edward III was able to make his challenge. In May 1350 royal ships

were equipped and in July other ships and mariners impressed. Edward then moved with a large and distinguished company to the Channel coast. On 29 August the Castilians were sighted and the two fleets joined battle. Throughout the remainder of the day they fought off Winchelsea the engagement known as Les Espagnols-sur-Mer. The Castilians lost a number of vessels before drawing off.[12]

The consequences of this English victory were in no way equal to the manner of its achievement. Certainly, the Castilians had been rudely dealt with and the first Franco-Castilian excursion into joint naval enterprise had merely given occasion to Edward III to demonstrate his confident superiority. But it was not this check that put an end to Franco-Castilian endeavour at sea; the death of Philip VI just before the battle was fought and the death of Alphonso XI in the same year brought new kings to the thrones of France and Castile. Although the treaty was renewed between the two countries in July 1352 Pedro I was too deeply involved in the struggle with his bastard brother Enrique of Trastamara to be able to send any help to John II. That king, while attentive to the building up of the royal fleet during the periods of truce in the early 1350s, had little time to take any real initiative at sea before he was captured at Poitiers in September 1356. Apart from the abortive expeditions of 1355 and the brief season of cross-Channel raiding in the spring of 1360 just before the treaty of Brétigny ended all official hostilities, there was little activity at sea during the 1350s. The sea-fight off Winchelsea in August 1350 closed ten years of successful English endeavour: when the war was reopened in 1369 it had no doubt become a fond memory, and as such it would have to serve amidst the reverses endured by the English in the 1370s.

One of the major causes of English discontent during that decade was the insecurity of the Channel coast. Canterbury West Gate, Cooling and Bodiam castles still survive to witness to that insecurity and the defensive measures taken to counter it.[13] It was the squadrons of Castilian galleys put at the disposal of the French which were responsible for much of the ravaging of the south coast of England. The galley was ideal for such raiding operations; its shallow draught and the fact that it was powered by oars (as well as sails) meant that it could penetrate inshore and was not as dependent on the favour of the wind for coming and going as a ship which only had sails to drive her. Both England and France had galleys in the fourteenth century, France in far greater quantity than England which only had a handful at any one time. It is, however, likely that the English vessel called a 'balinger' was a substitute for the galley. The balinger of the later fourteenth and fifteenth centuries was a shallow-draught vessel which also had oars as well as sails and the development of this type of vessel may have been in response to the evident success of the Castilian galleys in the 1370s. The balinger was not always differentiated from the barge in this period and it seems, therefore, that the barges and balingers that increasingly figure in French and English naval accounts in the second half of the fourteenth century are a northern compromise between the essentially Mediterranean galley and the ship, a recognition that this type of vessel was most suitable for the cross-Channel raiding which becomes such a feature of naval activity at this time.[14]

Nevertheless, both England and France also hired galleys from time to time from those southern countries which had them and the mariners experienced and skilful in their management. Until the late fourteenth century Genoese galleys served both sides on various occasions, though more frequently France than England, while the galleys of the Iberian kingdoms – Castile, Aragon and Portugal – were sought after by both countries. Hiring was expensive: ten Genoese galleys for three months and a ligne (a smaller galley-type vessel) for five months in 1373 cost the English government £9550;[15] the French government paid 40,000 florins for Cerda's ships in 1350 and the service of some twenty Castilian galleys in the summer of 1380 cost them over 50,000 francs.[16] It is obvious that expenditure on this scale was a burden and was not regularly to be borne, particularly in a sector that was not central to the war effort of either country. If, however, they could obtain the use of these galleys to supplement their own resources in some other way than by paying the full amount for them, this might give them a powerful advantage at sea. Competition between France and England for influence in the Iberian Peninsula, therefore, had as one of its motives this desire to augment their naval striking power, and 'since the chief prize at stake was the royal fleet of Castile it was natural that the main efforts of both English and French diplomacy should have been concentrated on the central kingdom in particular'.[17] None the less, it seems that English and French diplomatic and military involvement in Castile from the early 1360s was not as single-minded in intention as has been suggested. The bringing into action of the Castilian fleet in the Bay of Biscay and the Channel might alter the balance at sea to the extent of giving one side or another a decided superiority, for the stiffening given to the French naval effort by the small number of galleys that were sent during the 1370s and 1380s was real enough. But that the Castilian fleet might decide the course of the Hundred Years War[18] and that the French and English acted on that assumption seems a less sound supposition. As the war was simply the extension of diplomacy by other means, and the campaigns and battles on land and at sea an attempt to bring one's opponent to his reason (that reason being equivalent to the reason of one's demands), the more damage one could do and the more pressure one could bring to bear, the more successful one was likely to be. It is unlikely, however, that enough could be achieved at sea or in attacks from the sea by either France or England to bring the enemy to his knees and to his senses; the sea remained a secondary theatre in terms of decision. What France, even with Castilian aid, could win at sea was not going to be sufficient to lose England the war. The battle of La Rochelle in 1372, for example, when the Castilians first sent their galleys north and they entirely defeated an English fleet, 'was not the naval disaster it has been thought to be'.[19] England suffered in the 1370s but her sufferings were never severe enough for her to make peace; far from it, the defeat at La Rochelle only led her to redouble her efforts in naval affairs. Whatever the motives for the struggle in Spain, however, it was certainly a consequence of France winning that struggle that the galleys of Castile were at her disposal.

These galleys made a major contribution to French naval power in the 1370s and a still significant one to the less single-minded efforts of Charles VI's government between 1380 and 1389. They were most effective in raiding the English coast and an indication of the impact that their hit and run attacks had is to be found in the licence of 1385 granted to the men of Swanage and Studeley in Portland: the king allowed that they might pay ransom for the safety of their towns, for (it was stated) their exposed situation did not permit them to be saved in the event of the sudden arrival of enemies, particularly enemy galleys.[20] This might serve too as a fitting comment on the English government's response to the constant enemy pressure of the twenty years between 1369 and 1389. But it is not the whole story. Crippled as the government was for most of that time by the collapse and then the dissensions of its leaders, it was not paralysed. Whatever the eventual failure of Gaunt's schemes in Spain, for example, he at least had shown imagination in the 1380s in trying to eliminate Castilian help to France by attacking her directly, in alliance with Portugal. Moreover, the small number of Portuguese galleys in English service between 1384 and 1389[21] – one of the tangible benefits of the *chemin d'Espaigne* – while never as effective as the Castilian galleys which served France, were a help in a time of need. Enterprise was what was most needed on England's part in this period, for during it, particularly while Charles V reigned in France, she had to face a determined and organised enemy.

Aside from the assistance obtained from the Castilians and the Genoese, Charles V and Charles VI had two sources upon which they could draw for the supply of ships: their own naval establishment and the vessels of shipowners and merchants which they had the right to impress when required. The impressment of private vessels was never as dependable a source for French kings as it was for the kings of England: 'I do not deny that the king had the right to arrest the vessels of his subjects; but it can be seen how unwillingly the shipowners lent them compared with the situation of our enemy where it was an accepted practice.'[22] The great muster of one hundred and sixty-seven impressed ships from Norman and Picard ports, compared with thirty-two royal vessels and the small squadron of just three Genoese galleys, at Sluys in June 1340, was unusual.[23] Thereafter, impressed shipping never played so substantial a role in French as it did in English naval activity. Nor did the French have any equivalent to the service of the Cinque Ports to call upon. The obligation of those ports to supply at their own cost fifty-seven ships, each manned by twenty-one men, for fifteen days once a year was by the second half of the fourteenth century of little use to the English Crown in that form. However, the service in some modified form, usually fewer and larger ships for a somewhat longer period, was sometimes required, for instance six barges for a month's service in 1372. More frequently, small squadrons from the Cinque Ports served at the royal expense, for example in each year between 1372 and 1375 and in 1378.[24]

Where the kings of France had the advantage over the kings of England was in their own naval resources and their organisation. They had in the Clos des Galées at Rouen a naval base far superior to the English royal establishment centred on the Tower of London and at Ratcliffe below London Bridge. Modelled on the naval arsenal at Seville, and constructed between 1294 and 1298 by Genoese workmen under the supervision of the admiral of Castile, the Clos des Galées was on the left bank of the Seine opposite the city. It appears to have comprised a basin supplied with water from the river by a system of locks so that it could be filled or emptied as required. Round this, and within a defensive wall and ditch, were covered slipways for the building and repair of galleys and other vessels, workshops, warehouses and stores for equipment and armaments. Here, under the official known as the garde du Clos des Galées, the king's ships were built and maintained, munitioned and supplied, their crews gathered and paid off; and here, during times of inactivity, the vessels were laid up. The royal galleys were always stationed here; the royal barges, on the other hand, were often distributed among ports on the seaside like Harfleur, Boulogne and Dieppe, especially at Harfleur which at times became an advance base for the Clos des Galées at Rouen. Thus between 1298 and 1419 the French kings had a central base and organisation, which the English, rather more empirical in their approach to such matters, lacked.

The number of vessels in the royal fleet and the efficiency with which they were administered from the Clos des Galées of course varied throughout that period. This depended upon the interest and energy of particular kings, and upon their oversight of the admirals, who had immediate command of naval activity and of the gardes du Clos des Galées. Philip VI, John II and Charles V all showed concern for the royal fleet, and it was not until the 1380s and increasingly thereafter, with the disintegration of the central government, that the royal fleet declined in effectiveness. Until then the number of royal vessels of all types was generally between forty and fifty; the thirty-two at Sluys may not have represented the full complement of the royal fleet as there were only three galleys among them. In the early 1350s there were some twenty-two royal galleys and at least twenty-four other vessels, and in the 1370s about twenty-five galleys and more than twenty barges and ships.[25]

It was this royal naval establishment that was at the centre of Charles V's effort against England in the 1370s. During the first period of this phase of the war, until the truce of June 1375, Charles V showed considerable care for the state of his navy: ships were bought, barges and galleys were built, vessels kept in good repair and supply depots established at Dieppe and Harfleur. During these years the war at sea was one of constant attack and counter-attack by both sides, on each other's commercial shipping and each other's coasts. But since, as was generally the case throughout the war, the major efforts of each did not coincide, there were no engagements of any note between warships on the high seas.

The two years of truce were years of intensive preparation for Charles V. He had already appointed admiral, on 27 December 1373, Jean de Vienne, whose leadership at sea would be comparable to the constable's on land.[26] Under Vienne all was made ready for the time when the truce would run out on 24 June 1377. At Harfleur on 25 June he passed in review the fleet that was to attack England: thirty-five royal vessels with 4000 French troops aboard, eight Castilian and five Portuguese galleys. On 29 June this fleet led by Vienne attacked and captured Rye and a few days later defeated a force led by the prior of Lewes; they then burnt Lewes itself and sailed off westwards. Vienne had not attacked Winchelsea, which, unlike Rye, was walled and which had been promptly garrisoned by the abbot of Battle; nor had he retained Rye as a base from which to raid inland. He seems to have sailed as far west as Plymouth and burnt that port before returning to Harfleur. In August the fleet sailed out again. The Isle of Wight was overrun but an assault on Southampton was beaten off by Sir John Arundel who had been sent to defend the town with a strong force in July. An attack on Poole was also resisted, and as Vienne sailed back eastwards along the now well-defended coast he had no further success, save at Hastings, where he burnt the town. He then sailed for Calais, which was being invested by land by the duke of Burgundy; neither, however, made any serious attempt against that place and both withdrew in mid-September. It was a disappointing end to a campaign that had begun so well. And once the French had left the seas the English, whose naval preparations had been interrupted by the death of Edward III on 21 June,[27] but whose defensive measures in the summer had been effective enough, moved into action. The earl of Buckingham's expedition, driven back by the November winds, eventually sailed in December and relieved Brest in January 1378, Sir Thomas Percy captured part of a convoy of Spanish merchant vessels and Sir Hugh Calveley emerged from Calais to attack Boulogne. If there had been a chance of bringing England to submit that summer the French had not grasped it.

For the remaining three years of Charles V's reign the war at sea continued as before, the French and their Castilian allies retaining the initiative but with the English mounting frequent tactical offensives. Activity at the Clos des Galées was maintained; in 1379 seven 'grans barges' were under construction and fourteen other barges were being extensively repaired.[28] This was in great contrast to the English royal fleet at this time, which had sunk to a mere five vessels. But there was no French breakthrough, and even in 1380 when the French and Castilian raiding culminated in the sack of Winchelsea and the burning of Gravesend, an expedition led by Buckingham crossed to Calais and marched through France to Brittany. For all his enterprise and despite his many real achievements the end of the war was not in sight when Charles V died in September 1380. Nor did the dying king's last act, the abolition of the war taxes, show great concern for the continuing task of his successor.

The Clos des Galées suffered. The accounts of the *maistre et garde*, Jehan Champenois, survive for the two years from September 1382 to September 1384.[29] They present a dismal picture. By September 1384, of the ten galleys that remained three were said to be twenty-seven years old and all required extensive repair if they were to be made seaworthy. Little had been done to them during the two years of account. Some half a dozen barges, no doubt those under construction in 1379, remained unfinished and were rotting away for lack of attention; four other old barges were in bad condition. At least four barges had been given away in 1381–2. Although the Clos des Galées continued to function during the later 1380s – there were five galleys being repaired there in the spring of 1389 for example[30] – its contribution to the French naval effort was limited and was not, and would never again be, on the scale of the 1370s.

In a time of reduced naval and military activity which followed the death of Charles V in 1380, the chief French effort against England was in 1385–7 and it consisted of a plan and preparations for invasion, a threat which the English had not faced since 1340. In 1385 and 1386 the French postponed the invasion for reasons which are now obscure. During the winter months of 1386–7, however, concentrations of men, material and shipping were still being made in northern France, while in England the earl of Arundel was appointed admiral and in February 1387 named commander of a naval expedition for which preparations were put in hand. He was at sea by the middle of March with a fleet of over fifty vessels and a retinue of nearly 2400 soldiers[31]. His major exploit was the capture of a great number of Flemish merchant ships laden with wine; but by the time he had finally returned home in mid-September the French had called off their invasion once again and this time for good.

The last full season of campaigning in 1388 found both sides at sea in force. The Franco-Castilian fleet raided in the area of the Isle of Wight and the Solent and the earl of Arundel was again in command of a large expedition: 3500 soldiers in over sixty vessels.[32] He did considerable damage along the Biscay coast and in Normandy, arriving home early in September. Thus ended twenty years of hostilities; a stalemate had been reached and a truce for three years was agreed in June of the following year.

In the period from 1369 to 1389 the war at sea had been undertaken

by both sides with energy and sometimes with imagination. Effort had
been almost continuous; apart from the years of truce between June
1375 and April 1377 and from January 1384 to May 1385, and the
slackening of pace in the early 1380s, when revolts and lack of money
prevented both governments from attempting much, virtually every
season saw fleets or squadrons at sea, raids and counter-raids, merchant
shipping attacked. If, generally, the initiative was with the French,
the English were not slow to respond and towards the end of the period
the earl of Arundel was restoring a morale that had been much under-
mined in the years between 1377 and 1380. We have seen that the
French effort, when at its most vigorous in the 1370s, was based on the
organisation and strength of the royal fleet at the Clos des Galées,
supplemented by the Castilian galleys. What then were English
resources?[33]

In England private shipowners bore by far the greatest part of the
contribution to the naval war effort. Until 1380 the Crown made no
payment to the owners of impressed ships; in that year, after pressure
by the Commons in the Parliaments of 1373, 1376, 1378 and 1380 for
some compensation, the government granted (until the next Parliament)
a payment of 3s 4d per quarter per ton of carrying capacity; this was an
act of grace and was for maintenance. The matter was raised from time
to time in succeeding Parliaments, for example October 1385, 1386,
1388, October 1404 and March 1416, and payments seem generally to
have been made after 1380, though from 1385 at only 2s. The wages of
sailors of impressed ships were, of course, always paid by the Government; but all too often ships arrested for an expedition had to wait at
the rendezvous for weeks, even months, before that expedition got away,
and their crews had to be paid. Such was the case in 1386, when ships
arrested for Gaunt's voyage to Spain were held at Plymouth from April
till July.[34] As the orders for the impressment of these vessels had been
issued in January, there was not only the expense of the delay at the
port of embarkation but also that of the 'longe comyng togider of
the shippes'.[35] And it was this that often caused friction between the
government and shipowners, for although sometimes (as in 1386)
wages were paid from the time of arrest, on other occasions vessels were
detained without payment for long periods, as in 1372 when the crews
of twenty-four ships were held for 105 days before their wages began.[36]
Thus, while impressed shipping was essential to any major and sustained naval effort, the whole process of getting a fleet of such ships to
sea was a long and costly one, inconvenient to the government, even

dangerous if a speedy response was what was demanded, and not only a nuisance to shipowners but sometimes involving them in direct financial loss.

The English Crown did, however, have other resources to supplement that of impressed ships. We have already noticed the Cinque Ports service, the Portuguese galleys which served between 1384 and 1389 and the occasional hiring of Genoese galleys, for example in 1338 and 1373.[37] The longer the war went on the less important these particular sources became, and after 1389 they were but seldom resorted to. Another expedient was the building of barges and balingers by selected towns at their own cost. In the Parliaments of November 1372 and October 1377, the government, with the support of the Commons, ordered certain towns each to build a barge (in 1377 specifically a balinger of forty to fifty oars); in 1377 these were to be at the disposal of those who had borne the cost of their construction once the forthcoming campaigning season was over. In both cases the augmentation of the resources at the disposal of the government was neither long term nor particularly great. Some fourteen vessels were ready by the summer of 1373 and served that season, many of them the next and some of them thereafter in the later 1370s. The thirty-two balingers demanded in 1377 were to be ready by March 1378: 'a substantial number of new balingers served at sea in 1378; they are hard to identify in later years, but some were certainly employed again'.[38] Nevertheless, in the 1370s they must have been welcome to a hard-pressed government. A similar scheme mooted by the Crown in January 1401, when fifty-five barges and balingers (a somewhat excessive figure) were demanded from a wide variety of towns, ran into opposition in the Commons when Parliament met at the end of that month, and the order was withdrawn.[39]

This might serve as an example of the power of the Commons during this period. It also shows the concern of the Commons with naval affairs. This is an aspect of the war at sea which would repay detailed examination, for it is evident that in Parliament there was much discussion of what should be done at sea and how it should be done. In the earlier part of the war the Council chose to consult separately with representatives from the ports, in 1341, 1342, 1344 and 1347 for example, and again in November 1369; in May 1374 it was masters of ships who were singled out for consultation.[40] As Parliament became the forum for such and much other discussion in the later fourteenth century, it was there that the Council met criticism, heard advice, and there that plans and schemes were made for the better keeping of the seas, as the phrase ran. Nor was it only in the Commons that the mercantile and shipowning interest was represented, for with so many of the lords owning one or more ships of their own they too had a care to such matters and no doubt words they felt needed saying. In the Parliament of April 1379, for example, in response to a Commons petition, Henry Percy, earl of Northumberland and the mayor of London, John Philipot, were nominated to treat with the merchants in the Commons concerning the safety of Scarborough and the security of the northern seas. The scheme they drew up, and given the Commons' assent, was for two armed ships, two barges and two balingers to patrol in the North Sea and to be financed by a levy on merchant ships, fishing boats and colliers sailing those waters. Sir Thomas Percy, the admiral of the North and four others from Scarborough and elsewhere were made responsible for levying this rate and overseeing the whole operation, and collectors were appointed in London and the more important east-coast ports. The scheme was to run until 25 November.[41]

This elaborate scheme illustrates that gap between intention and result which is characteristic of medieval, and for that matter much of modern, legislation, for nothing seems to have come of it. The citizens of Scarborough petitioned again in the autumn Parliament of 1383; having purchased a barge and a balinger they asked for a levy similar to that of 1379 (though less wide in its application) in order to man and equip them.[42] They received an unfavourable reply on this occasion and nothing was done. They would, like so many others whose living was on or by the sea, have to help themselves.

The government too, although looking to others to supply the greater part of its naval resources, had one means of self-help. The king's ships are the remaining component of English seapower which we have to examine. While it has been quite rightly said that 'had the government been dependent on them as the backbone of its seapower much less could have been attempted than was in fact the case',[43] it is nevertheless true that during certain periods the king's own vessels played a significant part in the war at sea. How significant their contribution was during the first phase of the war has yet to be revealed. It would seem likely that at Sluys in 1340 and off Winchelsea in 1350 Edward III's own ships played a leading role, but an assessment of their contribution to the more mundane measures of England's naval effort in the years down to the 1350s requires a more detailed examination of the public records than has yet been undertaken.[44] As the number of royal ships during this period would appear to have been about forty, it may be that their role was like that of a similar number of vessels between 1369 and 1375. During the latter period they formed small squadrons which frequently went on patrol; in 1369 twenty-seven royal ships were at sea for varying periods between June and December, and they supplemented impressed ships in more imposing fleets, in 1374, the expedition of Sir William Nevill and Sir Philip Courtenay included thirteen king's ships – about one-third of the full complement.[45] This first role, that of patrolling, was perhaps the most valuable they could perform, and it was on this task that they would chiefly be employed when the king's ships again reached thirty in number during the reign of Henry V.

The king's ships were his own property, as much so as the Crown jewels or the royal demesne, and they could, therefore, be sold to pay his debts or given away to satisfy his creditors. Moreover, as the personal capacity of the king was what counted in medieval government, the quality of the royal ability was as crucial in small matters as in great ones and as important for the state of the king's ships as it was for the conduct of politics. Thus the accession of a minor had far-reaching effects upon the king's ships and the men who were concerned in their welfare; so it was in 1377. By September 1378 when Robert Crull handed over to John Lincoln as clerk of the king's ships only five of the forty or so king's ships of 1369–75 remained.[46] During the next two years some £387 was spent on them by Lincoln, but in October 1380 the four that then remained were ordered to be sold (at the best prices possible) in order to pay off certain of Edward III's debts.[47]

It was not until 1393–4 that Richard II acquired any ships of his own, and in August 1394 the first clerk of the king's ships since 1380 was appointed. By the end of the reign the number of king's ships had increased to four.[48] During the reign of Henry IV there were about half a dozen at any one time, although in 1408–9 only a couple, and little money was spent on them.[49] Preoccupied with revolts, and with money hard to come by, Henry had neither the means nor the time to pursue the war against France with any sustained determination. Nor were the French able to take the opportunity afforded them by Henry's difficulties in England and Wales, for with Charles VI intermittently mad the struggle between the dukes of Burgundy and Orléans became ever more intense until in 1410 civil war broke out.

This is not to say that there was not war at sea; that a state of truce existed did not prevent hostilities continuing. There were raids and counter-raids, commercial shipping was continually being pillaged, piracy flourished. But the greater part of all this was, in fact, undertaken on private initiative; little was done by either government.

With the accession of Henry V in March 1413 all this was to change. English military intervention in the French civil war had already begun in 1411, but Henry V's continuation of this policy was altogether on a different scale and it involved England in a war effort both by land and on the sea, the like of which she had not undergone since the 1340s nor indeed was to undergo again until the reign of Henry VIII. Henry V, however unheroic his ambitions, knew what he was at. The role English seapower now had to play would be a crucial one, but one subordinate to that of English armies. For if the war was to be won it would be in France, not at sea, however many raids were made or victories gained. Seapower, then, was to be employed essentially for defensive purposes, for the safety of the English coast and English merchant shipping, and to give security to the movement across the Channel of men and supplies for the armies in France. The deeper the English reached into France, the more secure the Channel became; the conquest of Normandy was the best security England and English shipping could have.[50] The only time that either of the combatants during the war achieved anything like a command of the seas was during Henry's reign, and that English control, never total by any means, was gained both by the presence of English squadrons at sea during every campaigning season from 1415 to 1421 and by the acquisition of northern France. And none of this would have been possible without the alliance of Burgundy.

Henry V's strategy was an assured one. Even if seapower was to play an auxiliary though proper part in that strategy, this still involved a sustained and costly naval programme. Part of that programme was the development of the king's own resources. The six king's ships of 1413 had doubled by 1415, by February 1417 they had more than doubled again, and by August 1417 there were thirty-four royal vessels; for the remainder of the reign the figure at any one time was between thirty and thirty-four. Within four years of his accession Henry had at his command a balanced fleet, obtained through purchase, capture and building: some seven carracks, all Genoese prizes from the victories of August 1416 and June 1417, about a dozen ships ranging from 200 to over 700 tons and fifteen or so barges and balingers, mainly balingers and most of them new built. This rapid expansion was directed by two men, William Catton, appointed keeper of the king's ships in July 1413, and William Soper of Southampton, who succeeded him as keeper in February 1420. Soper, however, was playing an active part in the administration of the king's ships long before he became keeper. From February 1414 onwards he was particularly engaged on the construction of ships, and it was under his close supervision that Southampton became a naval base of the first importance, much like the Clos des Galées at Rouen had been in the 1370s. At Southampton itself a dock and a storehouse was built, while just down the Solent at Hamble two other storehouses were established and wooden defences constructed for the safety of the ships lying up there. Soper's tasks were not restricted to the supervision of shipbuilding and refitting, he was also responsible for providing vessels for transport and patrolling duties, for equipping them and for paying their crews. So great was the amount of work to be done that Catton, the nominal head of the establishment, could not cope alone; he required the assistance of this wealthy merchant for the proper performance of the duties attaching to his office. The revolution that had been effected was acknowledged in 1420 when Soper was appointed keeper with a fee of £40 a year, more than double the 1s a day the clerks of the fourteenth century had received.

They, however, had been given benefices to support themselves, and the clerkship was but one of the offices that fell to them during a career in the civil service. Robert Crull, for instance, clerk from 1359 to 1378, went on to become treasurer of the Exchequer in Ireland in 1389, an office he continued to hold in the early part of Henry IV's reign, while John Lincoln, clerk from 1378 to 1380, eventually became the king's secretary in 1396.[51] John Chamberlain, clerk from March 1399 to July 1406, seems to have been the first layman in that office but he too was a civil servant.[52] The appointment of Soper, neither cleric nor civil servant but a man who owned and understood ships, was therefore a recognition of the professionalism that was now deemed necessary for the management of the king's ships.[53] This development of the royal navy was, of course, expensive. Certainly it was money well and carefully spent, for we can be sure that Henry himself took note of what was being done. The pious renaming of the carracks captured in June 1417[54] is as typical of that many-sided man's attention to detail as the fact that William Catton made almost as much from the hiring out of the royal ships between 1413 and 1415 as he received from the Exchequer. Henry and his clerk were not even above hauling coal from Newcastle and selling it at a profit in London.[55]

That all this was worth while is shown not only by the success of Henry's use of seapower but by the role of the king's ships in the naval activity of the reign. The advantages of having a fleet of around thirty vessels, a similar number of experienced king's mariners to captain them and an efficient organisation to maintain them are obvious. One did not have to endure the delays and frustrations almost invariably to be associated with the employment of impressed shipping. And as the speed with which one could get a force to sea was essential for the proper exercise of seapower, an already available and quickly fitted out royal fleet was clearly a powerful instrument of policy.[56] If, therefore, Henry's ships formed a substantial proportion of the sea-keeping expeditions sent out during his reign, then it may be argued that he had grasped this aspect of naval strategy as firmly as he had most aspects of military strategy.

Much detailed work needs to be done on the composition of those expeditions before that can be known, but it seems likely that most of the squadrons sent out between 1418 and 1421 did comprise a high proportion of king's ships. A typical patrolling squadron was that under John Cole and Thomas Treverak which was out from the end of July to the end of September 1418; it was a small affair of 180 soldiers in eight vessels: six royal balingers and two ships, the *Julian* owned by William Soper and the *Nicholas* of Newcastle.[57] Even the much larger force of 1500 soldiers under the command of Hugh Courtenay, earl of Devon, which was at sea from May to early November 1420, sailed in fourteen royal vessels, ten of them balingers, and a 200-ton ship from Dartmouth, possibly Courtenay's own.[58] In the earlier part of the reign, when the king's ships were fewer and Catton and Soper were still feeling their way, impressed vessels formed the greater part of these squadrons. In 1415, for example, Sir Thomas Carew's 180 soldiers sailed in four vessels, two from Bayonne and two from Dartmouth, and in 1417 the 988 soldiers under his command were in six or seven impressed ships, his own barge the *Trinity*, a Venetian carrack and two or three royal ships.[59]

During the years 1415 to 1417 there was too great a demand for shipping for the king's ships to be able to meet it. During this period there were not only defensive patrols, but transport fleets required for the campaign of 1415 and the invasion of 1417, as well as battles to be fought. The duke of Bedford's expedition of 1416 was a grand one, and its main purpose was the relief of Harfleur, besieged and blockaded by the French. In a hard fight on 15 August he dispersed the French and Genoese blockading fleet and thus was able to run in supplies to the garrison.[60] On 29 June of the following year the earl of Huntingdon, out on patrol, ran into the enemy fleet – composed of the Genoese and

Spanish vessels that had got away from Bedford the previous year as well as French ships – and defeated it.[61]

These two victories, the sustained patrolling between 1415 and 1421, and above all the fall of Rouen in January 1419 and the occupation of the Normandy ports, virtually destroyed French seapower. Effective command of the Channel, unobtainable by naval action alone, had been achieved in the only way possible: by the capture of the enemy's bases and the destruction of his resources. How permanent this might have become had Henry V lived we cannot tell, but to the Council, after Henry's death in August 1422, with the dual kingdom established and the Burgundian alliance remaining firm, it must have looked permanent enough. The time of great and costly effort, at any rate at sea, seemed and was indeed over. Henry's fleet had served its purpose and idle ships were a financial liability. Moreover, debts had to be paid.

It is against this background that the sale of the greater part of that fleet between 1423 and 1425 has to be seen. Nineteen of the thirty ships were disposed of. The 1000 marks that Henry V had stipulated in his will should be realised from selling his ships were duly handed over to his executors, and Soper was paid some of the money owing to him. Nevertheless, as nearly £1000 was made from the sale, perhaps the Council went too far in their brief, and may be criticised for parting with almost all of the balingers which were in good condition. A small force of these handy vessels would have been useful. The four big ships which had been built to fight the Genoese carracks in French pay were not sold; the *Jesus, Trinity Royal, Holigost* and *Grace Dieu* were kept in repair for some years, but by 1435 they had all been dismantled and been left to rot.[62] By that time only one other royal ship remained. The dissolution of Henry V's navy by his successors had been as total as that of Edward III's by his, even if in the circumstances of the 1420s it was more excusable. Thus by 1435, when English fortunes turned round and there was the prospect of increasing hostilities at sea, the English government was once again dependent on the resources of its subjects.[63]

Yet the French would never again be a power at sea while the war lasted. After the invasion of Normandy and the destruction of the Clos des Galées at Rouen[64] the French did little at sea. The recovery of France was slow, Charles VII hesitant, his energies concentrated on the erosion of the English position within France. As England held on to the greater part of northern France in 1435–7, when it looked most likely to be lost and the duke of Burgundy failed to take Calais during the summer of 1436, Charles VII remained cut off from the bases and resources essential to any effort at sea. Unlike Charles V, he could only strike at the English in France, and thus did not dissipate his resources as his grandfather had done in his raids on England in the 1370s. Thus, although England lost her initiative at sea in the 1430s, she did not experience any attacks on her coasts such as those she had in that decade. The English government also concentrated on the military situation in France; it did little at sea to combat the growing number of attacks on English commercial shipping by the Burgundians and by French privateers. The pressure for a strong sea-keeping policy came from a number of quarters, and in the writer of the *Libelle of Englyshe Polycye*[65] it found its most articulate apologist. In the Commons too voices were raised. Hard pressed by its critics and lacking funds, in 1436 the government resorted to an inexpensive method of sea-keeping: licences were granted to shipowners and merchants to keep the sea at their own cost. This government experiment was as unsuccessful as a Commons scheme for sea-keeping by merchants had been in 1406; friendly shipping suffered as much as that of the enemy.[66]

In 1442, however, the government accepted a Commons petition which outlined a plan for the keeping of the sea.[67] Eight selected ships, each with an accompanying barge and balinger, were to patrol at sea from 15 May to 15 November 1442, and then again from 1 March to 1 November 1443. The cost of this (over £10,000 in all) was to be met from the grant of tonnage and poundage. Eight knights or esquires were to be chosen to command the eight ships, one of them to be their chief captain. What actually happened was far less than this, but the government certainly tried. It was not until 26 June that Sir Stephen Popham indented with the Crown to serve with 565 soldiers for three months' service to begin on 1 August. His indenture noted that he, two other knights and two esquires had been appointed to keep the sea in the last Parliament, but that as they were neither present nor ready the indenture was being made with Popham alone. One of the knights disappears at this point, but Popham and the others received money from the Exchequer for their retinues, and commissioners to take the muster of their troops were appointed on 18 July. On 29 July the government had to remind the four commanders of the terms of their indentures; on 21 August the place to assemble was altered from the Camber to the Isle of Wight; on 2 September new commissioners were appointed and finally at Southampton on 13 September the muster was made. One knight and his company appear to have been missing and

Popham and the two esquires mustered 1344 men between them, only just over half the 2260 stipulated in the original plan and specified in the muster commission of 2 September. The muster-roll names five ships; if each of these was accompanied by a barge and balinger the total of fifteen vessels would have been sufficient to carry the depleted expedition. What it achieved, if anything, we do not know. No force went out in 1443.[68]

This was altogether different from the reign of Henry V: the long-delayed muster, the diminished force, the government writing round to various ports asking them to provide guns and war material.[69] It is no wonder that the *Libelle* dwelt nostalgically on Henry V and his fleet.[70] Those days had departed for ever and the problem now was how to make peace not war. The talking had begun in 1439, and in 1444 the truce of Tours was agreed. When war broke out once more in 1449 the French rapidly overcame English resistance in Normandy, taking the last English stronghold, Cherbourg, on 12 August 1450. The conquest of Gascony was equally rapid and by the summer of 1451 the whole territory was in French hands. Although John Talbot would be sent to Bordeaux in the following year, the government's reaction to the situation in France between 1449 and 1453 was a frantic rather than a determined one.

England, though she took long to reconcile herself to it, had lost. Gascony had gone, the Scots remained as much of a nuisance as they had been a hundred years before, English ships and English merchandise were as insecure as ever they were on the high seas. Yet the English still had Calais and they would still from time to time cross the Channel and march about northern France, while the French would never invade England. So it had been throughout the previous hundred years. Seapower had less to do with this, it seems, than the nature of the war itself. For the English, it was after all an offensive war which had continually to be carried into France; for the French, it was a war for the extension of the French kingdom within France and for the expulsion of the duke of Aquitaine. But as king of England he could not be kept out of France, for he had too many points of entry along French frontiers: through Flanders and Brittany as well as Gascony, Calais and the long coastline of Normandy. These entrances could not all be stopped up. Even in 1452 there was this problem; Charles VII strongly garrisoned Normandy, but Talbot got into Bordeaux.[71] On the other hand, the French had much less to gain from invading England; the Scots and the Welsh were not as useful to them as the Bretons and

Flemish were to the English, nor were their hearts really in, nor their minds really set upon such a course.

What one could achieve at sea, other than honourable feats of arms, the winning of plunder, the raising of one's morale and the lowering of the enemy's, was therefore little related to what one was able to do on land. Apart from the pressure brought to bear on the enemy by raids on his coasts, attacks on his shipping and the valuable assistance a fleet could bring to besieging or besieged troops, seapower was most strategically deployed when it was used for limited, defensive purposes – as it was by Henry V. Victory or defeat at sea in the Hundred Years War had none of those far-reaching consequences that they had when France and England fought out that other long conflict between the seventeenth and nineteenth centuries.[72]

BIBLIOGRAPHICAL NOTE

Charles de la Roncière, *Histoire de la marine française*, (6 vols, Paris, 1899–1934), is essential for the French side of the conflict at sea. Whereas La Roncière made extensive and excellent use of unpublished record material in his magisterial work, Sir Nicholas Harris Nicolas in his *History of the Royal Navy* (1847) did not; this and the fact that his two volumes only cover the period to 1422 make that work much less valuable. Nevertheless, it is important as a narrative account. For the English navy M. Oppenheim, *A History of the Administration of the Royal Navy* (1896), the Introduction on 'The navy before 1409' remains indispensable. On Henry V's reign particularly useful is W. J. Carpenter Turner, 'Southampton as a naval centre, 1414–1458', in *Collected Essays on Southampton*, ed. J. B. Morgan and P. Peberdy (Southampton, 1958), and J. H. Wylie, *The Reign of Henry V*, ii (Cambridge, 1919), ch. xlv has much information. On the ships themselves there are numerous articles in *Mariner's Mirror* and an important paper by G. V. Scammell, 'English Merchant Shipping at the end of the Middle Ages: some East coast evidence' in *EcHR* 2nd ser., xiii (1961). For the later stages of the war see C. F. Richmond, 'The Keeping of the Seas during the Hundred Years War: 1422–1440', *History*, xlix (1964), and the same writer's 'English Naval Power in the Fifteenth Century', *History*, lii (1967), which also has some general ideas on the nature of war at sea. Crucial to an understanding of that subject are the two perceptive articles of J. W. Sherborne, 'The English Navy: Shipping and Manpower 1369–1389', *Past and Present*, 37 (1967) and 'The Battle of La Rochelle and the War at Sea, 1372–5', *BIHR* xlii (1969).

NOTES

1. James Campbell, 'England, Scotland and the Hundred Years War in the Fourteenth Century', in *Europe in the Late Middle Ages*, ed. J. Hale, R. Highfield and B. Smalley (1965), pp. 188–91; Charles de la Roncière, *Histoire de la marine française*, i (Paris, 1899), 390–2, 421 ff. Where no specific reference is

given the events described are to be found in the work just cited and in Sir Nicholas Harris Nicolas, *A History of the Royal Navy*, ii (1847).

2. *CPR 1354–1358*, p. 608.
3. G. Dupont, *Histoire des Cotentin et ses Iles* (Caen, 1885), pp. 268 ff.
4. In 1338 for example: *CPR 1334–1338*, p. 564.
5. S. W. Roskill, *The Navy at War, 1939–45* (1960), p. 270.
6. May McKisack, *The Fourteenth Century* (Oxford, 1959), p. 129; E. Perroy, *The Hundred Years War* (English trans. W. B. Wells, 1951), p. 106; K. Fowler, *The Age of Plantagenet and Valois* (1967), p. 56.
7. J. W. Sherborne, 'The Battle of La Rochelle and the War at Sea, 1372–5', *BIHR*, xlii (1969), p. 28, The relevance of this important article is far wider than its title suggests.
8. S. W. Roskill, *The Strategy of Sea Power* (1962), p. 184.
9. *Rymer's Foedera* (20 vols, original edition, 1704–35), v, 231, trans. from the Latin. For further discussion of these ideas see *History*, lii (1967), 1–6.
10. J. Lemoine, 'Du Guesclin à Jersey (1373–76)', *Revue historique*, lxi (1896), 45–61.
11. La Roncière, op. cit., i, 495–7; G. Daumet, *Étude sur l'alliance de la France et de la Castile au xive et au xve siècles* (Paris, 1898), pp. 17–18; P. E. Russell, *The English Intervention in Spain and Portugal in the time of Edward III and Richard II* (Oxford, 1955), pp. 7–9.
12. Froissart's description of the battle is one of his most vivid passages; the most recent translation is *Froissart: Chronicles*, ed. and trans. G. Brereton (Penguin Classics, 1968), pp. 113–19. Another excellent description of fighting at sea is to be found in the chronicle of the Castilian galley captain Don Pedro Niño who led his galleys against England in 1405–6; *El Vitorial*, trans. Joan Evans under the title *The Unconquered Knight: A Chronicle of the Deeds of Don Pedro Niño* (1928), pp. 161–6.
13. B. H. St J. O'Neill, *Castles and Cannon* (Oxford, 1960), ch. 1.
14. J. W. Sherborne, 'The English Navy: Shipping and Manpower 1369–1389', *Past and Present*, 37 (1967), 168. In France Philip VI seems to have had built barges of this type: La Roncière, op. cit., i, 407.
15. PRO, Exchequer, Various Accounts, E. 101/612/52, an undated indenture witnessing that Jacob de Provan had received this amount from the Exchequer; it is no doubt related to the service of Genoese galleys put under the command of Provan in November 1372: *Foedera*, vi, 753.
16. La Roncière, op. cit., i, 495–7; Terrier de Loray, *Jean de Vienne, amiral de France, 1341–96* (Paris, 1877), appendix no. 71.
17. Russell, op. cit., p. xxi.
18. Ibid., p. 6.
19. Sherborne, 'La Rochelle', loc. cit., p. 28; the article demonstrates this conclusion.
20. *CPR 1381–1385*, p. 554.
21. Russell, op. cit., pp. 376, 415–16, 527–8.
22. La Roncière, op. cit., i, 410. His passage (pp. 399–412) on French naval organisation is admirable and has been followed in this paper and by F. Lot and R. Fawtier, *Histoire des institutions françaises au moyen âge*, ii (Paris, 1958), livre v, ch. ii.
23. La Roncière, op. cit., i, 439–42. The royal fleet comprised seven ships, twenty-two barges and three galleys.
24. Sherborne, 'Shipping and Manpower', loc. cit., pp. 167–8.
25. La Roncière, op. cit., i, 501–2; ibid., ii (Paris, 1900), 71.
26. On Jean de Vienne see Loray, op. cit., which has a valuable appendix of

documents. For another French historian's assessment of Vienne see R. Delachenal, *Histoire de Charles V*, v (Paris, 1931), 23-4.

27. Although begun late, a naval expedition under Gaunt was in preparation at this time and by 20 June a large number of ships had been impressed. As the young prince of Wales was also to go on this voyage the death of Edward clearly put an end to all plans: A. F. Alexander, 'The War in France in 1377' (London Ph.D. thesis, 1934), pp. 40-5.

28. Loray, op. cit., appendix, nos. 55, 56, 57, 61, 66.

29. Published by C. Bréard, 'Le compte du Clos des Galées de Rouen pour 1382-1384', in *Mélanges Société de l'Histoire de Normandie*, 2nd ser. (Rouen, 1893), 53-154.

30. La Roncière, op. cit., ii, 100.

31. Sherborne, 'Shipping and Manpower', loc. cit., p. 174.

32. Ibid.

33. For the period 1369-89 see ibid., pp. 163-75. For the period just prior to the opening of the war see *The English Government at Work, 1327-1336*, ed. J. F. Willard and W. A. Morris (Camb., Mass., 1940), i, part viii, ch. 6.

34. Russell, op. cit., pp. 411-19.

35. Quoted in *History*, lii (1967), p. 6.

36. Sherborne, 'Shipping and Manpower', loc. cit., p. 165.

37. *CPR 1334-1348*, p. 564 and p. 10 above.

38. Sherborne, 'Shipping and Manpower', loc. cit., p. 169.

39. *CCR 1399-1402*, p. 238; *Rot. Parl.*, iii, 458.

40. *CCR 1341-1343*, p. 107; *Rymer's Foedera* (Record Commission edition), ii, 1193; *CCR 1343-1346*, p. 349; *Foedera*, v, 548; *CCR 1369-1374*, p. 109; *Foedera*, iii, 1002.

41. *Rot. Parl.*, iii, 66; *Foedera*, vii, 220-1.

42. *Rot. Parl.*, iii, 162.

43. Sherborne, 'Shipping and Manpower', loc. cit., p. 167, with reference to the period 1369-89.

44. For the first phase of the war we await the results of a thesis on 'The English Navy under Edward III, 1336-48' being undertaken by Miss J. Linda Proom.

45. Sherborne, 'Shipping and Manpower', loc. cit., pp. 166-7.

46. PRO, Exchequer, Various Accounts, E.101/38/13.

47. PRO, Exchequer, Foreign Accounts, E.364/20, m.C dorse; *CPR 1377-1381*, p. 543.

48. *CPR 1391-1396*, pp. 266, 420, 489, 511, 519; PRO, E.364/39, m.F.

49. The clerks of the king's ships accounts: PRO, Exchequer, Foreign Accounts.

50. cf. *History*, xlix (1964), 283-5.

51. *CPR 1388-1392*, p. 103; *CPR 1399-1401*, p. 445; *CPR 1391-1396* p. 685.

52. His salary seems to have been augmented accordingly: *CPR 1396-1399*, p. 476; *CPR 1399-1401*, pp. 87, 121 185.

53. For Soper and the royal navy see the works cited in *History*, xlix (1964), 298 note. One looks forward to the results of Mrs Susan Rose's thesis on 'The navy accounts of Henry V and Henry VI'.

54. PRO, Chancery, Signet Warrants, C.81/1366/17-18; *CPR 1416-22*, p. 142. The carrack had replaced the galley as the principal Genoese vessel at the turn of the fourteenth century: J. Heers, *Gênes au XVᵉ siècle* (Paris, 1961), pp. 268-79.

55. PRO, Exchequer, Various Accounts, E.101/44/24. The ships were chiefly engaged in carrying wine from Bordeaux.

56. This is the gist of *History*, lii (1967), 1–15.

57. PRO, E.101/49/25.

58. PRO, Exchequer, Issue Roll, E.403/643, m.19; R. A. Newhall, *The English Conquest of Normandy, 1416–1424* (New Haven, 1924), p. 199.

59. PRO, E.101/48/9; E.101/48/14.

60. La Roncière, op. cit., ii, 220–4. He had indented to go on the keeping of the sea with 1050 soldiers for three months on 14 April; the musters were to be taken at Sandwich on 12 May: PRO, E.101/71/821. This was not a large force and would have required only about fifteen ships.

61. La Roncière, op. cit., ii, 226–7.

62. The visit of a Florentine galley captain to the *Grace Dieu* in 1430 has not been noticed in the most recent paper on that vessel: M. W. Prynne, 'Henry V's *Grace Dieu*', *Mariner's Mirror*, liv (1968), 115–28. For the visit of Luca di Maso degli Albizzi see M. E. Mallett, *The Florentine Galleys in the Fifteenth Century* (Oxford, 1967), pp. 258–9. I wish to thank Dr Mallett for the translation that follows:

On Tuesday 31 January I went with William Soper, customs officer of Southampton, to see the great ships of the king of England which are in the Hamble about 4 miles from Southampton. The largest they said was of 3000 *botti* burden, and some said more than 3300, and truly I have never seen so large and splendid a construction. I had the mast measured on the first deck and it was about 21 feet in circumference and 195½ feet high. From the galley of the prow to the water was about 50 feet, and they say that when she is at sea another corridor is raised above this. She was about 176½ feet long and about 96 feet in the beam. Near by was a ship of 1600 *botti* and another of about 1200 *botti*. We lunched on this ship and Soper and his companions did us great honour.

The *bota* is equal to something under half a ton. The other ships were the *Holigost* and the *Trinity Royal*.

63. For the sale and the period 1422–40 see *History*, xlix (1964), 283–98. There were ten councillors present when the order for the sale was made; they included the admiral of England, Thomas Beaufort, duke of Exeter: PRO, Exchequer, Council and Privy Seal, E.28/39, 3 March 1423.

64. With the remaining royal ships it was destroyed by the Rouennais to prevent it falling into English hands: La Roncière, op. cit., ii, 233.

65. Ed. Sir George Warner (Oxford, 1926).

66. *History*, xlix (1964), esp. 292–5; G. A. Holmes, 'The "Libel of English Policy"', *EHR* lxxvi (1961), 193–216. For the siege of Calais see now also: M.-R. Thielemans, *Bourgogne et Angleterre . . . 1435–1467* (Brussels, 1966), pp. 90–107.

67. *Rot. Parl.*, v, 59–60.

68. C. F. Richmond, 'Royal Administration and the Keeping of the Seas, 1422–1485' (Oxford D.Phil. thesis, 1963), pp. 213–26.

69. PRO, E.28/70, 26 June 1442.

70. Lines 1010–60.

71. M. G. A. Vale, 'The Last Years of English Gascony, 1451–1453', *TRHS*, 5th ser., xix (1969), 124–5.

72. I wish to thank Robin Studd for his patient help with this paper.

5. The English Aristocracy and the War

MICHAEL POWICKE

To most beginning students the 'Hundred Years War' is associated with the *Chronicles* of Froissart, and rightly so. Although Froissart is strictly limited in his value for the historian seeking the causes and sequences of events, he gives an incomparably vivid picture of the leaders and their activities and outlook during the first half of the war. He depicts the war as an essentially aristocratic conflict, dominated by the ideas of chivalry, while he fully recognised both its cruelties and the special contribution of the English archers.[1] Froissart wrote from an intimate knowledge of the courts of England and the Low Countries. This close association with the English and Netherlands courts, combined with his zest for narrative, and his eye for picturesque detail, qualify him as the best 'original' guide to the ethos of the war. It will soon be borne in on the reader that he cares more for the qualities of prowess in battle and for the code of honour of late medieval chivalry than he does either for the hereditary aristocracy or the administrative logistics of the war.

Chandos or Manny figure as largely as the Black Prince or John of Gaunt in his pages. Yet it is their chivalric valour rather than their mercenary self-interest (though he recognises the latter) that he reveres. The 'code' of aristocracy is prevalent. We are led to ask to what degree the aristocracy – i.e. the peers and barons – predominated in the English leadership during the war. The answers suggested in the following pages are only meant to be provisional in a still fluid area of study.

The execution of the war rested firmly in the hands of the king and his executive officers. The dominance of the household, i.e. Wardrobe and special officers such as the 'keeper of victuals', is demonstrable for the first stages of the war. Unfortunately, the executive arm for the later stages still remains largely unexplored. The termination of Wardrobe control left a gap, which the known records have left as yet unfilled. Fifteenth-century administrative history remains little-exposed terrain, perhaps because the sources are difficult and fragmented.

From the outset, Edward III seems to have recognised the need for baronial support. As early as 1330 he announced his intention 'that the matters which touch us and the estate of our realm are to be disposed of by the common counsel of the magnates of our realm'. This support was sought, in the opening stages of the war, in Parliament. This has been established, in spite of the absence of the principal parliamentary records, by E. B. Fryde. Further, as Parliament won control of both special taxation and of customs, its consent became more and more essential to the prosecution of the war. Its expression, in the form of appropriation, appointment of war treasurers, accountability, lie outside the scope of this study. But it should be kept in mind. What is more, the Lords, as the senior group in Parliament, with a multiplicity of undefined and probably undefinable ties to the Commons, influenced this parliamentary consent both directly (as the senior chamber), and indirectly, through inter-cameral committees and direct influence on the knights, esquires and burgesses of the 'Lower House'.[2]

Clearly, the evolution of Council and Parliament in the period of the war is crucial to an understanding of aristocratic control of the war. Unfortunately, no good study of either institution exists for these years. Pollard's *Evolution of Parliament* is preoccupied with special pleadings, while Baldwin's *King's Council* is bedevilled by the author's unwillingness to distinguish between different forms of the Council. Only Roskell's studies of the Commons stand out in this dreary picture. The general conclusion of these studies would seem to be that, as far as present knowledge goes, the king, depended, first, on officials; secondly, on the Lords; and thirdly, on the Commons, in decisions about peace and war.

The Council's role was crucial. It grew in influence steadily, as it grew in aristocratic composition, until the last decade of the war. Initially, the aristocratic component of the Council (known, at an as yet undetermined point, as the 'Lords of the Council'), did little but defend the war. The Lords were united behind the royal claims, either to royal sovereignty or to independence within their holdings, with regard to the Valois kings of France. To oppose the Plantagenet and Lancastrian claims was to be against God.

In supporting, and implementing, the royal claims, the Lords fell far short of the declaration of the ordinances of 1311 that 'the King shall neither go out of the Kingdom nor undertake an act of war against any one, without the assent of his baronage, and that in parliament'. They began to approach this notion of aristocratic assent towards the end of the fourteenth century, though in practice, if not in legal form, the need for the assent of the peerage long antedated the 'formal' procedures of the later period. In 1392 and 1395 predominantly aristocratic councils discussed diplomatic and military relations with France. In 1399 the Lords in Parliament agreed that Henry IV should go in person against the Scots. A Council of 1401 debated whether war should be declared on France, and whether parliamentary support for such a step should be sought. Another Council of the same year apparently counselled war with France and Scotland. Council for the remainder of Henry IV's reign was preoccupied with domestic affairs, until in 1411 it sanctioned Arundel's expedition against the Orléanists, and less certainly that against the Burgundians in 1412. It should be remembered, that at least in part in response to Commons' initiative, the Council was becoming more aristocratic and less official during these years.

Henry V restored royal initiative in its full vigour. This had an ambivalent effect on the Lords' support of the war. His initial moves in 1414 and 1415, were at least put before the Council, though aristocratic support was perhaps more emotional than institutional. The aristocratic conciliar and parliamentary support dwindled after 1415, when Henry V settled down to the piecemeal conquest of Normandy.

The death of Henry V put England in a dilemma. The medieval notion of a militant, leading, monarch, was still deeply ingrained, but now England had at first a child, and after 1437 a religious, peace-loving leader as king. Inevitably, a giant step forward in conciliar government followed. In all aspects, domestic and foreign alike, the Council predominated in English affairs from 1422 until a 'court' party emerged in the late 1430s. Even after that, Council still emerged occasionally as the forum of decision-making until the débâcle of 1450.

The conciliar debates after 1422 were overwhelmed by the conflict between Gloucester and Beaufort, and later between York and Suffolk. Nevertheless, Council 'contained' these rivalries, and postponed the outbreak of civil war, besides enabling energetic warriors like Bedford, Fastolf and Talbot to hang on to the English lands in France. Council discussed extensively Henry VI's 'coronation' expedition to France of 1430-1. Gloucester put forward far-reaching, if far-fetched proposals regarding the war in a Council of 1434. Bedford, too, in his last days, put forward to Council his ideas on the direction and financing of the war. As Council waned, Parliament again became a forum of acrimonious accusations and defence – e.g. in 1433 (Bedford's defence). Somerset's expedition of 1443 was preceded by lengthy conciliar debate. It was in Council and Parliament that he sought sanction for his peace negotiations in France, and it was in the latter that he was charged with treasonable dealings with Orléans and Charles, charges which led to his death. Once Suffolk was so violently removed, York carried his argument with Somerset to the country. Herein lay the first skirmishes of the 'Wars of the Roses'. Thus the last stages of the Hundred Years War saw the irruption of aristocratic interest, via Council and Parliament, into the decision-making process. It is nevertheless true, that for the war as a whole, the king with his chief ministers and advisers, was the supreme authority. The king, with aristocratic support, was well-nigh invincible; the reverse situation was, *per contra*, disastrous.[3]

Aristocratic influence on the financing of the war was much less direct. Early in the reign of Edward III, the Commons established a controlling voice in the voting of taxes. This they never lost. Therefore, the Lords' control was reduced to that which they exercised through joint committees. Attempts by the king to negotiate directly with the Lords, as in 1407, were sharply repudiated. Of course, the highly disrupted question of Lords' control of the Commons through indenture and affinity remained. Suffice it to remark here that this influence was a fact of late medieval political life, but involved much 'labouring' and pressure, as against direct control.

The war was characterised by innumerable exchanges of diplomats between the two sides, with the papacy at Rome or Avignon, and with the Church Councils of the early fifteenth century. These exchanges reached a high point on certain occasions when a truce, or even peace, was being sought, as in 1359–60, 1374, 1396, 1435 and 1444–5. The bulk of this diplomatic work was carried out by the clergy and the knights of the household. The usual embassy of an English king consisted of a bishop or two, a few knights and squires of the household and the occasional herald. It was exceptional for a Gaunt (in 1374) or a Suffolk (in 1444) to play the leading part. It was more likely for a Stratford, Beaufort or Kemp, from the bench of bishops, to lead the English delegations. The catalogue of L. Mirot and E. Déprez underscores this observation. One must set against this learned work the fact that magnates often served unpaid, and therefore earned no mention in the financial records on which the list is based. Nevertheless, the fact that magnates made up less than 10 per cent in this list of about 660 embassies is not without significance. Detailed studies of such diplomatic encounters as those at Bruges in 1374 and at Arras in 1435 underline this secondary role of the magnates in the conduct of diplomacy.[5]

When we turn from decision-making and foreign negotiations to the leadership of the war itself, we find a dramatic reversal of roles. The aristocracy were the war leaders *par excellence*, excelled only for limited periods and in limited areas of warfare by the professional adventurers. The commanders of the armies usually bore titles of prince, marquis, duke or earl, and the contingents under the direct control of these lords were the most numerous. These men, second only to the king himself, were responsible for the dramatic one-sided victories on the field of battle, for the most far-ranging and destructive *chevauchées*, and for the static commands of provinces under Plantagenet or Lancastrian control.

A review of the major campaigns and commands will illustrate these general remarks. The earl of Derby was among the captains in the opening campaign of 1337, and was in command of the Auberoche campaign of 1345. Credit for the victory of Morlaix (1342) must be shared between William Bohun, earl of Northampton and Robert of Artois. At Crécy (1346), the 'battles' into which an engaged medieval army were divided, were commanded respectively by King Edward III, Prince Edward (The Black Prince) and the earl of Arundel, supported by Bohun. Each of these commanders was in turn supported by sub-ordinates drawn principally from the aristocracy; the earls of Warwick and Oxford served under Prince Edward; lords Say and Audley under Arundel and Bohun; Robert de Ufford, earl of Suffolk and William Montagu, earl of Salisbury were commanders in the king's battle. The leadership at Crécy, and at the subsequent siege of Calais, was almost entirely in the hands of the English aristocracy.

A contrary movement set in after Crécy and Calais. The ensuing decade saw the rise of mercenary captains, usually drawn from the lesser nobility and 'gentry'. This 'class', if it can be so designated, was to play a greater or lesser part in the remaining years of the war; in fact, their tendency to resort to independent warfare in intervals of truce or peace was to make war a much more continuous experience for large parts of France than any of the national leaders intended. Among the early captains to lead English forces were Sir Thomas Dagworth (who succeeded the earl of Northampton as commander in Brittany), Sir Walter Bentley, Sir Hugh Calveley, Sir John Chandos (one of the few non-aristocratic individuals to become king's lieutenant in France) and the notorious Sir Robert Knowles. It was the activities of these men which supplied Froissart with many of his stories of chivalric heroism, such as the famous 'battle of the Thirty'. It is ironical that these men, whose fortune-hunting proclivities are well attested (though none so fully demonstrated as those of their fifteenth-century successor, Sir John Fastolf) were the darlings of chivalric literature.

At Poitiers, the 'professionals' sank back into second place. In that engagement, the 'battles' were commanded by the Black Prince, the earl of Warick and the earl of Salisbury. Subordinate commands were also mainly in the hands of aristocracy: the earls of Oxford and Suffolk, and lords Audley, Cobham and Willoughby. True, alongside them fought such captains as Chandos and Loring. The 'Northern' force led by Henry of Lancaster, with which Edward had probably hoped to link up, was similarly aristocratic in make-up.[6]

The 1360s, with desultory fighting following the treaty of Calais, were again dominated by the 'free companies'. This was the hey-day of Chandos, Calveley, Knowles and the Captal de Buch. Many of these followed the Black Prince into Spain to win battles and lose a war; though, at Nájera (1367), two of the customary three 'battles' were under aristocratic command (Prince Edward and Sir Thomas Percy, later earl of Worcester; the third was under the Captal de Buch). In general, the pattern of the years of 'truce' and the 'official' fighting which followed 1369, was of major enterprises under great princes and lords, but innumerable lesser commands and much illegal combat in the hands of the professionals.

After 'full-scale' war was resumed in 1369, the English efforts consisted of a series of *chevauchées*, devastating marches over French territory, while Charles V, ably seconded by Du Guesclin and Anjou, quietly reabsorbed most of the previous English gains by a combination of diplomacy and military 'nibbling'. The English *chevauchées* were led for the most part by great English lords. John of Gaunt led the greatest in 1373, and had led an earlier one in 1369. Others were led by the earl of Cambridge and the earl of Buckingham. Only one, in 1370, was under the command of a professional, Sir Robert Knowles; and aristocratic commanders failed to support Knowles. These dreadful marches were intended to terrorise the French into accepting Plantagenet rule, and to reward English participants with loot. It is significant that they came at a time when the English monarchy was at a low ebb, and hence must cast serious doubt on the capacity of the lords, unaided, to wage intelligent war. In defence of their failure, it must be remembered that the French monarchy was at the very same time experiencing a short-lived renaissance.

When war was resumed, tentatively in 1411–12, and on a national scale in 1415, the *de facto* power of the lords in the central direction of public affairs had been converted into an institutional form in the dominance of the 'Lords of the Council'. Hence Henry V, even more than Edward III, was able to take the bulk of his magnates with him in his bid for the French Crown; first, in the great *chevauchée* which culminated in Agincourt, most stunning of the great 'set-piece' victories of the English kings, and later (1417–20) in the slow, grinding, process of reducing Normandy, castle by castle, town by town. Needless to say, this latter form of war was less attractive, in spite of the new possibility of acquiring French fiefs, and both aristocratic and 'middle-class' support had begun to fall off somewhat before Burgundy's dramatic defection brought to Henry all he had hoped for (treaty of Troyes, 1420).

After Henry V's death in 1422, the English effort in France continued to be largely aristocratic, and was, of course, now decided more and more by the 'Lords of the Council'. Rifts were now appearing in the aristocratic front, occasioned in the main by social dislocation in England, but also by the new leadership which confronted the Lancastrians in France. France continued to offer handsome rewards to the unscrupulous, as the record of Sir John Fastolf amply demonstrates. Victories continued to be won under Bedford, and the English staying-power was remarkable. Bedford provided a princely, if not a royal leadership. With his passing, and the defection of Burgundy (1435), the increasingly spasmodic aristocratic support for, and leadership in, the war proved inadequate. A tendency to revert to the discredited *chevauchée* appeared in the military efforts of such men as Somerset, Suffolk and York. The 'middle class' of gentry increasingly lost interest, and armies had to be put together from a few loyal magnates leading a mass of bowmen. A marcher baron, John Talbot, ennobled as earl of Shrewsbury in 1442, provided some brilliant leadership. It needs stressing that this curious patchwork of rival lords and largely yeoman soldiers held on to the English gains until the very end of the war. The French victories of 1449–50 were a sudden, overwhelming reversal of previous 'stability'. The magnates, in a rather unimpressive way, had 'kept faith'.[7]

In the foregoing pages, we have been mainly concerned with leadership on campaigns. Besides their predominance in this area, the lords supplied the great majority of the lieutenants who ruled provinces (Aquitaine, Normandy, Brittany), and for considerable periods the whole of occupied France, on behalf of the king or Council. Most of these governors were, in point of fact, royal princes. Edward III's sons almost monopolised these posts in the fourteenth century: the Black Prince, John of Gaunt, Edmund Langley and Thomas Woodstock. The only non-royal leader of equal stature was Henry of Grosmont, duke of Lancaster. When war was resumed, the sons and grandsons of these princes continued the tradition: the Beauforts, York and Clarence. More of the non-princely aristocrats were now brought in: Thomas Montagu, earl of Salisbury, Richard Beauchamp, earl of Warwick and William de la Pole, earl of Suffolk. Lieutenants, particularly for Brittany which had its native princes, were occasionally drawn from outside the aristocracy. Such professionals as Dagworth, Bentley, Chandos and Knowles held lieutenancies. In the fifteenth century, John Talbot's career belongs half-way between that of a great aristocratic governor and a professional captain. In the fixed offices, then, as in the more transient expeditionary commands, the aristocracy were the right arm of the monarchy throughout the war. Perhaps a decline in calibre, and certainly a development of rivalry, must be included in any assessment of the ultimate débâcle.[8]

The motives and purposes of the aristocracy in so strongly supporting the royal claims in France can be largely deduced from their actions. Yet in two areas, those of 'ideals' and of profitability, it may be possible to carry the story a little further. As regards the first, one may note the persistence of feudal ideas. The elaborate machinery, and tedious procedures, by which all the English kings, from Edward III on, sought to justify the war; the insistence on the claims to homage and service; the repudiation of homage to the Valois; all the 'legal' debate which preceded and accompanied the war, was associated with the king's right to the feudal allegiance of both English and 'foreign' allies. Related to notions of homage and feudal allegiance were those chivalric notions which exalted 'prowess', 'courage', and similar values, especially on the battlefield. These 'chivalric' values were embodied, more than anywhere else, in the romantic stories which were staple reading for the aristocracy. Just which stories and episodes they preferred, and whether there was a distinctive English taste in romance, I do not know. Some writers have noted the relatively minor place occupied by 'courtesy' or 'romantic love' in English writings. One thing is certain, that the successful English kings – Edward III and Henry V – encouraged chivalric sentiment. The Arthurian legend both fostered, and was fostered by, the Order of the Garter. This Order, unlike the other great Order of the late Middle Ages, that of the Golden Fleece, played no part in politics. Perhaps the English took the whole charade of knightly entertainments, oaths, baths, tourneys and so on with a grain of salt. Nevertheless, as a reward for outstanding service, the Garter helped to foster devotion to the monarch and his military enterprises.

The dawn of a 'national chivalry', in which service to the nation replaced individual deeds of prowess, has been traced by A. B. Ferguson. This 'Indian Summer' of chivalry involved romances in English, the development of heralds and heraldry, the refinement of the tournament and much else. The highest expression of this notion of chivalry as handmaid of public policy was William of Worcester's *Booke of Noblesse* at the very end of the war. The absence of any but a solitary manuscript must make one sceptical about the influence of this treatise. Perhaps this manuscript may be considered as marking the end of an era, a final cry for a public-spirited military nobility in a time of defeat and compromise. Perhaps, by the middle of the fifteenth century, the sentiments of Gower, who argued that a true knight would prefer peace to war, or of the author of *Mum and Sothseyer* who saw the aristocracy's role as political rather than military, were dominant among the English nobility. But the arguments of Gloucester in Council and the discussion of 1449 in Parliament make this unlikely.[9]

To turn from the realm of ideas and legal rights and duties to that of profit and finance would at first seem to confirm Huizinga's view of the deeply divided nature of late medieval man. Froissart, surprisingly enough, supplies a connecting link. He wrote: 'The English will never love or honour their king unless he be victorious and a lover of arms and war against their neighbours and especially against such as are greater and richer than themselves. Their land is more fulfilled of riches and all manner of goods when they are at war than in times of peace. They take delight and solace in battles and slaughter. Covetous and envious are they above measure of other men's wealth.' Thus the glorifier of English chivalry! The question of the search for wealth and the success of the English in obtaining it has engendered a fair amount of historical discussion. The opinions of kings and lords, inasmuch as they have survived, are certainly more concerned with rights, feudal and dynastic, than with profit. Even the 'bourgeois' *Libelle of Englyshe Polycye* wrote of economics as a means towards power rather than as an end itself. So, while not writing off Froissart's view (and he expressed far more views of a contrary kind), it is unlikely that search for profit was a dominant, or even important, feature of the English aristocracy's involvement in the war.

A different question is whether the war actually was profitable or not. Here a great number of pieces of evidence have been examined, but no agreed conclusions have emerged. This is partly because, with the exception of Fastolf, detailed evidence for any one participant has not been forthcoming. Incidental information, such as Walsingham's observation on Knowles's 100,000-crown profits, would seem to confirm that the professional soldiers of the fourteenth as of the fifteenth century, made substantial gains from the war. But studies of noble families such as the group analysed by Dr Holmes, or the Percies, do not suggest that war was an item of substantial income; if anything, the reverse. Historians have, therefore, fallen back on deductions from general evidence, and have reached diametrically opposed conclusions. The late Mr K. B. McFarlane, who probably knew more about the late medieval aristocracy than any scholar past or present or in the foreseeable future, drew up a list of the sources of profit which make it likely, in his view, that lords and knights emerged substantially wealthier than when the war started. The lords received more from their tenants than they paid into the Exchequer by way of subsidies, though the considerable profits of the years before 1334 were lessened thereafter by the increased frequency of such grants and by difficulties of collection. The higher customs tax on wool exports was passed on to the foreign buyer rather than borne by the home producer. The 'spoils of war' were a direct gain, though they have not left quantities of evidence. Under this heading one can list loot, ransoms (multiplied by a profitable trade therein), profits of office, taxes levied on the French, indemnities, charges for capitulation, bribes received to leave places unharmed, and accumulation of fiefs in France. While not so fully evidenced as in the case of the professional captains, there are plenty of examples of these profits accruing to the nobility. Thus Clarence, in 1412, was bought off at Buzançais for 210,000 écus. Others' researches have shown that in the fifteenth century the size of French fiefs granted to Englishmen increased with the recipients' rank. Examples of such land acquisition are Clarence, granted the *vicomtés* of Auge, Orbec and Pontaudemer; the earl of Salisbury, granted the county of Perche and other lands; the duke of Exeter who got the county of Harcourt and the castle of Lillebonne. Revenues flowed from French lands into the English coffers of Humphrey of Gloucester and Richard of York. In fact the 'way of cession' pursued by Suffolk probably increased Yorkist support.

Indirect evidence is to be seen in the increasing standard of living of the aristocracy, summed up by Mr McFarlane as 'more building, more ostentation . . . increased expenditure on luxuries of all sorts'. The likelihood that the war was the source of the money so spent is increased if one considers the evidence of such writers as Dr Holmes for a decline (for at least part of the war) of domestic income.[10]

Against this impressive list of gains from the war, Professor M. M. Postan has listed an almost as striking a catalogue of war losses. The unprofitability of many French offices (e.g. that of king's lieutenant) is noted. However, if Humphrey, duke of Gloucester, was owed vast sums for his Calais expenses of 1449, much the same could be said of many domestic office holders. Arrears in pay were endemic in the fifteenth century. Another piece of evidence, the payment of annuities to the lieutenant and seneschal of Aquitaine, does not necessarily mean that they were suffering greatly. The poor yield of French estates, as Dr Allmand has shown, varied greatly with the date: it was about 1436 that the shrewder of English landholders began to sell out. Professor Postan's list of ransoms paid by captured English lords will hardly impress the student who considers the vastly superior number of French lords captured by the English. The argument that the lords' gain were largely in the form of grants from the English Crown, rather than direct profits, constitutes a useful corrective, but does not invalidate the main burden of Mr McFarlane's arguments. In sum, the case for the profitability of the war for the English lords as a whole must be considered, at present, to have the upper hand. Yet there is no doubt that a much fuller, more sophisticated, study of this whole problem is deeply needed. We are dealing here very much with probabilities.[11]

In summing up, we may argue that the English aristocracy played a predominant role in the war, but a role which varied in terms of policy-making, diplomatic activity, military leadership, and the polarities of ideas about the war and crude profitability. It was, overwhelmingly, a royal war. But a king who had the backing of the aristocracy in Council and Parliament, in relations with the adversary, and in military leadership, was far more able to achieve success than one who lacked enthusiastic support, let alone grudging adherence.

BIBLIOGRAPHICAL NOTE

REFERENCE AND SOURCES

The Complete Peerage, ed. G. E. Cokayne, new ed. V. Gibbs (1910–59). The major work on individual families and lords, with occasional general studies.

Dictionary of National Biography, ed. L. Stephen and S. Lee (1885–90); still useful.

L. Mirot and E. Déprez, 'Les ambassades anglaises pendant la guerre de Cent ans. Catalogue chronologique', *BEC*, lix–lxi (1898–1900). Invaluable, but as based on financial records, not exhaustive.

Rymer's Foedera. Includes chief treaties, some delegations and political documents.

N. H. Nicolas, *Proceedings and Ordinances of the Privy Council* (7 vols, Record Commission, 1834–7). Essential for the later stages of the war.

Rotuli Parliamentorum . . . (*Rot. Parl.*), 6 vols. Almost equally valuable.

E. Perroy, 'The Anglo-French Negotiations at Bruges, 1374–1377', *Camden Miscellancy*, xix (1952).

E. Perroy, 'The Diplomatic Correspondence of Richard II', *Camden Third Series*, xlviii (1933). Both articles essential for late fourteenth-century diplomacy.

GENERAL WORKS ON THE WAR

C. Oman, *A History of the Art of War in the Middle Ages*, ii (1898). Still the best introductory survey.

A. H. Burne, *The Crecy War* (1955); *The Agincourt War* (1956). However imprecise in scholarship, the only modern account of the actual fighting.

E. Perroy, *The Hundred Years War* (English trans. W. B. Wells, 1951). The best guide to the politics of the war.

K. Fowler, *The Age of Plantagenet and Valois* (1967). Supersedes much of the above. Magnificently illustrated.

MORE SPECIFIC STUDIES

H. J. Hewitt, *The Black Prince's Expedition of 1355–1357* (Manchester, 1958). The best monograph on a single expedition.

R. A. Newhall, *The English Conquest of Normandy, 1416–1424* (New Haven, 1924).

J. G. Dickinson, *The Congress of Arras, 1435* (Oxford, 1955). The best study in Hundred Years War diplomacy.

A. B. Ferguson, *The Indian Summer of English Chivalry* (Durham, North Carolina, 1960).

K. B. McFarlane, 'The Investment of Sir John Fastolf's Profits of War', *TRHS* 5th ser., vii (1957).

K. B. McFarlane, 'War, the Economy and Social Change', *Past and Present*, no. 22 (1962).

M. M. Postan, 'The Cost of the Hundred Years War', *Past and Present*, no. 27 (1964).

A. E. Prince, 'The Strength of English Armies in the Reign of Edward III', *EHR* xlvi (1931).

C. T. Allmand, 'The Lancastrian Land Settlement in Normandy, 1417–1450', *EcHR* 2nd ser., xxi (1968).

COUNCIL, PARLIAMENT, AND WAR

J. F. Baldwin, *The King's Council in England During the Middle Ages* (Oxford, 1913).

E. B. Fryde, 'Parliament and the French War, 1336-1340', in *Essays in Medieval History Presented to Bertie Wilkinson*, ed. T. A. Sandquist and M. R. Powicke, (Toronto, 1969).

K. B. McFarlane, 'Parliament and Bastard Feudalism', *TRHS* xxvi (1944).

J. S. Roskell, *The Commons in the Parliament of 1422* (Manchester, 1953). By far the best introduction to late medieval Parliaments in all their aspects.

A. R. Myers. 'A Parliamentary Debate of the mid-fifteenth century', *Bulletin of the John Rylands Library*, xxii (1938).

M. R. Powicke, *Military Obligation in Medieval England* (Oxford, 1962).

The following works may also be found of value:

J. H. Ramsay, *The Genesis of Lancaster; Lancaster and York* (2 vols, Oxford, 1892).

W. Stubbs, *The Constitutional History of Medieval England*, ii and iii.

B. Wilkinson, *The Constitutional History of Medieval England*, ii, iii and iv.

Encyclopaedia Britannica, 11th ed., s.v. 'Chivalry'.

NOTES

1. Froissart, *Chronicles*, trans. Lord Berners.

2. For particular studies, see E. B. Fryde, 'Parliament and the French War, 1336-1340, in *Essays in Medieval History Presented to Bertie Wilkinson* (Toronto, 1969); J. S. Roskell, *The Commons in the Parliament of 1422* (Manchester, 1953); K. B. McFarlane, 'Parliament and Bastard Feudalism', *TRHS* xxvi (1944).

3. See *Rot. Parl.*, vols. ii–v, *passim*; N. H. Nicolas, *Proceedings and Ordinances of the Privy Council* (7 vols, Record Commission, 1834–7). W. Stubbs, *Constitutional History of Medieval England*, ii and iii gives a useful account.

4. McFarlane, 'Parliament and Bastard Feudalism', loc. cit.

5. L. Mirot and E. Déprez, 'Les ambassades anglaises pendant la guerre de Cent ans. Catalogue chronologique', *BEC* lix-lxi; E. Perroy, 'The Anglo-French Negotiations at Bruges, 1374-1377', *Camden Miscellancy*, xix (1952); J. Dickinson, *The Congress of Arras* (Oxford, 1955); also confirmed in E. Perroy, *The Diplomatic Correspondence of Richard II*, Camden Third Series, xlviii (1933). K. Fowler's study, *The King's Lieutenant: Henry of Grosmont, First Duke of Lancaster, 1310-1361* (1969), amply illustrates the role of the great lords and princes in diplomacy. See also S. Armitage-Smith, *John of Gaunt* (1904), pp. 118–202.

6. For the Black Prince's expedition of 1355–7, we are fortunate in having H. J. Hewitt's special study.

7. Baronial commands are noted by chroniclers, but also, for the earlier period, by Wardrobe Books, and for the latter, by Indentures of War. The general surveys by C. Oman and A. Burne need to be supplemented by the works of A. E. Prince, R. Newhall and M. R. Powicke listed above.

8. See K. Fowler, *The Age of Plantagenet and Valois*, espec. ch. iii and iv.

9. Ibid.; A. B. Ferguson, *The Indian Summer of English Chivalry* (Durham, North Carolina, 1960); A. R. Myers, 'A Parliamentary Debate of the mid-fifteenth century', *Bulletin of the John Rylands Library*, xxii (1938).

10. K. B. McFarlane, 'War, the Economy and Social Change', *Past and Present*, 22 (1962); C. T. Allmand, 'The Lancastrian Land Settlement in Normandy, 1417-1450', *EcHR* 2nd ser., xxi (1968).

11. M. M. Postan, 'The Cost of the Hundred Years War', *Past and Present*, 27 (1964).

6. The French Nobility and the War

PHILIPPE CONTAMINE

I

'EVERYONE knows that in all Christian and in all heathen countries there are three estates, that is the clergy, the nobles and the people.'[1] Thus writes Philippe de Mézières in his *Songe du Vieil Pelerin*, which was completed around 1389. In 1461, at the time of Louis XI's solemn entry into Paris, the Saint-Denis Gate was surmounted by a 'silver ship, in which there was a bed from out of which arose a king guarded by two angels, and at the foot of this bed stood persons representing the Church, the Nobility and Labourers'.[2] At the meeting of the Estates of Tours in 1484, in reply to a lawyer from Troyes who had questioned the fiscal privileges of the nobility, messire Philippe de Poitiers, knight, deputy for the same *bailliage* declared:

> The distinction of the estates and of those concerned with the public good is well known to everyone, according to which it is prescribed that the Church should pray for others, give counsel and exhortation; that the nobility should protect others by the exercise of arms, and that the people should nourish and support them by paying taxes and by tilling the soil. And this shall not be done for the particular advantage of anybody, as this lawyer seems to imagine and describe it, but only for the public good, in order that everyone, in fulfilling his particular office, should proceed and strive to work not only for his own, but for everyone's benefit, in such a manner that if one usurps the office of one's associate, or if one imposes one's burden on to another, one does not show regard for the common good. Neither women nor young men, even those with only a smattering of education, are ignorant of the specificity of these functions.[3]

The tripartite division of society, an ancient but long-lived myth, seemed so obvious that it was soon adopted, in France, at the time of the convocations of general and provincial Estates, although to begin with these assemblies were nothing more than an enlargement of the *Curia* or the Council, which brought together, not the orders of which society was composed, but individuals and collectivities – prelates, barons, and the most important urban communities – who had the necessary authority or influence to be obeyed and followed by their subordinates or by their equals.

Nevertheless, such a division of society was too summary and simple not to tempt certain minds to loosen and refine it. Witness the aforesaid Philippe de Mézières, who proposes the following quadripartite division:

Estates	Church	Nobility		People
Order or hierarchy	1	2	3	4
Upper level	Prelates and abbots	King, 'royalty', great princes, barons and great lords	Judges and justiciaries: *presidents* and secular judges, *baillis*, *vicomtes*, *prévôts*	Wealthy Parisian burgesses and those from other good towns; merchants
Middle level	Archdeacons, deans, provosts, canons, chaplains, priests and parish priests	The chivalry and rank and file of nobles: esquires and men of gentle birth	Advocates, notaries and procurators	*Chefs des métiers* of the kingdom and tradesmen
Lower level	Monks and friars	Army chiefs and captains of towns, castles and fortresses	Treasurers, royal officers and receivers; *élus*; sergeants	Labourers and humble people from good towns and the flat country

One of the interesting features of this classification is the importance attached to men concerned with finance, the law and administration, 'officers' whose functions expanded precisely in the later Middle Ages, and who, by their social origins, sometimes belonged to the nobility and were sometimes commoners.[4]

However that may be, at both the beginning and the end of the Hundred Years War, in the documents from that time – chronicles and didactic treatises, customaries and *ordonnances*, judicial, administrative or financial sources, and accounts of eyewitnesses – in each case a distinction is to be found between the nobles and the nobility, *les gentilshommes* and *la gentillesse*, on the one hand, and *le peuple, la populaire, le commun, les communes, les plébéiens, les roturiers, les coutumiers, les bourgeois* and *gens de pôté*, *les bourgeois* and *gens de basse condition*, or, more frequently, the non-nobles, on the other. There is no evidence in France during this period of an antithesis comparable to that which existed in fifteenth-century England between the nobility and the lords, on the one hand, and the knights, esquires, gentlemen and gentry, on the other. Most certainly the vocabulary of the time frequently distinguishes the *gentilshommes* and *simples gentilshommes* from the *seigneurs* or *grands seigneurs*; but in 1358 the nobles of Picardy and of Normandy addressed the king of Navarre, Charles the Bad, as the *plus gentilhomme du monde*,[5] and as late as the sixteenth century Francis I did not hesitate to style himself the *premier gentilhomme* of his realm. If there was any difference between the *gentilhomme* and the noble, it is, in the strictest sense, in so far as the latter could only be an ennobled person: 'A gentleman [*gentilhomme*] is someone who from time immemorial is the issue of gentlemen and gentlewomen', whereas nobility is only 'the beginning of *gentillesse*'.[6]

On the whole, despite all the shades and subtleties of vocabulary and despite regional differences, it may be assumed that around 1340, in the kingdom of France, the nobility corresponded to a sufficiently well-defined social reality for the historian to trace its contours and to study its structure.

II

It is first necessary to consider the absolute number of nobles and noble families and the ratio between them and the population as a whole. Taking into account the mass of documentation that has been preserved, an answer – at least an approximate one – is in itself not impossible; but it would call for detailed regional investigations of a kind that have not so far attracted much research. All that can be done here is to gather together some data which are of necessity fragmentary.

Take, for instance, the example of Forez, whose archives have been utilised with admirable sagacity by M. Perroy. This small province, which roughly corresponds to the present *département* of the Loire, was made up of 230 to 250 parishes. It is possible to locate 215 noble lineages there throughout the thirteenth century, although it is doubtful if more than 150 were in existence at any given time; however, since the lineage was more numerous than the family proper, it can be assumed that there was an average of one noble family per parish.[7] Let us leave the kingdom for an instant to consider the situation in the county of Provence. There were 3000 noble households there in 1271, 6 per cent with rural and 1–2 per cent with urban hearths; nobles accounted for 3·7 per cent of the total population.[8] In 1295, in the barony of Lunel, which is made up of some 15 communes of the present *département* of Hérault, an investigation enumerates – without counting the clergy – 1688 hearths 'of the common *taille* of non-nobles' ('de la taille commune des non nobles'), 285 were exempted from the *taille* because of poverty, 28 hearths were held by Jews and 56 by nobles; the proportion of the last mentioned here amounts to 2·7 per cent.[9] In 1337 the nobles and feoffees of the *bailliage* of Amiens offered Philip of Valois the services of 13 bannarets, 1102 armed and mounted men, and 462 foot soldiers armed with a hauberk and a bascinet: altogether 1577 men, when nine years earlier the *bailliage* numbered 1144 parishes and 115,716 hearths. Assuming that these 1577 men accounted for the same number of noble hearths, one ends up with 1·3 noble hearths per parish and 1·3 per cent nobles of the total population. A fiscal document from 1356, concerning 58 parishes in the district of Clermont-Ferrand in Auvergne, shows that there were 84 noble hearths among a total of 5385 (1·4 per cent), and there were 226 clerics (3·4 per cent of the total).[10] These few examples reveal the existence of rather marked regional variations; the different provinces of the kingdom were far from containing the same proportion of nobles. But taken together the proportion of nobles to the total population appears quite high, clearly exceeding 1 per cent in each case. If one accepts the figure of 15 million inhabitants for the population of the kingdom of France in 1328, one would certainly have to concede that 200,000 of these were nobles from approximately 40,000 to 50,000 families – clearly more than one noble family per parish, since there were then 32,500 parishes in the kingdom.[11]

This was the situation during the first half of the fourteenth century; but what about the following century? A document from that period states that in 1413 in the duchy of Brittany – which is composed of 5 *départements* and 35,000 square kilometres – there were 3 counts, 9 great barons, 18 bannarets and 4700 lesser nobles.[12] Now, some twenty years earlier the total population there numbered between 1,000,000 and 1,250,000 inhabitants.[13] The proportion of nobles thus amounted to 1·7 per cent. In 1477, in the same province, among a population of 1,300,000 to 1,500,000 inhabitants,[14] the nobles, who then numbered more than 8000, accounted for 2·3 per cent of the total.[15] According to the rolls of the *ban* and *arrière-ban* for 1467–71, at least 2500 nobles in Anjou, Poitou, Saintonge, Angoumois, Limousin, Marche and Combraille – an area comprising approximately 55,000 square kilometres –

owed military service by reason of their fiefs; during the same period there were at least 283 in Nivernais (5000 square kilometres), 167 in the *bailliage* of Berry, 127 in that of Troyes, 574 in those of Caux and Gisors, and slightly more than 1000 in Dauphiné (22,000 square kilometres). In 1474 six *bailliages* in the duchy of Burgundy – approximately 15,000 square kilometres – numbered more than 500 tenants-in-chief, sub-tenants and those holding lands in seigniorial freehold.[16] If these different data are related to the size of the kingdom, it can be estimated that there were 30,000 to 40,000 noble families around 1470, that is 1–1·6 per cent of a total population of 10–12 million. Two conclusions can be drawn from this. On the one hand, that regional divergencies continued to exist, permitting the definition of areas with a high density of nobles – Brittany, Anjou, Maine; those with an average density – Poitou, Saintonge, Limousin, Quercy; and those with a low density – Berry, Nivernais, parts of Burgundy and of Champagne. On the other hand, it appears that in spite of plague and other causes of mortality, wars, famines, political and social upheavals and economic difficulties, the number of nobles does not appear to have fallen more than that of the population as a whole.

All the same, it is not certain that the demographic characteristics of noble society were identical with those of the rest of the population. In particular, it is possible – although there are still no detailed studies dealing with this matter – that they married earlier, had larger families and remarried more frequently; inversely, might they not have had a significantly higher percentage of children who were without issue because they went into the Church?[17] Finally, although it is probable that, in the midst of this relatively privileged group, the mortality caused by deprivations and epidemics was lower than elsewhere, it may be assumed that this was evened out by the greater ravages wrought among the nobility by war.

In the fourteenth and fifteenth centuries nobility was normally transmitted by blood: those who were the legitimate issue of a noble father were nobles. Certainly, it was more honourable to have two noble parents, but it was not essential; indeed, as *Le Songe du Vergier* comments, 'if a woman who is not of noble birth marries a noble, she becomes noble'.[18] Nevertheless, there was an exception to this rule; in Champagne and Barrois nobility through the mother was recognised and perhaps even essential: in 1367 Charles V confirmed the noble status of two persons who had served him 'on the frontiers of Lorraine' and in the *bailliage* of Sens, and whose forefathers, themselves

nobles, had married women who were not of noble birth.[19] But elsewhere, the nobility of the mother was only one argument among others
to obtain ennoblement: in 1455, two brothers, Fauconnet and Pons de
Bervigier, probably hailing from the south-west of France, asked
Charles VII to ennoble them, in view of the fact that they were noble on
their mother's side, that they lived like nobles, and that they had exercised the profession of arms.[20]

On the other hand, from the later Middle Ages the bastards of nobles
did not necessarily retain the rank of their father;[21] for them, everything depended on their style of living, their financial resources and the
rank of their parents: the illegitimate son of a great lord who had
obtained a fief, even a modest one, and who at the time of his succession
lived in the manner of a noble, and who married a girl of noble birth,
had a good chance of having his noble rank recognised and passed on to
his descendants without contestation.

However, the transmission of nobility by blood does not in itself
explain the survival of noble society, since there exists an inexorable
'law of extinction',[22] which has been documented not only for the later
Middle Ages, but also for earlier and for later periods. Of the 215
lineages in thirteenth-century Forez identified by M. Perroy, 66 or
30·7 per cent had disappeared before 1300, when only 149 remained,
and of this number 80 or 53·6 per cent vanished between 1300 and 1400;
of the remaining 69, a further 38 were lost between 1400 and 1500, and
the process continued during later periods: immediately before the
French Revolution there were only 5 lineages with direct male succession dating from the thirteenth century.[23] How can this diminution,
averaging 50 per cent per century, be explained?

It is difficult to believe that it was solely due to a hypothetical excess
of deaths over the number of births. On the other hand, it did largely
result from the fact that in the system adopted there was no succession
through the female line. One must also take into account the hardship
suffered by the nobility as a result of exceptional circumstances. For
instance, in 1358, threatened by the Parisians, a noble of long-standing,
Robert de Lorris, lord of Ermenonville, knight and chamberlain of the
king, renounced his nobility and declared himself a burgess of Paris in
order to save his life.[24] In certain regions of real serfdom, it seems that a
noble could lose his rank by receiving the inheritance of a serf.[25] Or
again, a noble defeated in a gage of battle lost 'his goods, his honour,
his arms and his name', as also did his children born after the forfeiture
in which the gage of battle resulted.[26]

Yet another idea intervened: that of derogation,[27] by virtue of which a whole range of professional activity was judged incompatible with nobility. 'A noble who engages in trade or tilling the land, or in any other manner lives as a commoner by mechanical arts, commonly and manifestly, without in any way behaving like a noble, exercising or frequenting arms and noble deeds, shall not enjoy the privilege of a noble', says, for example, the customary of Poitou, compiled in 1417.[28]

Nevertheless, it may be noted that in theory it was possible to be a noble and not to enjoy the privileges of nobility, and that in fact many nobles pursued manual or commercial activities. 'There are some who are noble through their father', states a text from the beginning of the fourteenth century, 'who live and have for long lived as merchants selling cloth, grain, wine and all other things of merchandise, or as tradesmen, furriers, shoemakers or tailors.'[29] An Act of Charles VI, dating from 1405, notes as a current fact that nobles are 'engaging in public trade'.[30] In 1456, an *ordonnance* of the duke of Brittany mentions 'nobles of lineage' who trade wholesale and retail, keep taverns, engage in the service of others and fatten cattle on other people's lands'.[31]

However, the fact remains that, with the exception of Brittany, the further the fifteenth century advanced, the more the idea of derogation hardened and was more clearly defined. In a process in Parlement dating from 1409, the advocate of one of the parties, whose nobility had been called into question because of the activities in which he engaged, answered that his client had done nothing but sell wines and grain issuing from his inheritance, which implies that if he had sold goods that he had not produced himself, his nobility could come under legitimate suspicion.[32] A burgess from Bordeaux, Bernard de Garos, who was ennobled in 1445, gave up commerce, leaving only his brother at the head of the business that their father had made prosper.[33] One might conclude that, even without there being any formal incompatability between nobility and merchandise, it would be difficult for a noble, who permanently devoted himself to trading, to later regain his privileges and obtain exemption from the *taille*: he would then run up against opposition from the non-nobles in his town or parish, anxious not to see any decrease in the number of tax-payers, and he would not be supported by other nobles who disapproved of all types of commerce. A noble who traded, or – at least in certain areas[34] – practised as a lawyer, procurator or scrivener (*avocat, procureur, tabellion*), no longer led the life of a noble and lost touch with his original milieu; by force of circumstance he cut himself off from the nobility. As *Le Songe du Vergier* puts it, 'nobility can be acquired or lost by habit and by breaking habits'.[35] In these conditions the arrangements made by Louis XI in an Act of November 1470 appear all the more remarkable. By this Act the king collectively ennobled all the non-nobles who had acquired fiefs in the duchy of Normandy and, to make it possible for them to enjoy the privileges of nobility, they were required 'to comport themselves in all ways like the other nobles in the said country', so that if they did 'anything derogating nobility' they would have to pay the *taille*, but if they stopped acting in this manner they would at once regain their privileges and recover the plentitude of their new condition.[36] In any case, a noble forced by poverty to get employment, and who had alienated his noble possessions or only kept a small part of them, lost practically all chance of preserving his rank; in a generation or two his origins would be obliterated.

How could the gaps thus created in the midst of noble society by demographic disequilibrium, lineages dying out on the male side, voluntary abandonment of the noble way of life, or, most frequently, under the pressure of necessity, be filled?

One of the means of access to the nobility was to obtain patents of nobility (*lettres d'anoblissement*), often for a consideration.[37] The first of these known to be issued by the king of France date from 1285 and 1290. Their appearance indicates that from that time onwards the nobility could be clearly defined; indeed, it could be said that there was no nobility, properly speaking, before the existence of patents of nobility.

The attitude of the French monarchy during the fourteenth and fifteenth centuries was that 'only the king should issue and grant . . . patents . . . of nobility'.[38] This extreme point of view, which was in fact virtually untenable, took into consideration the political structure of the kingdom. *Le Songe du Vergier*, partly inspired by the Italian civil lawyers, Bartolus of Sassoferrato and John of Legnano, advances a more diversified theory: only a 'prince' could make a 'commoner' into a 'noble', considering that 'political and civil nobility' arise from the law of nations (*jus gentium*), 'the which depends upon and is authorised by the prince'. In this way, one could be ennobled not only by the emperor or the king, who did not recognise any temporal sovereign, but also by a 'territorial lord' having 'power to make laws, for if he has the power of making laws he can confer ennoblement',[39] in other words, by a territorial prince. In fact, during these last two medieval centuries, the dukes of Burgundy, Brittany, Orléans and Berry, and the count of Armagnac, granted patents of nobility without always asking the king of France to confirm them.[40]

Patents of nobility issued by the king had to be registered by the Chancery and the Chambre des Comptes. Thus it is possible to get an approximate idea of the frequency with which they were issued. In the registers of the Trésor des Chartes there are 180 for the twenty-two years of Louis XI's reign and a comparable number for the first ten years of Charles V's reign.[41] This indicates that recruitment by patents of nobility was important, and if one includes ennoblements by the princes, they can be estimated as several hundred per generation. Moreover, a prince also had the right to create or change armorial bearings and the exclusive privilege of creating or changing great noble titles. According to Antoine de la Sale, it seems that only an emperor or a king could 'create a duke', but a territorial prince could confer the titles of count, *vicomte* or baron on any of his vassals.[42] However, such conferments were still rare in late medieval France: examples are Charles IV creating the duchy of Bourbon, Philip of Valois that of Orléans, John the Good those of Anjou, Berry and Touraine, and Charles VI those of Valois and of Alençon.[43]

Unlike ennoblements by patent, ennoblements by office were very rare prior to the reign of Louis XI; only three cases of *noblesse de cloche* or municipal nobility are known before 1461: La Rochelle and Poitiers, from the reign of Charles V, and Toulouse from 1420. Access was all the more difficult in that during the fifteenth century municipal offices tended to be monopolised by a small number of families, and sometimes, in order to continue to trade, certain of them renounced the privileges to which they were entitled.[44] Moreover, an Act of 1410 granted the king's sergeants-at-arms automatic access to the nobility on taking up office. On the other hand, except perhaps in Dauphiné,[45] there was no *noblesse de robe* before the beginning of the sixteenth century. 'In the fifteenth century there is only the *noblesse d'epée*.'[46]

But the most common method of ennoblement was by positive prescription. According to *Le Songe du Vergier*, those who have always performed 'noble deeds' and 'acted like nobles . . . for as long as it can be remembered' should be known as such.[47] Olivier de la Marche, although he was hampered by 'class' prejudices, gives evidence of even greater laxity: to 'maintain one's freedom', 'lead the honest life of a nobleman', 'bear arms as a man-at-arms and serve the prince gallantly and with valour throughout his wars', all this makes one noble.[48]

However, the fact remains that to acquire nobility by usage or a certain style of living was not easy; it entailed litigation and lawsuits and, in particular, at least from the end of the thirteenth century, possession of a noble fief was not sufficient to ennoble its holder. In Burgundy, the acquisition of a noble fief did not give an entitlement to enoblement until the third succession.[49] In addition to patience and tenacity, it was necessary to make use of one's connections and to silence all criticism. The most difficult thing was to get on quickly. But a family that combined the material resources to lead a noble life with the will to join the nobility would be almost certain to succeed within the course of two generations, either more or less rapidly. In the fourteenth and fifteenth centuries, legal arrangements, the weight of opinion, the political and social establishments, did not strictly form a barrier so much as a brake on access to the nobility, the efficiency of which varied according to the time, circumstances, regions and individuals concerned.

A study of patents of nobility allows an insight into the origins of the beneficiaries: burgesses and merchants, lawyers, physicians, soldiers, officials and familiars of kings or great lords. On the other hand, despite the great number of recruits into the nobility which they provided, there is no evidence in this type of source of either the wealthy peasant, acknowledged as a noble simply because of acquiring noble possessions, or of the petty seigniorial officer, utilising what meagre authority he possessed to ensure his promotion.

The text of the period differentiate from the rest of the nobility 'princes, dukes, counts, barons and lords of castle', or again, 'princes, dukes, counts, *vicomtes*, barons and other knights bannaret'.[50] Despite the moral and material distance separating these different dignities, it is permissible to regard them as what might be called the upper nobility. In order to appreciate their numerical importance, let us first examine the accounts of the treasury of wars. These list the cavalry units or *batailles* assembled at the end of the summer of 1340 by Philip of Valois in what his contemporaries called the 'host of Bouvines'. On 1 September, that is at the moment when the forces were at their maximum strength, the upper nobility comprised 303 persons compared with 18,620 knights bachelor and ordinary esquires, that is 1·6 per cent of the total.[51] It is, of course, probable that the upper nobility, whose service was directly solicited by Philip VI, responded more fully to the royal summons than did the lower and middle nobility; but, inversely, a certain number of non-nobles must have slipped in among the alleged esquires. In 1383, at the time of the host of Bourbourg, the upper nobility amounted to 113 persons as compared with 16,407 men-at-arms, that is 0·8 per cent; but this time there were many more men-at-arms of humble standing, as there was also at the time of the 'voyage du Mans' in 1392, when, of 7000–8000 men-at-arms, 77 belonged to the upper nobility.[52] If these percentages are extended to the entire nobility of the realm, the proportion of the upper level can be estimated at 1–1·5 per cent, that is between 400 and 800 families around 1340.

The most apparent distinction within the lower and middle nobility is that which existed between knights, on the one hand, and *damoiseaux*, *donzeaux*, *simples gentilshommes*, or, most frequently, esquires, on the other hand. What should be noted here is the slow but regular decrease in the percentage of knights. Among the men-at-arms responding to royal summonses, the percentage of knights fell from approximately 15 per cent in 1340 to approximately 10 per cent at the end of the fourteenth century. During the following century, the proportion of knights among the men-at-arms in the king's service is almost always less than 5 per cent. However, it should be noted that this development does not simply reflect a change taking place within the nobility; in particular, during the first half of the fifteenth century, many men-at-arms were in fact of non-noble origin. Moreover, while at the beginning of the Hundred Years War almost all the nobles retained by the king in his armies served as men-at-arms, from the beginning of the fifteenth century onwards a number of these served as bowmen. Finally, the armies were, by preference, mainly recruited from young men, whereas at the end of the Middle Ages, particularly among the lower nobility, people were frequently knighted late on in life. All of these remarks lead one to believe that between 1340 and 1460 there was undoubtedly an increase in the number of nobles who never became knights.

It also appears that there were considerable regional variations in the percentage of knights. In 1340 they were two or three times fewer among the men-at-arms from Languedoc, Savoy, the county of Foix or the *vicomté* of Béarn, as compared with those from Normandy, Picardy, the Île-de-France, Champagne and Burgundy. It looks as if knighthood, around this time, was more widespread among the nobility in the north of the kingdom than among that in the south; as with feudal usages, so also the rites of entry into knighthood were relatively unfamiliar to gentlemen from the south. Investigation of the rolls of the *ban* and *arrière-ban* for the reign of Louis XI demonstrates that the Hundred Years War did not result in the disappearance of these differences.

However, even then the title of knight preserved a great part of its significance, if not moral, at least social: it was mostly granted to nobles from the best lineages, but also to the richest. Noble society respected the precept of Antoine de la Sale that 'it is better to be a well-to-do esquire than a poor knight'.[53] Under Charles VII as under Louis XI, when the *arrière-ban* was convoked knights almost always served as men-at-arms, with complete armour and three mounts, and not as *brigandiniers*, who only had one or two horses at their disposal. Knights were preponderant among the delegates of the nobility at the Estates of Tours in 1484. The majority of the commanders in the French cavalry during the second half of the fifteenth century were knights. The title was far from being granted for anything to anybody.

In what circumstances did one enter the 'order of chivalry', and what was the procedure of becoming, according to the phraseology of the time, 'a new knight'? In the middle of the fifteenth century Antoine de la Sale enumerated several methods. Some became knights at the 'Holy Sepulchre of Our Lord', or else at that of 'Saint Catherine'; others followed the classic armed vigil spent in a church 'in great devotion', and went through a detailed ceremony loaded with symbolism; still others became knights 'before battle, assault or encounter, where there were banners of princes'.[54] The latter way of conferring knighthood, together with those that took place at a coronation, at the solemn entry into a town, and even during combat in a mine, are those which narrative texts most frequently evoke. Documentary evidence tells the same story. According to the accounts of the treasury of wars of Philip of Valois, 4 bannarets and 5 esquires were knighted at the time of the French expedition before Bordeaux in July and August 1339; the following year, during the host of Bouvines, 16 esquires bannaret and 216 simple esquires were knighted, and certain cavalry units – perhaps those which it was intended should be used first – saw particularly massive promotions: 82 in the *bataille* of the duke of Burgundy and 40 in that of the count of Armagnac. Nor did these newly created knights attain their new status on unimportant dates; 61 were created on 20 June 1340, at the time of the siege of Thun-l'Evêque, a place which was to surrender three days later, and 38 on 25 July at the time of a skirmish before Saint-Omer against the Flemings under Robert of Artois.[55] But even then a great many esquires did not benefit from these collective knightings. Was this due to refusal or indifference on their part, or rather because of a selection carried out by the commanders on the basis of birth, the patronage of a great lord and the military equipment of these men?

In the course of the formidable crisis of 1420–45 the practice of conferring knighthood during the course of military operations appears to have become particularly rare on the French side; but it again reached significant proportions in the last campaigns of the Hundred Years War. The Valois monarchy, at the same time as it undertook the reform of the army and, in a larger sense, the return to order of the State and society, deemed it appropriate to re-establish these old customs that had lapsed, and which it thought would reinforce the nature and structure of the nobility.

Are we to believe that all those who styled themselves knights had undergone these rights of initiation? Was there always a ceremony, even if in an extremely simplified form? Whatever the case, it does not seem that, at the end of the fifteenth century, the rank of knight had already become simply a rung in the noble hierarchy, inferior to those of count or baron.

III

There were various ties between the members of noble society, and it is appropriate to briefly examine their character and importance. The following example illustrates the situation at the beginning of the Hundred Years War. During the reign of Philip of Valois, Raoul de Brienne was a lord of very high rank. He was invested with the sword of the constable of France in 1329 and held that office until his sudden death, during the course of a tournament, on 20 January 1345. By reason of his numerous fiefs – the counties of Eu and Guines, and lands in Poitou, Saintonge, Artois, Burgundy and Nivernais – he was the vassal both of the king of France and of his son, the duke of Normandy, as well as of the duke of Burgundy and count of Artois, and of the count of Bar. Holding lands in England and in Ireland, he was also a tenant and sub-tenant of Edward III. Involved in European affairs, he stayed in England in 1331 and went to Lombardy in 1333. It is difficult to comprehend what these different allegiances meant to him. Certainly, he was first and foremost a vassal of the king of France, who called him to his Council, paid him a pension, and granted him high pay and considerable advantages when he took part in military campaigns; but this did not prevent him from conducting his own policies, which did not always coincide with those of the French monarchy.[56]

Besides being the vassal of several lords, Raoul de Brienne was also the lord of several vassals. The list of the most important nobles who served in his *bataille* and made up his 'retinue' during the host of

Bouvines in 1340 has been preserved. It reveals that a number of them were natives of the counties of Eu and Guines, while, with one or two exceptions, the others came from regions in which the constable held fiefs: Burgundy, Artois, Picardy, Beauvaisis, Boulonnais, Vimeu, Upper Normandy, Poitou and Saintonge.[57] This is a striking coincidence, and it is not unreasonable to conclude that many of the 500 men-at-arms who were then under his *gouvernement* were his vassals or his vassals' vassals; others, who had no feudal ties with him, held lands neighbouring to his own. The importance of family bonds is equally evident: as well as his son, Guillaume and Dreu de Mello, to whom he was related through his wife, Jeanne de Mello, served under him. Thus the three major forms of solidarity are evident: those of vassalage, regional and family ties. Nevertheless, a sharp divergence from classical feudal service may be noted. In effect, his vassals no longer performed unpaid service, but were paid through his offices at the same rate as others and with more or less the same delay and exactitude for the entire duration of the campaign, from the moment of departure from their castles or manors until their return there. In his turn, the count of Eu received from the king, through the offices of the treasurers of wars, the pay due for the services of all the combatants under his command.[58] On the other hand, there was no longer any question of the traditional forty days' service in the host, or of any geographical limitations which various customs imposed on feudal service. In other words, strictly speaking the king of France no longer utilised the feudal service of his vassals but, in the midst of a paid army, used that of the feoffees of his realm, whether or not they had done homage to him.

Finally, in this same *bataille* of Raoul d'Eu, the names of a number of men who had even more personal ties with their commander may be noted. Among these familiars, who formed a part of his *hôtel* or *ménage*, we find not only his chaplains, minstrels and sergeants-at-arms, but also Jean de Caieu, who received a life rent from the constable, assigned on his lands at Beaurains in Artois, Enguerran Quiéret, who received another in the county of Eu, and Geoffrey de Charny, who was wholly maintained by Raoul d'Eu.[59]

Thus, although family and regional relationships continued to play an important role, the importance of the bond of vassalage in terms of human reality progressively decreased. The formulae and rites remained, and the 'love, service and obedience',[60] due to the feudal lord were still observed, but this was often nothing more than window dressing, a façade. In their place other types of human relationship appeared or developed, also based on an oath, and also often giving rise to a written document: 'aliances, brotherhood and companionship in arms',[61] orders of chivalry. The king and the great lords multiplied the pensions granted to their protégés; as a sign of connection or dependence the latter frequently wore a livery with the device and colours of their patron. This amounted to a kind of domestication of lesser and greater nobles for the benefit of the king, the princes and high-ranking lords; but this domestication was thought honourable and its social and political role was to grow even more after 1450, to become one of the marked features of French society during the sixteenth century.[62]

IV

Historians are in agreement that because of economic and demographic difficulties – of low grain prices, shortage of labour and rising wages – as much as to political and military problems, the French nobility experienced a considerable decrease in their resources during the Hundred Years War. M. Perroy evokes his 'extreme impoverishment' around 1450, while M. Boutruche talks about the 'distress' of a great number of aristocratic families.[63] However, the total diagnosis calls for a certain amount of precision and nuances.

1. At the same time as their revenues melted away, the expenses of the nobility to some extent increased, either due to a greater desire to imitate the luxurious style of living of the princes or due to a lag between industrial and agricultural prices to the detriment of the latter, or above all because of the exceptionally high expenses resulting from the war. With the increasing impoverishment there was an increase in debts.

2. It has sometimes been thought that the economic decline of the nobility and, in a more general fashion, that of lay and ecclesiastical lords, was even more marked than that of the peasantry. According to M. Fourquin, the devastation wrought by routiers, brigands and other soldiers would, in particular, have had a more serious effect on the capital and revenues of the lords than on peasant resources.[64]

3. The difficulties of noble society were not provoked solely by the conditions prevailing in the period 1330–1460. They can be explained by factors already in existence earlier and which also continued after this period. Among these causes were religious and charitable foundations and bequests. It has been calculated that, in the Bordelais, the sum

of testamentary bequests from several lords in the middle ranges of the nobility amounted to between 1500 and 3000 *livres bordelaises* at a time when the annual income of a family of five to six persons from the same milieu amounted to 400 *livres*.[65] But there were also the practices of succession. On this subject, it has often been stressed that the insufficiency of the law of primogeniture in France constituted an important factor in the failure of noble lineages to survive; but it should still be noted that, according to the ideas of the period, to grant a part of the inheritance to each member of the family was to reinforce the cohesion and allow an extension of the lineage. The same thing happened here as with the *apanages* granted to younger sons of the royal family. Moreover, the rules of noble division varied greatly from region to region. Let us take the very simple case of a noble, only disposing of noble revenues and not seeking to give undue advantage to any of his three legitimate sons; when various bequests to the Church, to his friends and his servants had been subtracted, his estate amounted to 1000 *livres* rent, of which a 'principal manor' in itself yielded 100; this would result in the following division:[66]

Customary	Share of the eldest son (in livres)	Share of each younger son (in livres)
Artois	800	100
Anjou	700	150
Paris	550	225
Poitiers	400	300
Perche	333	333

In these circumstances it was inevitable that the economic problems of the nobility would be subject to regional variations.

4. Too few historians have attempted to establish the importance and specify the chronology of the variations in seigniorial income. Working on predominantly ecclesiastical sources, M. Fourquin concludes that between 1335 and 1340 and 1400 and 1410 there was a 50 per cent decrease in money of account, despite a partial revival in the intervening period.[67] In his study of the barony of Neubourg in Normandy, M. Plaisse discovered a catastrophic decrease in seigniorial revenue between the end of the fourteenth century and the period 1428–45. As late as 1470–80 the revenue, expressed in money of account, remained lower than what it had been eighty years earlier.[68]

5. More than any other section of society, the nobility suffered confiscations as a result of political and military events. For instance, a considerable section of the Norman nobility, that remained faithful to

the French monarchy, lost its fiefs when Henry V conquered that province.[69]

6. However, noble society did not take these menaces and disasters lying down. It showed the will to survive, and sometimes it even showed a great capacity to adapt itself. First of all, there were conservative measures, designed to defend or restore the lordship and its traditional rights. 'The crisis of the lordship is not synonymous with its downfall. The masters of the land make concessions but do not capitulate.'[70] The nobles also attempted to find alternative sources of income, from professional activities, marriages to the daughters of wealthy burgesses, pensions and wages offered by the prince or the king, and profits of war. The period of the Hundred Years War was marked by a considerable increase in receipts deriving from 'extraordinary' revenues; thus, directly or indirectly, a large part of these receipts were redistributed for the benefit of the nobles; the budget of the State was to some extent a budget of noble assistance.

7. Consequently, it is easier to explain the strength of the noble inheritance. What was the point of disposing of lands at low prices, even if their return was small, from the moment when income from other sources allowed their owners to keep up their style of living? Much better to hang on to real estate in the hope that it would one day regain its value. The bourgeoisie had not yet acquired a great deal of landed property in France. The convenient formulae of 'the decline of the nobility' and 'the rise of the bourgeoisie' are hardly applicable before the middle of the fifteenth century. At the end of the preceding century, in the *bailliage* of Senlis, bourgeois penetration was limited to narrow spheres; almost everywhere the lordships, small and large, remained in the hands of 'nobles of the traditional type, knights or esquires, bound to their lands, descended from them, and finding their livelihood from them or from war'.[71] The same was true of the Île-de-France until the end of the Hundred Years War, despite its proximity to the powerful capital of Paris.[72]

But is there not a contradiction between the rapid renewal of noble families, pointed out above, and this survival of great seigniorial fortunes? In fact, this contradiction is eliminated if we distinguish the extinction of families, on the one hand, from the sale of their possessions, on the other. From the thirteenth to the fifteenth centuries, the lordship of Laval, a county from 1429, passed from the main branch of the Laval family to the Montmorency-Lavals and then to the Montfort-Lavals.[73] During the same period the barony of Neubourg passed from the Meulans to the La Fertés, then to the Vieuxponts, after which it was confiscated by Henry V for the benefit of the earl of Salisbury, only to revert to the Vieuxponts in 1444.[74] In these two cases, despite these transfers, there was no opportunity for a newcomer to acquire these fiefs.

8. However, it is possible that average and mediocre seigniorial fortunes survived less easily, and that their holders were more frequently obliged to part with them.

V

The crisis of 1356-58, by its very acuteness, reveals the relationship between the authorities and the nobility, as well as the relations between the latter and other sections of society.

Surveyed over a period of twenty years, during the course of which the French monarchy experienced more set-backs than good fortune, more disappointments than success, the defeat at Poitiers and the captivity of King John gave rise to a great number of antagonisms and tensions which, up to then, had been more or less hidden.

For political as well as financial reasons Charles, duke of Normandy and dauphin of Viennois, eldest son and lieutenant of the king, convoked the Estates of Languedoïl in Paris in October 1356. Around 800 people assembled there, from whom were appointed a commission of 50-80 élus, made up of clerics, burgesses and nobles. This commission attacked, first and foremost, the 'councillors' of the Crown, the 'governors' of the kingdom and the 'officers' appointed by either of them. Up to then, there appeared to be nothing indicating a hostile movement against the nobility. Moreover, the attacks were conducted particularly vigorously against men of *petit estat*, recently ennobled, and whose origins had not been forgotten.

However, the measures proposed by the commission show that we must not be taken in by this false unanimity. Two councils were planned: one in charge of the conduct of the war, in which the nobles were to share responsibility with the burgesses and even with the prelates; the other, known as the 'great and secret council', was to comprise 28 members, of which 4 were to be prelates, 12 knights and 12 burgesses; the last-mentioned thus obtained 42 per cent of the places. Moreover, a subsidy was levied which taxed the privileged orders heavily. Some months earlier, in March 1356, it had been decided to levy a tax under the terms of which – to take an example – a noble with an income of 200 *livres* had to pay 6 *livres*, just like a burgess who had the same income or possessed 2000 *livres* in movables. By contrast, on this occasion nobles and clerics, on the one hand, and non-nobles, on the other, were taxed according to different scales. The former had to pay 15 per cent of their income, which would have meant 30 *livres* for the instance cited above. As regards the non-nobles, they had to pay an average of 1·8 florins per hearth, which seems a relatively modest amount.

This was a double set-back for the nobility, who regarded themselves as being over-taxed and lost their *de facto* quasi-monopoly of directing military operations. If they agreed to ratify such schemes it was under pressure of popular opinion that held them responsible for the defeat at Poitiers and was deeply hostile towards them.

Neither of the two councils planned ever came into existence, and only a handful of burgesses entered the royal council in March 1357. But the great *ordonnance* that was then promulgated maintained and preserved intact the fiscal plans formulated in October 1356. This time, the nobles kept their distance with regard to the Parisian movement and no longer participated in the struggle to obtain the reformation of a régime that had fallen into disrepute.[75] They refused to pay their taxes on the same grounds as did the clergy. In November 1357 it was no longer a question of the Estates, but of a Convocation attended only by deputies of the leading towns; at the Estates of January and February 1358, although there were still some prelates, the representation of the nobility was insignificant.

When the Dauphin Charles, by now regent of the realm, left the capital on 25 March 1358, it was in order to meet the nobles of Picardy, Artois and Upper Normandy. At a meeting of the Estates of Champagne, and later those of Compiègne, which had been called together by his fiat, the nobles, who were this time in the majority, led the proceedings. The fiscal decisions taken on this occasion reveal the sentiments of these assemblies. It was envisaged that the non-nobles should pay an average of 2·57 *écus* per hearth, in other words, more than in 1356 and 1357. For the serfs talliable each year at will – a category still existing in Burgundy, Nivernais and Champagne – the contribution decreased to an average of 0·9 *écus*; but this was in order to allow their masters to levy the seigniorial *taille*, which was thus added to royal taxes. The clergy were to pay 10 per cent of the value of their benefices. As for the nobles, they were taxed at 5 per cent of their revenues, from which they could deduct the sum of the servile *taille* as well as the sum of the wages that they paid to their officers. Thus, a noble with an income of 200 *livres*, of which 30 came from the servile *taille* and 30 was intended for his officers, would not pay more than 7 *livres*.[76]

Two weeks after the meeting of the Estates at Compiègne, the peasant rising known as the 'Jacquerie' began. It has been interpreted as a remote consequence of the wheat crisis at the beginning of the four-teenth century: the rich grain-growing plains in the region round Paris had witnessed considerable discontent since 1315.[77] This is pure hypothesis. In fact, the 'Jacques' did not go for the landholders, the lords, which would have meant that the clergy would also have come under attack; they went for the nobles, lesser and great, holders of castles as well as simple manors. Their revolt was very different from that in England in 1381. There do not appear to have been any religious aspirations, nor any desire to modify the land law or the legal condition of the people. At the level of conscious and expressed motivation two related ideas appear: on the one hand, the nobles had betrayed and were still betraying the kingdom; on the other hand, far from defending their men, which was their vocation and their duty, they acted like enemies, relentlessly pillaging the country people, the *rustici*. At the same time, the geographical distribution of the 'sedition' at once becomes clear. The regions involved were those in which the nobles responded to the regent's appeal, armed themselves and organised the defence of their places. In these circumstances, lacking money, they procured the necessary means for themselves by raiding the open country, the *plat pays*.[78] According to Froissart, only if the movement had been allowed to spread and prolong itself would the 'commanalty' have destroyed 'Holy Church' and 'all rich people'.[79]

The reaction of the nobility was commensurate with the intense panic which they had experienced. The gentlemen of Picardy and Normandy appealed to the king of Navarre, who defeated the army of Jacques. The latter had doubtless hoped to secure assistance from the burgesses, for, at the time, there were 'few towns, cities or other places in Languedoïl that were not against the *gentilz hommes*'.[80] But the majority of these offered only limited and reticent assistance to these rebels whom they both despised and feared. In this connection, the attitude of Étienne Marcel is revealing; in order to impose the reform of the State, of which he dreamed, he had to appear as the defender and spokesman of not only one class, milieu or town, but of all whom he had received into Paris – gentlemen included – when they fled the peasants' fury. For the same reasons, he described his partner, Charles of Navarre,

as the friend of 'the three estates of the realm', and as the enemy only
of 'the wicked'. Certainly the king of Navarre contributed more than
anyone else to suppressing the Jacquerie, but as soon as he gained his
victory he made every effort to limit the repression and to forbid all
unnecessary revenge. The regent, on the other hand, according to
Étienne Marcel had 'acknowledged' the war of the nobles against the
non-nobles; he was no longer the head of more than one of the three
Estates.[81]

But the passions among a large part of the nobility of Languedoïl
were such that they disapproved of the *rapprochement* between the king
of Navarre and Étienne Marcel. From the moment when Charles the
Bad accepted the 'captaincy of those of Paris', the 'gentlemen of
Burgundy', who had hitherto supported him, now abandoned him, not
wanting to be either against the regent or 'against the gentlemen'.[82]
Isolated, the king of Navarre had to resort to aid from the 'English' –
hence his fall from popularity among the Parisians.

The crisis of 1356–8 cannot thus be explained simply by the war, the
captivity of the king and the struggle between the Navarrese and the
partisans of the dauphin. It also shows the hostility to the royal officers
and the great organs of government, and it reveals the divergencies
between the towns and the open country, the split between the provinces and Paris. But above all else it demonstrates the opposition
between the nobles and the non-nobles, and the psychological gulf that
separated them.

VI

At the end of the Hundred Years War a large part of the nobility were
in a precarious financial situation. At the same time that their fiscal
privileges were recognised, first of all by the authorities and then by
public opinion, the notion of derogation developed, as a result of which
they found themselves almost completely cut off from the economy.
The lords of castles and those exercising *haute justice* had lost a great
deal of the power that they had once exercised over their men; while
their tribunals had not disappeared they had for the most part to com-
pete with those of the Crown. Whereas, as late as the middle of the
fourteenth century, the king had been obliged to obtain the approval of
the nobles when he wished to tax their subjects, this was only exceptionally the case a hundred years later. The right to private war had, in

particular, been checked. Briefly, the nobility had lost much of their 'feudal' independence. At the higher level, after the failure of the Praguerie, the princes did not, as they had hoped, succeed in controlling the Crown. The unimportant role played by the Estates – except in Languedoc – prevented the claims common to the whole of the nobility from being expressed or succeeding.

On the other hand, the noble style of living maintained its attraction for non-nobles; a burgess who made good normally tried to secure ennoblement, bought lordships and acquired or built a castle. The road to social and political success always lay via the nobility and the higher clergy. Even if noble society was sick or weakened, the idea of nobility survived intact. Moreover, the nobility preserved its military role. After set-backs it emerged victorious in the conflict with England. The chroniclers proclaimed that Charles VII had regained his 'lordship' 'with the help of God and his nobles'. Nobles were as numerous as ever among the officers of the king and the princes, and round the king emerged that new avator of the nobility: the courtier. Briefly, the nobility was not simply a privileged class,[83] still more it was not a governing class; but it was the *milieu par excellence* from which the political authorities could draw the leaders of which it had need.

Would a different evolution have been possible? Could the French nobility have changed its countenance, freely taking up remunerative activities, not expecting everything from the king's service, and turn itself away from traditions, prejudices and war? Certainly the force of habit and of attitudes, an inclination for ease, and immediate interests helped to make the French nobility into what it was in fact to become. To avoid it would have required strong action from the Crown, exercised in two particular directions. Firstly, the suppression of the fiscal privileges of the nobles; this would not only have alleviated the common burden, but would also have abolished one of the main barriers separating the nobles from the non-nobles. Secondly, the suppression of military service that burdened the feoffees; for even in the second half of the fifteenth century this service was exacting and costly, and it provided the nobles with a fatal orientation towards war. Neither of these two measures was possible for as long as the Anglo-French conflict lasted. But even afterwards it was doubtless too much to ask of a monarchy that was conformist by nature. Even a Louis XI, if he momentarily toyed with the idea, did not dare to carry it through.

BIBLIOGRAPHICAL NOTE

There is no overall study of the French nobility in the later Middle Ages. For two valuable recent works, see E. Dravasa, ' "Vivre noblement". Recherches sur la dérogeance de noblesse du XIVe au XVIe siècles', *Revue juridique et économique du Sud-Ouest, Série juridique*, xvi (1965), 135–93, and ibid., xvii (1966), 23–119; P. S. Lewis, *Later Medieval France, the Polity* (1968), pp. 187–237. The first volume of the *Bibliographie généalogique, héraldique et nobiliaire de la France, des origines à nos jours. Imprimés et manuscrits*, by G. Saffroy, was published in Paris in 1968; further volumes are to follow. In 'Projet d'une enquête sur la noblesse française', *Annales d'histoire économique et sociale*, 8ème année (1936), the count of Neubourg provides a preliminary investigation that is still valuable, despite its brevity. The best introduction to the major problem of the renewal of the nobility is to be found in E. Perroy, 'Social Mobility among the French *Noblesse* in the Later Middle Ages', *Past and Present*, xxi (1962). The articles by P. S. Lewis – 'Decayed and Non-feudalism in Later Medieval France', *BIHR* xxxvii (1964) and 'Une devise de chevalerie inconnue, créé par un comte de Foix? Le Dragon', *Annales du Midi* lxxvi (1964) – provide an excellent survey of the new ties that appeared at the time among the French nobility. The concise but useful book by J. R. Bloch, *L'anoblissement en France au temps de François Ier. Essai d'une définition de la condition juridique et sociale de la noblesse au début du XVIe siècle* (Paris, 1934), also deals with the earlier period. The political role of the nobility at the beginning of the Hundred Years War is largely dealt with in R. Cazelles, *La société politique et la crise de la royauté sous Philippe de Valois* (Paris, 1958), whereas the economic and social problems with which they were faced during the fourteenth and fifteenth centuries are very fully presented in R. Boutruche, *La crise d'une société: seigneurs et paysans du Bordelais pendant la Guerre de Cent Ans* (new edition, Paris, 1963), and G. Fourquin, *Les campagnes de la région parisienne à la fin du Moyen Age, du milieu du XIIIe au début du XVIe siècle* (Paris, 1964). The relationship between the nobility and the lawyers is dealt with in B. Guenée, *Tribunaux et gens de justice dans le bailliage de Senlis à la fin du Moyen Age, vers 1380–vers 1550* (Paris, 1963), and R. Fédou, 'Les hommes de loi lyonnais à la fin du Moyen Age, étude sur les origines de la classe de robe', *Annales de l'Université de Lyon* (1964), and the role of the nobility among the ranks of the higher clergy by B. Guillemain, *La cour pontificale d'Avignon (1309–1376). Étude d'une société* (Paris, 1962).

NOTES

1. 'Chacun scet que en tous royaumes des Crestiens et aussi des payens a troys estaz, c'est assavoir les gens le l'eglise, les nobles, et le peuple': Philippe de Mézières, *Le Songe de Vieil Pelerin*, ed. G. W. Coopland (Cambridge, 1969), i, 526.

2. A 'nef a façon d'argent, en laquelle avoit ung lis dont procedoit ung Roy gardé de deux anglez, et au pié de ce liz estoit l'Eglise, Noblesse et Labeur par personnages': C. Couderc, 'L'entrée solennelle de Louis XI à Paris (31 août 1461)', in *Mémoires de la Société de l'histoire de Paris et de l'Île-de-France*, xxiii (1896), 165.

3. 'La distinction des états et des membres de la chose publique n'est inconnue de personne, selon laquelle il est prescrit à l'Eglise de prier pour les

autres, de conseiller et d'exhorter, à la noblesse de protéger les autres par les armes, et au peuple de les nourrir et de les entretenir par les contributions et par l'agriculture; et cela non point pour l'avantage particulier de chacun, ainsi que le seigneur avocat paraît l'imaginer et le dépeindre, mais pour le seul but du seul bien public, que chacun, en accomplissant son office, doit poursuivre et rechercher, sans travailler seulement pour soi, mais pour tous ensemble, en sorte que, si l'on usurpe l'office de son associé, ou si l'on rejette son fardeau sur un autre, on s'occupe mal de l'utilité du bien commun. Cette spécificité des offices, ni les femmes ni les jeunes gens, pour peu qu'ils aient quelque teinture d'instruction, ne l'ignorent': Jehan Masselin, *Journal des États généraux de France tenus à Tours en 1484 sous le règne de Charles VIII*, ed. A. Bernier (Paris, 1835), p. 504.

4. Philippe de Mézières, op. cit., i, 446–623.

5. *Chronique normande du XIVᵉ siècle*, ed. E. Molinier (Paris, 1882), p. 172.

6. 'Le gentilhomme est celluy qui, d'ancienneté, est issu de gentilzhommes et gentilzfemmes', whereas nobility is only 'commencement de gentillesse': Olivier de la Marche, *Traité du duel judiciaire*, ed. B. Prost (Paris, 1872), p. 45.

7. E. Perroy, 'Social Mobility among the French *Noblesse* in the Later Middle Ages', *Past and Present*, xxi (1962), 27.

8. E. Baratier, *La démographie provençale du XIIIᵉ au XVᵉ siècle, avec chiffres de comparaison pour le XVIIIᵉ siècle* (Paris, 1961), p. 68.

9. F. Maillard, 'Une enquête sur Lunel et Rochefort en 1295', *Annales du Midi*, lxxiii (1961), 72.

10. R. de Belleval, *Rôle des nobles et fieffés du bailliage d'Amiens convoqués pour la guerre le 25 août 1337* (Amiens, 1862). Bibl. nat., lat. 17714; for Dauphiné, see also G. Giordanesco, 'La noblesse dauphinoise au temps du dauphin Humbert II: 1333–49', *École nationale des Chartes, Positions des thèses* (1969), pp. 49–59.

11. F. Lot, 'L'état des paroisses et des feux de 1328', *BEC* xc (1929), 306.

12. G. A. Knowlson, *Jean V, duc de Bretagne, et l'Angleterre, 1399–1442* (Cambridge and Rennes, 1964), p. 7.

13. H. Touchard, *Le commerce maritime breton à la fin du Moyen Age*, p. 55.

14. Ibid.

15. B.-A. Pocquet du Haut-Jussé, 'De la vassalité à la noblesse dans le duché de Bretagne', *Bulletin philologique et historique (jusqu'en 1610) du comité des travaux historiques et scientifiques* (Paris, 1966), p. 798, gives the even higher figure of 9336, which he obtains by multiplying by eight the figure drawn from an examination of the musters of the bishopric of Vannes, published by R. de Laigne, *La noblesse bretonne aux XVᵉ et XVᵉ siècles. Reformations et montres. Evêché de Vannes* (2 vols, Rennes, 1902). In fact, Brittany then comprised nine dioceses, of which that of Dol was very small. But it is not certain that all the other large dioceses had the same number of nobles as that of Vannes (cf. Bibl. municip., Saint-Brieuc, MS 34, fos. 206 ff. and MS 38, fos. 281 ff.); on the other hand, it is possible that certain of the individuals listed were only holders of noble fiefs and not nobles. I have thus slightly reduced the generous estimations of M. Pocquet du Haut-Jussé.

16. Anjou: Bibl. nat., français 32905, fos. 34–69 (1470). Poitou, Saintonge and Angoumois: *Rooles des bans et arrière-bans de la province de Poictou, Xaintonge et Angoumois* (Poitiers, 1667), pp. 23 ff. (1467). Limousin, Marche and Combraille: Bibl. municip., Poitiers, MS 407, and G. Clément-Simon, *Archives historiques de la Corrèze (ancien Bas-Limousin), recueil de documents inédits depuis les origines jusqu'à la fin du XVIIIᵉ siècle*, i (Paris, 1903), 50–85 (1470). Nivernais: *Inventaire des titres de Nevers de l'abbé de Marolles, publié par le*

comte de Soultrait (Nevers, 1873), cols. 392–5 (1470, n. st.). Berri: Bibl. nat., français 2919, fos. 79–87 (1491). Bailliage de Troyes: Bibliothèque de l'Institut de France, fonds Godefroy, 97, fo. 40 (*c.* 1465?). Caux and Gisors: G. A. de La Roque de La Lontière, *Traité du ban et arrière-ban, de son origine et de ses convocations anciennes et nouvelles* (Rouen, 1735), pp. 113–31 (1470). Dauphiné: H. Pilot de Thorey, *Catalogue des actes de Louis XI relatifs au Dauphiné* (3 vols, Grenoble, 1899–1911), ii, 187, n. 1, and Bibl. nat., nouv. acq. française 9813, fo. 115 (1473). Bourgogne: Arch. dép., Côte-d'Or, B 11725, fos. 1–60.

By way of comparison, it should be noted that according to Lavoisier there were 83,000 nobles in 1789 – of whom 18,323 were nobles and ennobled men capable of bearing arms – in the kingdom of France, the total population of which was then 25 million inhabitants (P. Sagnac, *La formation de la société française moderne*, ii, *La révolution des idées et des mœurs et le déclin de l'Ancien Régime, 1715–1788*, Paris, 1946, 216). But according to Sieyès there would have been 110,000 (G. Lefèbvre, *La Révolution française*, Paris, 1951, p. 47), whereas A. Goodwin, 'The Social Structure and Economic and Political Attitudes of the French Nobility in the Eighteenth Century', in *Comité international des Sciences historiques, XIIe congrés international des sciences historiques* (Vienna, 1965), *Rapports*, i, *Grands thèmes*, 356, estimates their number at between 160,000 and 400,000. These divergencies – sometimes fivefold – should make us cautious in our estimates for even earlier periods.

Writing around 1471–2, Thomas Basin estimated that the king of France could secure more than 50,000 knights from the nobility of the realm (Thomas Basin, *Histoire de Charles VII*, ed. and trans. C. Samaran ii, Paris, 1944, 32).

17. See, for example, the genealogy of the Conflans family in *Documents relatifs au comté de Champagne et de Brie, 1172–1361*, i, *Les fiefs* (Paris, 1901), 463–5.

18. 'Le Songe du Vergier, qui parle de la disputacion du clerc et du chevalier', in *Revue du Moyen Age latin*, xiii (1957), 18. This work, written by an unknown author, was first put together in Latin under the title of *Somnium Viridarii* (1376) and then published in French two years later.

19. Arch. nat., JJ 97, no. 7, fo. 10.

20. *Annuaire-bulletin de la Société de l'Histoire de France* (1883), p. 217.

21. *Le Songe du Vergier*, p. 186. See the case recorded in the *Ordonnances des Roys de France* (Ord. Roys), xix, 556.

22. Comte de Neubourg, 'Projet d'une enquête sur la noblesse française', *Annales d'histoire économique et sociale*, 8ème année (1936), pp. 246–7.

23. E. Perroy, op. cit., p. 31. See also his 'La noblesse forézienne et les ligues nobiliaires de 1314–1315', *Bulletin de la Diana*, xxxvi (1960), 193.

24. *Chronographia regum Francorum*, ed. H. Moranvillé (3 vols, Paris, 1891–7), ii, 273.

25. See the document published by P. Guilhermez in *BEC* l (1889), 522–36.

26. Olivier de la Marche, loc. cit.

27. According to G. Zeller, 'Procès à réviser? Louis XI, la noblesse et la marchandise', *Annales*, i (1946), 333, the word *dérogeance* had not come into use by the fifteenth century. In fact, the expression 'dérogant a la noblesse' appears in a text of 1462 (Arch. nat., JJ 200, no. 248, cited by R. Favreau, 'La condition sociale des maires de Poitiers au XVe siècle', *Bulletin philologique et historique, jusqu'en 1610, du comité des travaux historiques et scientifiques*, année 1961, Paris, 1963, p. 167). and *dérogeance* in a text of 1485: 'L'office de tabellion ou notaire ne devoit estre dit derogeance', *Ord. Roys*, xix, 556. The article by G. Zeller, 'Une notion de caractère historico-social: la dérogeance', *Cahiers internationaux de sociologie*, xxii (1957), 40–74, mainly deals with the modern period.

28. 'Ung noble qui use de fait de marchandise ou de labourage ou en autre manniere vit d'art mecanique rousturierement, communeement et notoirement sans aucunement se porter comme noble, exercer ou frequenter les armes et fait de noblesse, ne joyra pas de privilege de noble': *Le vieux coustumier de Poictou*, ed. R. Filhol (Bourges, 1956), p. 201, art. 566.

29. 'Il y a aucuns nobles de par le pere qui vivent et ont vescu longtemps comme marchandz de draps, blés, vins et de toutes autres marchandises, ou comme gens de mestier, pelletiers, cardonniers, tailleurs de robes': Cited by R. Cazelles, *La société politique et la crise de la royauté sous Philippe de Valois* (Paris, 1958), p. 290.

30. 'fait de marchandise publique': *Ord. Roys*, xii, 221–2.

31. M. Planiol, *La très ancienne coutume de Bretagne, avec les assises Constitutions de Parlement et Ordonnances ducales suivies d'un recueil de textes divers antérieurs à 1491* (Rennes, 1896), pp. 433–4.

32. A. Bossuat, *Perrinet Gressart et François de Surienne, agents de l'Angleterre. Contribution à l'étude des relations de l'Angleterre et de la Bourgogne avec la France, sous le règne de Charles VII* (Paris, 1936), p. 3.

33. R. Boutruche, *La crise d'une société: seigneurs et paysans du Bordelais pendant la Guerre de Cent Ans* (new edition, Paris, 1963), p. 373 and n. 4.

34. This was the case in the bailliage of Senlis: B. Guenée, *Tribunaux et gens de justice dans le bailliage de Senlis à la fin du Moyen Age, vers 1380–vers 1550* (Paris, 1963), p. 201. Investigations into proof of nobility are very instructive in giving a concrete notion of what contemporaries thought most important: first and foremost that the patrimony of a noble's parents had profited from 'partage noble', that he himself or his parents had borne and still bore arms, that he was allied with families of 'chevalerie ancienne', and that he had always been known as 'noble homme en tous ses contractz, lettres et autres affaires' (R. Favreau, 'La preuve de noblesse en Poitou au XVe siècle d'après les textes', *Bulletin de la société des Antiquaires de l'Ouest et des musées de Poitiers*, 1960, pp. 618–22).

35. 'noblesse si peut estre acquise ou perdue par acoustumance et par sa desacoustumance': *Le Songe du Vergier*, p. 185.

36. *Ord. Roys*, xvii, 337 ff.

37. These sometimes cost a lot: 300 *livres tournois* for the ennoblement of Joachim des Astars and his brothers and sisters in 1489 (Bibl. nat. MS français 7881, fo. 35r). If it cost nothing it was called an ennoblement *absque financia*. Ennobled persons were still not always exempted from paying the *taille* (J. Billioud, *Les Etats de Bourgogne aux XIVe et XVe siècles*, Dijon, 1922, p. 133).

38. 'au roy seul et pour le tout appartient donner et octroyer . . . lettres . . . de nobilitacions': *Ord. Roys*, v, 479–80, art. 6 (1372).

39. *Le Songe du Vergier*, p. 190.

40. R. Lacour, *Le gouvernement de l'apanage de Jean, duc de Berry, 1360–1416* (Paris, 1934), pp. 296–7.

41. R. Gandilhon, *Politique économique de Louis XI* (Rennes, 1940), p. 112; Bibl. nat., MSS français 22253 and 4834.

42. Antoine de la Sale, *La Salade*, ed. F. Desonay (Paris and Liège, 1935), pp. 231–4.

43. In *Le debat des herauts d'armes de France et d'Angleterre*, ed. L. Pannier and P. Meyer (Paris, 1877), pp. 41–2, which was written in the middle of the fifteenth century, the herald-at-arms of France draws attention, on this subject, to the contrast with the English practice of creating dukes who 'ne sont pas seigneurs de la ville ny du pays dont ilz portent le nom', so that 'c'est comme le pape fait les evesques portatifz et comme l'en fait les heraulx'.

44. On this point, see F. Bluche and P. Durye, 'L'anoblissement par charges avant 1789', *Les cahiers nobles*, nos. 23 and 24 (1962).

45. R. Fédou, 'Les hommes de loi lyonnais à la fin du Moyen Age, étude sur les origines de la classe de robe', *Annales de l'Université de Lyon* (1964), p. 427.

46. Guenée, op. cit., p. 413. See the whole passage, pp. 409–15.

47. *Le Songe du Vergier*, p. 185.

48. Olivier de la Marche, loc. cit. See also Jean de Bueil, *Le Jouvencel*, ed. Favre et Lecestre (2 vols, Paris, 1887–9), ii, 80. 'Quant aucun est passé deux fois en monstres, est deinceps reputé noble' (cited by A. Bossuat, loc. cit., although the following is also found there: 'porter le hauberjon n'est pas signe de noblesse').

49. J. Bartier, *Légistes et gens de finances au XVᵉ siècle. Les conseillers des ducs de Bourgogne Philippe le Bon et Charles le Téméraire* (Brussels, 1955).

50. 'princes, ducs, comtes, barons et seigneurs châtelains', or again, 'princes, ducs, comtes, vicomtes, barons et autres chevaliers à bannière'. On the other hand, the title of marquess was not used in the kingdom of France in the later Middle Ages, although it should be noted that the marquess of Saluces was a vassal of the dauphin and thus, from the middle of the fourteenth century, of the king's eldest son (the 'filz du marquis de Saluce' was present at the coronation of Louis XI in 1461: *Journal parisien de Jean Maupoint*, ed. G. Fagniez, Paris, 1878; *Mémoires de la société de l'histoire de Paris et de l'Île-de-France* iv (1877), 43, no. 1). The marquisate of Pont, which belonged to a prince of the House of Anjou in the fifteenth century, did not form part of the kingdom.

51. Bibl. nat., nouv. acq. franç. 9238–40. Among these forces there were many who were not subjects of the kingdom, but they came from areas approximately corresponding to present-day France. I have not deducted these from the sum total.

52. Bibl. nat., français 7858, fos. 221–54, and français 32510, fos. 256 ff. (1383); français 4482, fos. 167–236, and français 7858, fos. 309v ff.

53. Antoine de la Sale, op. cit., p. 234.

54. Ibid.

55. Bibl. nat., nouv. acq. français 9238–40.

56. See the biographical details in R. Cazelles, op. cit., pp. 137–9.

57. Bibl. nat., nouv. acq. française 9238, fos. 127v–32r.

58. See his account, Arch. nat., JJ 269.

59. Ibid., fos. 57r, 90v and 92r.

60. *Chroniques de Jean Froissart*, ed. S. Luce, G. Raynaud, L. and A. Mirot (14 vols, Société de l'histoire de France, Paris, 1869–1966), viii, 10.

61. Guillaume Cousinot, *Geste des nobles françois*, ed. Vallet de Viriville (Paris, 1859), p. 134.

62. For a discussion of these problems, see in particular P. S. Lewis, 'Decayed and Non-feudalism in Later Medieval France', *BIHR* xxxvii (1964), 157–84, and, for the subsequent period, J. Russell Major, 'The Crown and the Aristocracy in Renaissance France', *American Historical Review*, lxix (1964), 631–45. There are two recent articles on the role and character of Orders of Chivalry in France during the Hundred Years War: P. S. Lewis, 'Une devise de chevalerie inconnue, créé par un comte de Foix? Le Dragon', *Annales du Midi* lxxvi (1964), 77–84, and M. G. A. Vale, 'A Fourteenth-Century Order of Chivalry: the Tiercelet', in *EHR* lxxxii (1967), 332–41.

63. E. Perroy, *La guerre de Cent Ans* (Paris, 1945), p. 292; R. Boutruche, summarising his book, cited above in *Annales*, ii (1947), 344. C. Petit-Dutaillis, in *L'Histoire de France* of E. Lavisse iv, ii (Paris, 1902), 156, comments: 'In the fifteenth century the majority of nobles were hard pressed.'

64. G. Fourquin, *Histoire économique de l'Occident médiéval* (Paris, 1969), p. 335.

65. R. Boutruche, *Seigneurs et paysans* . . . , pp. 77, 280.

66. Artois: A. Tardif, *Coutumier d'Artois* (Paris, 1883), p. 87. Anjou: A. Joubert, *Histoire de la baronnie de Craon de 1382 à 1626* (Angers and Paris, 1888), pp. 398–400. Paris: O. Martin, *Histoire de la coutume de la prévôté et vicomté de Paris*, i (Paris, 1922), 344–54. Poitiers: *Le vieux coustumier de Poictou*, pp. 201 ff. Perche: C. Petit-Dutaillis, op. cit., p. 157.

67. G. Fourquin, *Les campagnes de la région parisienne à la fin du Moyen Age, du milieu du XIIIᵉ au début du XVIᵉ siècle* (Paris, 1964).

68. A. Plaisse, *La baronnie de Neubourg* (Paris, 1961). G. Duby, *L'économie rurale et la vie des campagnes dans l'Occident médiéval (France, Angleterre, Empire), XIVᵉ–XVᵉ siècles. Essai de synthèse et perspectives de recherches* (2 vols, Paris, 1962), may also be profitably consulted.

69. See, for example, H. de Frondeville, *La vicomté d'Orbec pendant l'occupation anglaise* (Caen, 1936).

70. R. Boutruche, *Seigneurs et paysans* . . . , p. 333. See the whole chapter, pp. 333–43. 'The lords have not abdicated', M. Fourquin similarly declares in his *Histoire économique* . . . , p. 336.

71. Guenée, op. cit., p. 70.

72. Fourquin, *Campagnes de la région parisienne* . . . , pp. 339–49.

73. Comte Bertrand de Broussillon, *La maison de Laval, 1020–1605, étude historique accompagnée du cartulaire de Laval et de Vitré, illustrée de nombreux sceaux et monuments funéraires par Paul de Farcy*, ii, *Les Montmorency-Laval, 1264–1412*, and iii, *Les Montfort-Laval, 1412–1501* (Paris, 1898 and 1900).

74. Fraisse, op. cit.

75. For a different view, see R. Cazelles, 'Les mouvements révolutionnaires du milieu du XIVᵉ siècle et le cycle de l'action politique', *Revue historique*, cccclxiv (1962), 279–312.

76. *Ord. Roys*, iii, 221–32.

77. Fourquin, *Campagnes de la région parisienne* . . . , p. 233, who thinks that compared with others, this was 'one of the least unimportant causes' of the Jacquerie.

78. The *Chronique de Richard Lescot*, ed. J. Lemoine (Paris, 1896), pp. 126–7, shows for instance the *agrestes incole*, repeating the same point: 'Insurgamus in istos nobiles proditores qui, regni defensionem postponendo, nil aliud intendunt quam plebis sustantiam devorare.

79. Cited by S. Luce, *Histoire de la Jacquerie d'après des documents inédits* (new edition, Paris, 1894), p. 61. The same conclusion is to be found in Philippe de Mézières, op. cit., i, 455.

80. 'pou de villes, citez ou autres en la langue doyl qui ne fussent meu contre les gentilz hommes': *Chronique des règnes de Jean II et de Charles V*, ed. R. Delachenal (4 vols, Paris, 1916–20), i, 181.

81. See the letters – not lacking in grandeur – that Étienne Marcel wrote to the *échevins* of Ypres on the eve of his downfall, on 28 June and 11 July 1358, reproduced in J. d'Avout, *31 juillet 1358. Le Meurtre d'Étienne Marcel* (Paris, 1960), pp. 303–10.

82. *Chronique des règnes de Jean II et Charles V*, i, 187–8. Although it is rather conformist and official, R. Delachenal, *Histoire de Charles V*, i (Paris, 1909), 245–470, remains the classical account of the crisis of 1356–8.

83. 'From being a ruling class, the nobility became a privileged class' (J. Calmette and E. Déprez, *Les premières grandes puissances*, Paris, 1939, p. 465). This phrase is in need of much modification.

7. The War and Non-combatant

C. T. ALLMAND

UNTIL fairly recently, the part played in the Hundred Years War by the non-combatant populations of England and France has been, if not underestimated, at least understudied. Historians have always known what contemporaries knew only too well, that the non-combatant was the chief victim of the war. But it is only as we study the war's less publicised aspects, and learn to understand it as involving the destinies of others than those who actually bore arms, that we come to appreciate its true significance. Perhaps, for better or for worse, we are influenced by events which have occurred within the lifetimes of living generations, who have observed how unarmed civilians can suffer appalling distress as a result of modern warfare. This is a factor to be considered in our attitude towards the study of the past. But the historian is also influenced by other factors, such as the materials that provide him with the story which it is his task to build up. The chroniclers and their works, many of them adorned by fine miniatures illustrating battles and sieges – the set-pieces of medieval warfare – are less used now than in former times. Other kinds of sources, legal, administrative, as well as literary, are not increasingly employed. As a result, none should be surprised if the perspectives of history are changing.

War should be seen in the round. This is specially true of the Hundred Years War for, however it originated, it soon became a conflict between two nations, involving two peoples in all its aspects. It was partly financed (although perhaps more so in England than in France) by grants voted in non-military assemblies: in Parliament and the Estates (both national and local); in specially summoned meetings of the merchant community; and in assemblies of churchmen called, in England, Convocation. What proportion of the finances needed to undertake the war's many campaigns came from such sources, it is difficult to estimate. The important point here is the obvious one: that the country was required to help pay for undertakings in which the whole nation, not merely an army fighting in the name of the king, was involved.

In course of time, too, it became the practice for kings to raise loans from their subjects to supplement the sums already raised at the national level. Such payments led not only to a theoretical involvement in the war: men began to expect, and on occasions to demand, a say in the way national affairs were run. Money voted in Parliament became public money, and the king and those who held office under him were expected to see that it was not misused, as the events of the Good Parliament of 1376 serve to remind us. Subjects would help pay for war and would follow their leaders; but they expected something in return – success. If this were not forthcoming, as the French rebels showed in the 1350s, and the English demonstrated both inside and outside Parliament in the 1370s, and again in the 1440s, somebody would have to answer for it.

Powerful economic groups might seek to further their own interests within the context of the war. The well-known tract, *The Libelle of English Polycye*, written in 1436, represents an attempt to influence English policy-makers to turn the conflict in the direction which might bring maximum advantage to the English merchant community.[1] On the opposite side of the Channel, the dukes of Burgundy were also, to some extent, subject to popular opinion. So important was the English connection to the prosperity of certain Flemish towns, that these could not bear to see trade with England cut off for long. If the dukes tried the use of economic forces against England, they were likely to find themselves in trouble at home. Not even the most influential of the dukes felt free to do as he alone willed, for he had it made very clear to him where the public interest lay and what policy he should follow.

Not all, however, were enthusiastic for the war nor, as Edward III discovered, would the Commons readily give advice as to how it should be waged, preferring to leave this to those whose training and position in society better fitted them for the task. As a consequence, it is hardly surprising to find that the period of the war witnessed a considerable development in the use of propaganda, designed chiefly to arouse involvement in the conflict against the enemy, as well as an increased awareness of national feeling and identity. The methods used to achieve this were various: the dispatch of letters home, describing progress and, if possible, success – letters which would be read publicly from pulpit and market cross; the publication of letters justifying a particular line of action, such as those published by Henry V before his first invasion of Normandy in 1415; the request that bishops order their clergy to recite special prayers for the successful outcome of a campaign, or organise processions to petition the Almighty to bless men's efforts when an important peace initiative was about to begin. To such simple forms of involvement were added more sophisticated kinds, whose chief purpose was to arouse in men, by pictorial illustration and the written word, an awareness of the legitimacy of the ruling dynasty (the English did this in France in the fifteenth century) and an emphasis on the need for support for a national policy.[2] The size and importance of this propagandist literature shows how clearly it was appreciated that only by general co-operation in the war could, for example, the French drive the English out of France, and thereby bring the conflict to a successful conclusion. This was to be everybody's war, and propaganda was increasingly designed to ensure this.

The point is underlined by what we know of the practice of war. No longer was it the duty of the soldier alone to be involved in military activity: those concerned with the preparations for war, the conveyance of troops, the carrying of supplies, as with the voting of taxes to pay for such necessities, all were concerned in that one over-all activity which is called war. The active involvement of the non-military elements in a society (both English and French) indicates that the history of war in the late medieval period must be extended beyond the impression gained from reading the chronicles alone. These give an inadequate picture of societies at war. To study war in terms of armies alone is bound to lead to an under-appreciation of the many problems which it brought in its wake.[3]

Late medieval writers were almost unanimous in their opinion that those whom the war had affected the most were not the soldiers, but the non-combatants. If the civilian population of England, except on a number of notable occasions, suffered but little, that of large parts of France suffered terribly from the effects of war. In part, this was due to the succession of English raids and invasions; in part, too, to internecine warfare caused in some measure by the weakness of the French Crown and the quarrels of an uncurbed and independently minded nobility. Which was responsible for what, it is not our task here to decide. Rather, we should ask why people suffered such material destruction, how it came to be inflicted, and, finally, what others thought and did about it.

In spite of the chivalric spirit which motivated Froissart and many of those whose exploits he described, this was an age of violence and uncertainty. Such is the message writ large in the chronicles and other literary works of the day. Acts of violence, legitimate in battle, less so when perpetrated against the non-combatant of whatever class or order, are frequently recorded in historical sources. Considering the length of the war, there were relatively few set battles between opposing armies. Had there been more, it is conceivable that the non-combatant might have escaped more easily.

Two main factors led to the infliction of war upon those who did not actually bear arms. The first was the physical nature of France itself, a country of many small towns with relatively open country in between. The towns, and especially the larger ones, were usually well fortified; walls and castles provided both protection for the peoples of the locality or region, and a military challenge which no enemy commander could for long safely ignore. This meant that any invasion of France by the English would be held up by the presence of such castles, so that the war was certain to be dominated, at the stage of invasion, at least, by siege warfare. This could only lead to a slowing down and protraction of the war. It would not be over quickly, and the longer foreign armies were present on French soil, the more all classes of French society were likely to suffer. Since, too, the towns and their attendant castles existed, in part, to provide cover for those who did not normally live within their confines, sieges were bound to bring calamity upon those who sought refuge within their walls. At best, life would be arduous, but relief would come; at worst, a town would be taken by storm and no quarter given. Even if the town surrendered, the fate of those within it was very uncertain. At no time were the prospects for the besieged at all rosy. The classic example, the siege of Rouen by the English in the hard winter 1418–19, shows how the innocent non-combatant might suffer if the besieger were determined and unrelenting.[4]

The second factor, closely bound up with and largely made possible by the openness of the French countryside, was the nature of the war which the English fought upon French soil. In the fourteenth century, part of its aim was to help demoralise the French population, thereby bringing pressure to bear upon the French king without having recourse to the near-ultimate sanction of a pitched battle. Great encounters were therefore avoided, and a form of petty war (but with a definite plan) was inflicted upon the French population. In addition to, and frequently surpassing the damage caused by the new artillery against military fortifications, were the ills caused to the usually unarmed non-combatants. These, sometimes ignorant of why they should be the victims of other men's quarrels, suffered physical violence, arson, theft, destruction of home, animals and crops, in addition to having to pay either protection money (*pâtis*) or ransom to a less than merciful soldiery. Towns and castles might afford succour to those in their vicinity; for those who lived in the open country there was little hope once the armed bands came in their direction.

If the fifteenth century saw a slight change in the way the war was fought, the non-combatant was still that war's chief victim. True, the English were now more determined upon conquest than they had been under Edward III, and for this reason were more likely to try to control the activities of their soldiers. Yet the fact remains that in August 1424, at the moment of the striking English victory at Verneuil, control of the English armies seemed to be slipping out of their commanders' hands, thereby forcing the duke of Bedford, Henry VI's regent in France, to issue the following directive:

> We wish and therefore command you that all men-at-arms who have come from England whom you may find living off the land or practising theft or extortion upon the poor people, should be taken by you and put into prison, where they shall be punished as was formerly ordered both by the king and by us.[5]

Nor were the English alone in practising violence and extortion. As was well recognised at the time, Norman patriots who had taken to the woods (the so-called *brigans*) committed crimes against the non-combatant population; against these, too, the English were obliged to take drastic but not always successful action.

But why, one may ask, was there such destruction? In part this was the result of the weapons employed in war. Fire, used both on land and at sea, could be devastating in its effects when so much, from houses to ships, was built of wood. But the development of the cannon, gunpowder and larger missiles also meant that destruction, even of strongholds built largely of stone, became more common. Considerable architectural developments were made necessary to combat the destructive effects of cannonball and gunpowder.[6]

But this is less than half the answer. More fundamental still were the soldier's attitude to war and peace, and what contemporary military practice permitted him to get away with. Of one thing we may be certain: in his attitude to the war the soldier, of whatever rank, was not normally motivated by patriotism alone. If the French soldier, especially towards the end of the period, saw it as his chief task to help expel the enemy from France, his English counterpart saw matters very differently. War abroad presented him, in an age of low wages and social unrest, with the opportunity, not merely of adventure, but of making more money (much more money, if he were lucky) in a shorter time than if he remained at home. Men, therefore, went to war for their country's advantage, but even more so for their own profit. A large variety of sources, covering the narrative accounts found in chronicles, the evidence of disputes found in legal records, and the terms of indenture, or contract, signed between kings and their subordinate commanders, show that the incentive motive, largely an economic one, was very powerful in gathering an army together. 'The desire for booty was a motive in all medieval warfare.'[7]

It was generally accepted that the profits of war were available to the soldier, be he noble or common, under certain conditions and at certain times. Laws, which were international in character, regulated this aspect of war, stating what it was proper to take and under what conditions.[8] The victor, as always, came out best, and to him most things were possible – and legally possible. He and his soldiers held the defeated enemy at their mercy; lives might be forfeit, and property would certainly be so. The picture which we have of the siege of Caen by Edward III's army in 1346 shows how a triumphant army could set to work to strip a prosperous town of its important inhabitants and worthwhile possessions which, in this case, were shipped back to England for sale and ransom. All this, it should be emphasised, was done by an army, led by the king of England himself, which had already, as Froissart reports, plundered Barfleur, Cherbourg, Valognes and Saint-Lô, helping itself to as much booty as it could carry. In the next century some of these Norman towns were to suffer a similar fate: as Charles VII wrote in 1450, the city of Caen underwent two changes of lordship within one generation, in 1417 when taken by the army of Henry V, and again in 1450 when recaptured by the French king.[9] Some years before, the Welsh chronicler, Adam of Usk, had already reported that the booty won by the victorious armies of Henry V was on sale all over England, following upon English successes abroad.

The temptations to go to war, in spite of the risks involved, must have been considerable. War, having its own rules, became a kind of game,[10] a chivalric game for those trained in the ways of chivalry, a dirty and underhand one for those disreputable elements who, as Froissart claimed and Dr Hewitt has since proved, existed in the armies of the time.[11] It was against these last that military leaders had to take strong action. To many, all was fair in war, and since the laws of war gave little protection to the undefended non-combatant, it was up to the leaders of armies and mercenary groups to see that the defenceless were not unduly molested. In an age when even officially recruited armies were badly paid, or paid tardily, or sometimes not at all, it needed a great effort on a commander's part to see that his orders were carried out. All medieval armies had to live, to a greater or lesser degree, off the land in which they found themselves; they had orders, if not always the means, to pay for what they took for their subsistence. It was when they broke this first rule that they incurred the odium of the non-combatant population. Whatever the laws of war might fail to do in providing sufficient protection for the men who did not fight, the writers and moralists of the age were in no doubt that the non-combatant should be left alone to pursue his peacetime occupation. In this they were supported by some of the historical writers of the day, who pointed out that few military leaders had sufficient moral courage to hold back men when looting and plundering were legitimately allowed them. When, however, they did so, Froissart, Eustache Deschamps and others went out of their way to give them an unsolicited pat on the back for having maintained a firm grip upon their soldiers' activities, thereby avoiding the all-too-normal excesses of war. Such firmness was indeed worth applauding. When considered along with the respect shown to a man such as Henry V for the strict way he disciplined his armies, this kind of comment goes far towards showing firstly, that strong and effective military discipline was needed to counteract the indiscipline likely to be caused when men were presented with the opportunity of gaining immediate material benefit in the form of booty and plunder; secondly, that such effective discipline was but rarely exercised; and thirdly, that all too frequently the non-combatant population was at the mercy of a victorious force or army.

It was men's attitudes to warfare, and the unchivalric practices thus encouraged, which lay at the root of the misery suffered by the non-fighting population. If the prospect of quick profit helped towards the recruitment of an army, it made it correspondingly more difficult to exercise effective discipline, as many commanders discovered. If the initiative slipped from the hands of the leaders into those of their men, then the non-combatant would be ever at the mercy of undisciplined armies. Assuming, therefore, a general need for discipline, contemporary writers and critics discussed at length how best to achieve it. In theory this was done, in English armies, by the publication of military ordinances by a succession of kings, from the time of Richard II onwards.[12] These well-intentioned attempts, however, did not always prove adequate, since they failed to take proper account of that which lay at the root of the matter: the need for adequate and, above all, regular pay. As long as men were uncertain of receiving their wages, they would seek to find them elsewhere, and discipline would consequently suffer. Soldiers were not angels, and the non-combatants were easy victims. This was an economic problem, whose long-term solution lay in the adequate provision of real, hard cash. To those who took part in it, war had become a commercial venture, with the result that it was easier to begin a war than to end it. The words which follow, those of the late fourteenth-century English Dominican, John Bromyard, were written about Italy, but they could as easily have been applied to France:

It is plain that the majority of wars fought in Lombardy are fought unjustly, and are not begun with the authority of the prince, but at the command of the strongest man in the city. Nor are they fought for any honest reason, but by partisans of the Ghuelf and Ghibelline parties; not out of good intention, but out of a desire for gain and an urge to lord it over others.[13]

Of the chief participants in the Hundred Years War, England was fortunate enough to suffer the least damage to property and morale. There were decided disadvantages in fighting abroad, but as far as the non-combatant was concerned this was the war's greatest advantage. Englishmen were thus largely spared the experiences which were the lot of much of the French population; almost, but not quite. The defence of the coast was something which mattered greatly in the eyes of those who lived within striking distance of the English Channel, and when the French were successful in making raids upon the coast of England, people demanded to know why the government had not been able to protect them. The threat of French attacks was ever present, except under Henry V and Henry VI, when control of the Channel was effectively assured by the presence of Englishmen on both its opposing shores. But in the fourteenth century the whole coast lived under this threat. In October 1338 it became a reality at Southampton, when a French galley fleet descended upon the port, causing the citizens to flee to the surrounding country. In the meantime, for one profitable day, the French controlled the town, hanged some of the unfortunate inhabitants who had not fled, and helped themselves to what they could carry, before being driven back into the sea by the levies of the neighbouring counties who, under cover of expelling the enemy, caused further considerable loss to the citizens of Southampton, and to some visiting Spanish merchants, before order could finally be restored. But this was mild when compared to what certain parts of the French population had to endure. During much of the war, the French were 'visited' not only by English royal armies, but by other groups of soldiers (some well connected and bearing royal approval for their activities, others little more than unauthorised bands of predatory soldiers) who did much to help achieve one of the aims of English policy, the demoralisation of the population and kingdom of France. It was to these bands that critics such as Philippe de Mézières were referring when they described the English as the scourge of God inflicting punishment upon the people of France for their sins. These men, whether officially recognised or not, whether known as Companies in the fourteenth century or as *Écorcheurs* in the fifteenth, were the bane of the countryside and of the defenceless people who lived there. They were an affront to order, and especially to the royal authority, which feebly did its rather limited best to rid France of this affliction which seemed to be at its most dangerous during the periods of truce which punctuated the long war.[14]

To list the activities of the soldiery, and to draw up a catalogue of their misdeeds, would be simple enough, but of little value for this essay. None the less, some kind of indication of the devastation wreaked at this period is called for. We have already seen how, at the successful conclusion of a siege, the conquerors normally divided the spoils and enriched themselves in this way. In battle, too, the taking of prisoners was considered to be of the greatest importance, above all if the person captured was either notable or rich (a king, perhaps, as happened at Poitiers in 1356), for he could then be put to a heavy ransom, and his captor might be considerably rewarded. Ransoms were sufficiently important for men to go to law over the settlement of a claim to capture, and the perseverance of certain litigants during the years which the courts sometimes took to reach a verdict indicates that ransoms and, indeed, less valuable material booty counted for a good deal in the eyes of the late medieval fighting man. That those taken into captivity and put up to ransom included both soldiers and non-combatants hardly needs to be emphasised here.[15]

The armies of the late Middle Ages were also responsible for much material destruction, which today might be termed 'vandalism'. Many are the instances reported by the chroniclers of armies looting and pillaging, before setting fire to the places which they had robbed. At times, whole districts might be held to ransom by the soldiery, who demanded the payment of *pâtis* in order that a particular district should not have to submit to depredation. Frontier regions were specially prone to blackmail of this kind.

One of the chief victims of the war was the Church, whose buildings – sacred or not – frequently attracted the attention of armies, to the loss of the Church's spiritual and temporal ministrations. Soldiers were hardly inclined to spare a church simply because it was a sacred building. The story of how Henry V caused one of his soldiers to be hanged for stealing a precious and sacred vessel from a church is well known; the fact that, only a short time before this incident, the king had ordered the publication of special ordinances granting the royal protection to all women, children and churchmen adds point to the story. The evidence of the St Albans chronicler who recalled that many Normans adopted a religious habit when coming into contact with Henry V's men, indicates clearly enough that, although the cowl did not necessarily make the monk, it was thought to afford a certain protection against the less-disciplined elements in the English army. That a clerical garb was far from always being adequate protection is emphasised by the fact that the Companies once held the pope and the papal court at Avignon to ransom. If such could befall a pope, what might not happen to lesser churchmen and their churches?

Ecclesiastics were specially vulnerable by the fact that they were large landowners. Their estates and their buildings, their crops and their flocks were at the mercy of a hostile army – with little that could effectively be done in their defence. As a consequence, and like the landed nobility all over France at this period, ecclesiastical institutions found themselves in difficulties because their estates were not providing them with the revenues required to maintain and repair them. Not only was there a lack of money; there was also a lack of incentive. The English had made several descents upon the French mainland, and the Companies and *Écorcheurs* were never all that far away. In such circumstances, there was lacking a positive desire to repair and to rebuild after destruction, since the same might soon occur again. There thus seems little doubt that French agriculture as a whole, and individual fortunes in particular, declined as a result of the war. About 1470, the ex-chief justice of England, Sir John Fortescue, noticed the desolation in which the land in the region of the Caux, north-west of Rouen, still lay after a rebellion which had taken place about thirty-five years, or more than one generation, before. This may appear as an extreme example but it indicated how, even in a rich agricultural region, war might have a devastating effect upon the fate, and above all the morale, of the non-combatant.

That the French population suffered a great deal, both psychologically and physically, cannot be doubted. Yet a reading of the evidence forces one to ask the question whether that evidence was not exaggerated, and whether it did not place too much emphasis on material destruction and the economic loss which inevitably ensued. Suspicions are certainly raised by the fact that we learn much about the losses incurred by the Church and churchmen from supplications sent to the papal court, seeking remission from certain ecclesiastical taxes, or the union of benefices which could no longer exist separately. Take, for instance, this example, selected at random:

Most Holy Father. Since the revenues and dues of the parish church of St Mary of Ardevone, and the chapel or leprosy of St Giles of the said place, both in the diocese of Avranches, are so terribly reduced that the said church, worth in time of peace some twenty gold ducats, is now, because of wars which have been raging in these parts for the past twenty years, worth scarcely six, and the chapel of St Giles, which used to be worth ten gold ducats, is now worth but four, from which revenues it is now only possible to maintain one person. Stephen de la Chesnaye, clerk, bachelor in canon law, priest of the said church of St Mary, supplicates that the two benefices be united. Granted, at St Peter's, Rome. 21 November 1433.[16]

In the secular sphere, similar demands, citing the losses caused by war, were made for exemption from rent or royal taxation. But on reading further, suspicions are allayed. This was no gigantic plot to deny pope and king of their revenues. It is the use of other evidence which convinces one that, over-all, the picture of devastation derived from this type of evidence is trustworthy. Thus the evidence about the region of the Caux, taken from Sir John Fortescue, agrees with that provided by administrative documents and other sources. Again, as regards the Church, we have the reliable testimony of Philippe de Mézières that the Church was one of the chief victims of the war in the fourteenth century. We have, besides, other forms of evidence which point in the same direction: the legal records of the Paris Parlement, and those of notaries in many parts of France (Tabellionage); the records of the reluctance of the French to pay taxes voted by the Estates, on the grounds that they had been impoverished by war; the more literary evidence of the works of Roland de Talent, the Italian humanist who lived in Normandy during the last years of the English occupation in the fifteenth century and who, as an outsider, was in a good position to study the situation without too much commitment; and the evidence, very different but strangely complementary, of Jean Juvenal des Ursins and Bishop Thomas Basin. Seen as a whole, such multifarious evidence is overwhelming.

As might be expected, a long period of hostility between countries found public opinion asserting itself against what were seen as the evil practices of war. Such opinion, showing how some men hoped to improve the lot of others, is also reflected in the practical measures advocated to avert those evils. Of those who wrote, we may distinguish two kinds: the chroniclers, who reflected opinion rather than formed it; and the social commentators and critics whose task it was to influence public opinion as far as such a thing was possible. Those who took steps to improve the situation were those who worked actively for peace, who strove to bring order to the military scene, and who helped alleviate suffering and hardship undergone by the more innocent of the war's victims. In all these ways men showed themselves aware of the situation which appeared to many to be worsening with every passing year.

No chronicler, if he collected his information assiduously, could fail to realise that war had its darker side. To a man like Froissart, the arch-exponent of the chivalric chronicle, such a realisation must have been distasteful. In his reporting of the war, we do not normally find that the worst excesses are committed by men of birth and breeding – the natural leaders – but by the riff-raff of society found in any army of his day. Yet, in spite of his leanings, Froissart did not ignore the realities of life, which he was at pains to describe. None the less, he clearly frowned upon acts of treachery and unnecessary violence, reserving praise for those who helped prevent such excesses.

If Froissart had both feet on the ground, and knew what went on between men in wartime, he nevertheless did not live so close to the earth and the ordinary people as did some other writers, of whom we may take the fourteenth-century French Carmelite, Jean de Venette, as an example.[17] Froissart, it is true, was a clerk, but Venette was a dedicated priest, and doubtless there was something of the priestly outlook reflected in his comments on the conduct of the war. Born a peasant, his social attitude was more humble than that of Froissart, and it is probable that he reflected with greater feeling and accuracy the sentiments of the French lower classes – especially of the non-combatant classes – towards the activities of the soldiery. He was also a sharp critic of the nobility for their failure to take a proper lead against the English, and for not protecting the people from some of the worst effects of war. Such criticism was not motivated by Venette's lowly birth, for the nobility had other critics, some of them more highly born than Venette had been. On the effects of war upon the French countryside and its unfortunate population, few could paint a more harrowing picture. Venette's liking for the purple passage, however, should not prevent us from realising that, in spite of his wordiness, he felt strongly about the desperate situation in the France of his day, and that he was acute enough to see, in part at least, where the roots of the trouble lay.

Social critics, not unnaturally, had a good deal more to say on the matter of war, and especially on its abuses. They are interesting, not only because they reflect a keen awareness of the troubles which afflicted Europe, and especially France, in the fourteenth and fifteenth centuries, but because they put forward solutions as to how best to bring them to an end. That these solutions bore considerable resemblance to one another should not surprise us, for each critic owed a debt to those who had preceded him; yet it would be wrong to assume that they copied one another blindly. The fact that their solutions seem to follow a close pattern indicates, rather, how valid their suggestions may have been.

In England there appears to have been considerable awareness, among the better informed critics at least, of the plight of those caught up, in spite of themselves, in the great French war. Not surprisingly, churchmen were among the strongest critics of the manner in which the war was being fought. Sermons were preached condemning the conduct of the war, if not the very policy of the war itself. Two well-known fourteenth-century bishops, Richard Fitzralph of Armagh and Thomas Brinton of Rochester, could openly state their doubts concerning the morality of fighting one's neighbour, Brinton expressing what was, for an Englishman, a very forthright opinion when he stated, about 1375, that the English were at that time being worsted by the French as divine punishment for their sins. This kind of opinion, more normally associated with French publicists, is most revealing as indicating the evils of war as they affected the non-combatant were the retribution which God levied upon a whole people for their sins. The notion that war envelops all is implied, if not stated.[18]

The violence of war, and the hypocrisy which it engendered, caused some to attack all forms of military aggression. If Langland was, in some sort, a pacifist, the chief exponent of this doctrine was to be John Wyclif who, with not a little justice, saw war as being waged 'for pride and coveitise', or for ambition and hope of advantage, as we might put it.[19] In his Latin work, *De Officio Regis*, Wyclif condemned war fought among Christians as being against the Commandment to love one's neighbour. How could a claimant to a kingdom (he plainly had in mind Edward III's claim to the French throne) know for certain that God had chosen him for it, and if not, how dare he risk so many lives for so great an uncertainty? War, he stated to add weight to his argument, was more dangerous in his day than it had been in Old Testament times. A bitter critic of his fellow clergy, Wyclif castigated them for giving financial support to a king who pursued a policy of war: no words, either, were strong enough to condemn the activities of Bishop Despenser of Norwich in leading a 'crusade' in Flanders against the supporters of the anti-pope, Clement VII, in 1383. Death, when it came to Wyclif at the end of the following year, must have been a welcome relief from so sinful a world.[20] But his influence lived on. In 1391 Walter Brut, who described himself as 'a sinner, layman, farmer and a Christian', denounced all war, as Wyclif had done, as being against both the spirit and the letter of the Gospel; while the opinions of William Swynderby who, like Brut, condemned war in strong terms, had to be refuted by two Cambridge theologians, who defended the right of the then king of England, Richard II, to attack the kingdom of France.[21]

One of the most interesting critics of the effects of war was another priest, the more orthodox Dominican, John Bromyard. In his *Summa Predicantium*, or notes for preachers, he expressed in several places what he saw as being wrong with war; his views have added interest in that they refer to events in both France and Italy, which he mentions more than once, in the second half of the fourteenth century. As became a priest, Bromyard was concerned with the morally degrading effects of war, both upon those who caused evils and those who suffered them. Soldiers, he asserted, came to look for money and, not finding it, they searched for their victims' best clothes. They who had been robbed now found themselves in such poverty, that necessity obliged them to steal and to use threats and violence to obtain even the minimum of what they needed.[22] War was, therefore, a source of moral danger for all concerned; death came quickly and unexpectedly, and the man who died in sin might be damned for all eternity.

But Bromyard also showed an awareness of the difficulties experienced by the non-combatant, together with much sympathy for him in his plight. The well-informed Dominican clearly realised that if the age in which he lived was dominated by war and its effects, this was largely due to the existence of badly paid soldiers, who encouraged and protracted aggression for their own benefit. They were the only men who knew how to use force with any effect, being accustomed to overriding the law and the courts, both secular and ecclesiastical, as the occasion demanded. Such men despoiled the Church and the poor as they went along, taking what they wanted as and when it suited them. But the poor had yet more to suffer, for not only did they expect the visitations of the soldiery and the Companies, but they also had to put up with the levying of dues and other taxes by their lords and the officers of the king, the money then being wasted on tournaments, the buying of horses for war, the paying of ransoms and the like. Behind this condemnation of many aspects of war was the recognition that men's thirst for *luxuria* lay at the root of the deceit, treason and violence by which war was now characterised.[23]

On the French side, much was naturally made of the physical sufferings brought about by war; 'the groans of poets Eustache Deschamps and Jean Meschinot are only too easy to hear'.[24] These present what may perhaps be seen as the popular view of the war. Later, in the fifteenth century, two Normans, Alain Chartier and Bishop Thomas Basin, also criticised the manner of conducting the war, and in this they were joined by the voice of the influential Jean Juvenal des Ursins. Basin was specially critical of Charles VII for not defending his people, blaming it chiefly on the lack of control which the king had over his army, which was allowed to do much as it, not as the king himself, willed.

The most interesting of the French social critics of the late fourteenth century was Philippe de Mézières, whose *Songe du Vieil Pelerin* contains much that is pertinent to our problem. Not surprisingly, he echoed several criticisms which have already been mentioned, while citing other abuses whose existence is confirmed by the surviving historical records of the day. He was much concerned with the fate of the Church, all the more so since that institution was in the grips of the Great Schism at the time that Mézières was writing. Like Wyclif, with whom he would not be naturally associated, he was more than once critical of the English clergy who appeared to him to be giving their support to the continuation of the war; he even singled out certain bishops for being too concerned with the cares of the world. In his own France, churchmen were experiencing other difficulties; their churches were frequently ruined and they were finding it difficult to obtain possession of their livings, being obliged to have recourse to the courts, where they frequently encountered the obstructionist tactics of petty officialdom. When writing of the suffering, physical and moral, experienced by the non-combatant, Mézières made it clear that what his own country needed was an authority which could control its own officials and curb the excesses of the *gens d'armes*, chiefly by paying them properly, and by demanding of them the implementation of their obligations. It is significant that he should have been against the granting of letters of marque, as these derogated from the king's right to make war and apply justice, thereby giving encouragement to those who wished to take the law into their own hands for their own advantage.[25]

Turning to those who took active steps to improve the lot of the non-combatant, it is well to mention a few writers who dealt more specifically with military affairs. The late fourteenth-century French priest, Honoré Bonet, whose treatise, *L'Arbre des Batailles*, concerned problems which any soldier might encounter, showed himself keenly aware of the tragic effects of the war, and of its evil influence upon men of his day, although some may object that his legal background caused him to consider these problems in formal, rather than in human terms.[26] Yet these were precisely the qualities which made his work influential and well known; the popular early fifteenth-century writer, Christine de Pisan, leant heavily on him. Their joint popularity is reflected by the fact that Henry VII was to lend William Caxton his manuscript of Christine's work, with orders to translate it into English; the work finally appeared from Caxton's press under the title of *The Book of Fayttes of Armes and of Chyualrye*.[27] In a part of the third book, which dealt with some of the practical considerations of war, Christine asserted that a king, before he ever engaged in war, should ensure that he could pay his army adequately, in order to prevent pillaging the common people who, unless they were found helping the enemy, ought to be left in peace. We are once again in the presence of the much-advocated answer to violence: discipline and control based upon ability to pay an army.

Much the same form of argument was to be employed by the Englishman, Nicholas Upton, who compiled his *De Studio Militari* from the fruits of practical experience gained in the French wars of Henry VI. Upton had no doubts that the non-combatant must remain unmolested. All religious persons, those concerned with farming and agriculture, pilgrims, merchants, surgeons and barbers (the physicians of the day) and (as Christine de Pisan would have added) university students travelling to and from their place of study – all these should be allowed to go freely. From his own experience Upton agreed that 'onrewly couetousnes [is the] mother of stryffes, enemy of peace [and the] occasion of grutche and malice'. Taking this view Upton would punish soldiers for action that 'ys not reputyd for a sowdier' by 'correction by the purse'.[28] This, at any rate, was action which the ordinary soldier understood, and was in fact used in Normandy by the duke of Bedford, who ordered that soldiers who, against orders, did not pay for goods which they took, would have their value deducted from their wages. The good intended from this measure is obvious. Yet the fact remained that although the soldier concerned might be punished, the embittered civilian remained uncompensated for the theft.

We have now returned to the realities of life. The social critics, the poets and the chroniclers might express the views of society, and its sympathy for those who suffered from the war. Yet how effective were such comments? Rulers were not unaware of the problems, but were limited in what they could do to solve them. The English military ordinances, which constituted the shadowy line of demarcation between legitimate military and civil interests, and the development of the court of chivalry at this period, were two attempts to impose effective military discipline. In France, the Cabochien revolt of 1413 was partly provoked by a desire to solve the military problem, but the Ordinances were too short lived to have any lasting effect.[29] The necessary order in the military sphere could only be achieved as part of a more general resurgence of royal authority. That the effective military reforms of the reign of Charles VII should have coincided with this resurgence was no accident. From then on matters improved, and France began her slow recovery from the effects of war.

The Church, too (*pace* Wyclif), did not always speak tongue in cheek when it had occasion to bemoan the spilling of Christian blood by other Christians. It could, mainly through the sermons of its clergy, draw men's attention to the many moral problems of war, and to the calamities which conflict brought with it. The Church could help, too, in peace negotiations; on more than one notable occasion the papacy (and during the Conciliar period, the Councils, especially that of Basel) was represented at the international meetings convened to solve the deadlock which existed between the main protagonists, England and France. In one now well-known case, about 1340, Pope Benedict XII sent a gift of 6000 gold florins as war relief to the inhabitants of the terribly devasted region around Cambrai, in north-eastern France. That this instance of Christian bounty in the face of hardships experienced by an almost defenceless civil population should be needed at all was largely due to the fire-raising excesses of Edward III's army in the first major campaign of the Hundred Years War. This was bad enough, but as we now know, matters would get worse before they got better.[30]

Thus, although steps were taken to improve the deteriorating situation, they had but little practical effect. The fourteenth century, for a variety of causes, saw the broadening out of the war into several theatres; over much of France, into Spain and Portugal, not to mention the war at sea. The English could not afford to give adequate pay to those who went to fight on these expeditions. Nor could the French, so often on the defensive in different quarters, do any better. Military leaders fully realised this, taking it upon themselves to lead expeditions against the enemy on condition that a blind eye be turned to their misdeeds and those of their soldiers. Badly and irregularly paid, sometimes not paid at all, they had to fend for themselves. As Nicolas de Clémanges wrote to Jean Gerson, sometime after 1408, this meant that any man, simply by making promises, could gather round himself a group which would set out to seek its own fortune; inevitably, this led to the situation in which that group would not fight against the country's real enemies, but rather against its own citizens and inhabitants. Dismissing the system whereby soldiers were not properly paid as rotten, Clémanges condemned it as the root of all the evils from which the France of his day was suffering.[31]

Such was one of the great problems which faced men in late medieval France, a problem which, as events were to show, would only be solved by a successful reassertion of the monarchy's power. But the monarchy could not do everything alone. There were attitudes to be conquered, and those of the seasoned soldier were the hardest to change. In 1435, in a well-known memorandum, Sir John Fastolf advocated a scorched-earth policy as the best way of defeating the French because they had, he claimed, rejected the suggestion that the war be fought 'alonly betwixt men of werre and men of werre'. Since this relatively humanitarian approach had been spurned, Fastolf was prepared to support the harshest methods. Groups of soldiers should go through northern France 'brennyng and distruynge alle the lande as thei pas, both hous, corne, veignes and all treis that beren fruyte for mannys sustenance, and all bestaile that may not be dryven, to be distroiede'.[32] It is revealing that, in spite of showing an awareness of the plight of the non-combatant,

Fastolf should have advocated the destruction of his goods, crops and cattle, everything, in fact, that he had to live on. Fastolf, the hardened soldier, had a clear idea as to how the war should be fought. The non-combatant should be spared; but in the name of military necessity he must be prepared to lose his all.

Less than twenty years after these words were written, the English had been expelled from France, and many of the reasons which lay behind the sufferings experienced by the non-fighting populations disappeared with them. Yet, in spite of it all, few seem to have adopted strongly held anti-military attitudes; a man like Bonet was not against war as such. The predominating feeling, as the fifteenth century advanced, became one of lassitude and fatalistic resignation. All too frequently men attributed the loss of goods or property to 'la fortune de la guerre', a force against which they felt powerless to act. Demoralisation was what leaders in both Church and State had to contend with, since generations had grown up who had never known any condition but that of war, a condition which the poet Deschamps described as that of 'damnation'. War now joined famine and the plague as the signs of divine disfavour from whose tribulations men prayed to be spared: *A fame, bello et peste, libera nos, Domine.*

BIBLIOGRAPHICAL NOTE

The majority of the important and normally accessible works with a bearing on this subject have been cited in the footnotes. For an essay of this kind, information must be sought in a large number and variety of sources, few of which, however, contribute an outstanding amount of material.

A valuable discussion on 'war' is to be found in Bede Jarrett's *The Social Theories of the Middle Ages, 1200–1500* (1926), while an interesting if somewhat short chapter on war is contained in E. Perroy's *Le Moyen Age* (Histoire generale des civilisations, iii; Paris, 1957), pp. 458–66.

Some articles may be found useful. E. B. Fryde, 'Parliament and the French War, 1336–1340', in *Essays in Medieval History Presented to Bertie Wilkinson*, ed. T. A. Sandquist and M. R. Powicke (Toronto, 1969) shows clearly the element of consultation which existed between Edward III and Parliament over the French war in the 1330s. In 'War Propaganda and Historiography in Fifteenth-Century France and England' (*TRHS* 5th ser., xv, 1965), P. S. Lewis discusses the value of propagandist literature and its place in war during part of the Hundred Years War. The reality behind the chivalric façade in the war is described by M. H. Keen, 'Brotherhood in Arms', in *History*, xlvii (1962), while in a brilliant *exposé*, the late K. B. McFarlane revealed how certain

Englishmen looked upon war as a business ('A Business-Partnership in War and Administration, 1421–1445', in *EHR* lxxviii, 1963). The link between profit and discipline is very usefully brought out and discussed by K. A. Fowler, 'Les finances et la discipline dans les armées anglaises en France au XIVe siècle', *Actes du Colloque International de Cocherel, Les Cahiers Vernonnais*, iv (1964).

NOTES

1. *The Libelle of English Polycye*, ed. Sir George Warner (Oxford, 1926).
2. B. J. H. Rowe, 'King Henry VI's Claim to France: In Picture and Poem', *The Library*, 4th ser., xiii (1933); J. W. McKenna, 'Henry VI of England and the Dual Monarchy: Aspects of Royal Propaganda, 1422–1432', *Journal of the Warburg and Courtauld Institutes*, xxviii (1965).
3. This is amply borne out by the study of Dr H. J. Hewitt's *The Organization of War under Edward III* (Manchester, 1966).
4. See John Page's poem on the siege, in *The Historical Collections of a Citizen of London in the Fifteenth Century*, ed. J. Gairdner (Camden Society, 1876).
5. *Chronique de Mont-Saint-Michel, 1343–1468*, ed. S. Luce (Société des anciens textes français, Paris, 1879), i, 145. The original text is in French.
6. On this question, see B. H. St J. O'Neil, *Castles and Cannon: A Study of Early Artillery Fortifications in England* (Oxford, 1960); J. R. Hale, 'The Early Development of the Bastion: An Italian Chronology, *c.* 1450–*c.* 1534', in *Europe in the Late Middle Ages*, ed. J. R. Hale, J. R. L. Highfield and B. Smalley (1965).
7. D. Hay, 'The Division of the Spoils of War in Fourteenth-Century England', *TRHS* 5th ser., iv (1954), 91.
8. The best over-all coverage is to be found in M. H. Keen, *The Laws of War in the Late Middle Ages* (1965), *passim*.
9. Arch. dép., Calvados, D 27.
10. J. Huizinga, *Homo Ludens. A Study in the Play-Element in Culture* (English trans., 1949), ch. v, 'Play and War'.
11. Hewitt, op. cit., pp. 28 ff.
12. F. Grose, *Military Antiquities* (1788), ii, 79 ff.
13. Johannes de Bromyard, *Summa Predicantium* (various editions), under 'Bellum'.
14. A. Tuetey, *Les Écorcheurs sous Charles VII* (Montbéliard, 1874).
15. Some cases took many years to settle. See E. Perroy, 'L'affaire du comte de Denia', in *Mélanges d'histoire du moyen âge dédiés à la mémoire de Louis Halphen* (Paris, 1957), and A. Rogers, 'Hoton versus Shakell: A Ransom Case in the Court of Chivalry, 1390–5', in *Nottingham Medieval Studies*, vi (1962); vii (1963).
16. H. Denifle, *La désolation des églises, monastères et hôpitaux en France pendant la guerre de Cent ans* (Paris, 1897), i, 78. The original text, now in the Vatican Archives, is in Latin.
17. *The Chronicle of Jean de Venette*, trans. and ed. J. Birdsall and R. A. Newhall (New York, 1953).
18. On this, see G. R. Owst, *Preaching in Medieval England* (Cambridge, 1926: reprinted New York, 1965); *Literature and Pulpit in Medieval England* (Cambridge, 1933: new edition, Oxford, 1961).

19. *The English Works of Wyclif, hitherto unpublished*, ed. F. D. Matthew (Early English Texts Society, 1880), p. 91.

20. *Tractatus de Offcio Regis*, ed. A. W. Pollard and C. Sayle (Wyclif Society, 1887), 262, 272, 276; *English Works*, pp. 90–1.

21. *The Register of John Trefnant, Bishop of Hereford (1389–1404)*, ed. W. W. Capes (Hereford, 1914).

22. *Summa Predicantium*, under 'Ministratio'.

23. *Summa Predicantium*, under 'Lex' and 'Bellum'. Wyclif (*De Officio Regis*, p. 271) had said that money spent on war could be more profitably employed in other ways.

24. P. S. Lewis, *Later Medieval France, the Polity* (1968), p. 16.

25. Philippe de Mézières, *Le Songe du Vieil Pelerin*, ed. G. W. Coopland (2 vols, Cambridge, 1969).

26. Trans. and ed. G. W. Coopland, under the title of *The Tree of Battles of Honoré Bonet* (Liverpool, 1949).

27. Ed. A. T. P. Byles (Early English Texts Society, 1932 and 1937).

28. *The Essential Portions of Nicholas Upton's 'De Studio Militari'*, ed. F. P. Barnard (Oxford, 1931), pp. 4, 5, 28–9, 33, 46.

29. See A. Coville, *L'Ordonnance Cabochienne* (Paris, 1891), especially pp. 172 ff.

30. Hewitt, op. cit., 124–5.

31. *Jean Gerson. Oeuvres Complètes*, ed. P. Glorieux (Paris, 1960), ii, 121–2.

32. *Letters and Papers Illustrative of the Wars of the English in France*, ed. J. Stevenson, Rolls Series, ii, pt 2, 580–1.

8. Truces

KENNETH FOWLER

'TRUCE', wrote Honoré Bonet in his *Tree of Battles*, which was completed in 1387, is 'a royal surety.' It 'signifies three things or three benefits; for first, it gives surety to persons, secondly to goods, and thirdly, hope of peace, for during the truce ways and means of reconciling and pacifying the two sides are sought'.[1] This essay is concerned with the truces of the Hundred Years War, with their mediation and negotiation, and the problems of enforcement which confronted those who made them and were included in their terms. It will investigate the difficulties encountered by the protagonists in their attempts to bring about a cessation of the hostilities, and will underline a number of the problems discussed in previous chapters.

The importance of this virtually unexplored aspect of the war is evident. Apart from nine years of incompletely ratified peace between 1360 and 1369, England and France were in a state of either war or truce from 1337 to 1492. More than half of the 116 years between 1337 and 1453 were taken up by periods of general truce. In the 83 years down to the treaty of Troyes in 1420 there were 55 years of general truce, while major campaigns occupied little more than 25–6 years, during which the fighting was often intermittent. In the 63 years between 1337 and 1400 major campaigns took place in little more than 18 years, there were less than 9 years of incompletely ratified peace, and 29 of general and 7 of local truce. This essay is principally concerned with these 63 years of the fourteenth century; for by 1400 all of the more important disarmament problems had presented themselves to the protagonists, and such solutions as seemed possible within the framework of a truce had been formulated. An examination of the years between 1337 and 1400 will thus demonstrate the nature of the problems and show what progress had been made in solving them; for during the course of the fourteenth century statesmen in both England and France persistently tried, but were unable to end through the channels of diplomacy, a war which became increasingly endemic and outwith royal control.

I

It is, of course, impossible to totally dissociate the negotiation of the truces from the negotiations for peace; for as Bonet remarked, one of the principal purposes of a truce was that it paved the way for peace discussions. Down to 1377 the truces were almost entirely mediated by the papacy which, 'acting through its accredited representatives, or sometimes by personal intervention, was in this sphere the equivalent of the modern United Nations'.[2] However, the mediation of a truce was primarily regarded by the papacy as a necessary preliminary to the discussion of a peace. Hence the ambassadors who met to conclude a truce were often empowered to treat of peace; when they met to conclude peace they invariably had to fall back on their procurations to negotiate a truce, or the extension of an existing one. But the advent of the Great Schism in 1378 put paid to the role of the papacy as mediator and, by dividing off France and her allies from England and hers in allegiance to two rival popes, constituted yet one further impediment to the conclusion of peace. Thereafter, agreement had first to be reached on who was to fulfil this important office; either side agreed to the archbishop of Rouen in 1381–2, the Emperor Wenzel of Luxemburg sent the imperial chancellor and a team of Germans to offer his good offices in 1384, these were disputed with those of the duke or duchess of Bavaria in 1385 and, most unlikely of all, the king of Armenia offered his services in 1386;[3] but although he worked hard and impartially to bring the two sides to an accommodation which he hoped would lead on to a Crusade in which he would recover his distant kingdom, it was without success. During the following ten years they had to manage as best they could without any outside mediation.[4]

Prior to the fall of Calais in 1347 truces were concluded to end a campaign: at Esplechin in the Low Countries in 1340, in the church of Malestroit in Brittany in 1343, and beneath the walls of Calais in 1347.[5] Successive prolongations of the last agreement until June 1355,[6] and the constant endeavours of the papacy to convert it into a peace, led to an almost permanent conference at work, under the chairmanship of Cardinal Guy de Boulogne, in tents pitched on the frontier between Calais and Guines. From 1381 onwards regular meetings took place in the church of Leulinghen, a tiny hamlet situated in the desolate and wind-swept landscape half-way between Calais and Boulogne-sur-Mer. These resulted in two partial truces to last from 26 January 1384 until 1 May 1385, and a general truce concluded on 18 June 1389, which was renewed three times, until 29 September 1398, and replaced by a long truce sealed in Paris on 9 March 1396, which was intended to last from 1398 to 1426.[7] Occasional truce and peace conferences also took place elsewhere (at Bordeaux in 1357, Brétigny and Calais in 1360, Bruges in 1374–7, and in Guyenne and elsewhere at other times) and some of these resulted in both general and local truces;[8] but the main centres of activity during the fourteenth century were undoubtedly on the military frontier in the Pas-de-Calais in the forties, fifties, eighties and nineties, and it was to this 'no man's land' that English, French, Scottish, Flemish, Castilian, Portuguese and other embassies gravitated to discuss the problems of peace in western Europe and to try to arrange a cessation of hostilities on their frontiers and within their marches.

II

In the fourteenth century governments did not employ permanent, resident ambassadors. Diplomacy was consequently a matter of *ad hoc* embassies, the more important of which always included a quorum of high-ranking noblemen, who had extensive powers to conclude treaties on behalf of the sovereigns whom they represented. Much of the real work was done by legal experts, a body of ecclesiastics and king's councillors presided over by a bishop or archbishop, often the keeper of the king's privy seal or his chancellor, and who formed an ambassadorial council responsible for preparing the ground for the main negotiations or, when more routine matters only were being discussed – such as the extension of a previously negotiated truce – had powers to conclude an agreement on their own.[9] Sometimes, the presence of nobles was intended solely to give the negotiations such importance and urgency as might be desired; but more often than not they took an active and leading part in the discussions, with considerable powers to interpret their royal and conciliar instructions as they saw best.[10] In the 1340s and 1350s the chief noblemen on the English side were the first duke of Lancaster and the earl of Arundel, and the lord of Offémont and the count of Montfort on the French.[11] The principal ecclesiastics who presided over the ambassadorial councils during the same period

were William Bateman, bishop of Norwich, for the English, and
Hugues d'Arcy, bishop of Laon, who was succeeded by Pierre de la
Forêt, bishop of Paris and subsequently archbishop of Rouen, for the
French.[12] It is probable that, on the French side, the ecclesiastics
played the most important role in these earlier negotiations. For
whereas the English embassies always had to include an earl or a duke
along with Bateman, the French embassies often did not include a high-
ranking nobleman, and only the presence of a senior ecclesiastic was
required for a quorum.[13] But in the 1380s and 1390s the dukes of
Lancaster and Gloucester for England, and of Burgundy and Berry for
France, were undoubtedly the chief men in the negotiations at Leulinghen, arriving at Calais and Boulogne respectively in retinues of upwards
of 500 men for the more important discussions.[14] Only four to eight
persons for either side were actually involved in the negotiations,
returning from Leulinghen to Calais and Boulogne each night,[15] and
on at least one occasion (in 1384) the councils were unable to prepare
the ground for the royal dukes to leave their respective bases; they
could not agree whether to meet at Leulinghen or near-by Marquise,
the English would not give a safe-conduct to the Scottish representatives (Cardinal Walter, bishop of Glasgow, and the chancellor John,
bishop of Dunbrelden), and the councillors had to content themselves
with representing their respective cases before the ambassadors in
Boulogne and Calais.[16]

All of this, and much more besides, is known to us from a *dossier* kept
by the chairman of the French ambassadorial council in the 1380s,
Nicolas Dubosc, bishop of Bayeux.[17] It reveals a great deal about the
actual conduct of the negotiations: of how it was necessary to secure
safe-conducts for all concerned, and sometimes conclude a local truce
for Picardy, before the negotiations could proceed; of the delays –
deliberate and otherwise – in the issue and conclusion of these and in
the arrival of envoys, which had the effect of holding up and sometimes
preventing the discussions; of the instructions given to the ambassadors
by the king's council and of the contacts which they maintained during
the course of the negotiations; of the difficulties encountered over
procedure, protocol, the location of the talks and the representation at
them of the allies of either side. Along with a *dossier* kept by the papal
nuncios at the negotiations at Bruges in 1374–7,[18] it provides a unique
insight into the nature of fourteenth-century diplomacy and the
problems encountered and created by the ambassadors responsible for
negotiating the truces.

III

Once a truce had been concluded, arrangements had to be made for its publication and proclamation. Occasionally, sergeants were sent from the conference ground to announce the terms of a truce,[19] but the usual procedure was for one of the envoys to notify them to the king and council, who then instructed the chancellor to have them published under the great seal and to issue instructions for their proclamation.[20] On the English side, these were usually sent to all the sheriffs, to the two admirals of the fleet or their lieutenants, to the constable of Dover and warden of the Cinque Ports and, in France, to the English authorities in Aquitaine and the captains of Calais and other coastal fortresses.[21] On the French side, similar instructions were sent to the *baillis* and *sénéchaux*,[22] and in the frontier regions *vidimi* were issued by officers specially appointed for the purpose.[23] Since many of these officers were themselves military captains, directly involved in the war, in exceptional circumstances special commissioners were sent to the trouble spots to see that the terms of a truce were properly proclaimed.[24] The difficulties which could arise if they were not, are well illustrated by an instruction given to one of Charles VI's councillors, Nicolas Paynel, who was sent on a mission to Richard II in August 1398.[25] Charles complained that, although he had had the truce proclaimed in all the places to which it appertained, Richard had only had it proclaimed in the marches of Picardy, and not in Guyenne, and that according to the terms of the truce it was to be proclaimed everywhere before 29 September 1398, when the four-year truce concluded at Leulinghen on 27 May 1394 ran out. Consequently, Charles complained, many Anglo-Gascon captains in Guyenne publicly boasted that they would renew the war on that day. Worried about the whole business, Charles had already sent two embassies to Richard to require him to have the twenty-eight-year truce proclaimed, but of no avail. He had no alternative, therefore, but to point out that if the English began hostilities at the end of September, the French would reply in kind. Charles wanted to make it quite clear that he did not wish this to happen, but he must know what Richard's intentions were – for he had had two years to have the truce proclaimed – without further delay. Since time was running out, to get it proclaimed by the required date by *gens d'estat*, as the truce required, Charles suggested that Richard should send responsible messengers, equipped with letters to all concerned, requiring them not to take any military action until more high-ranking envoys arrived.

There can be no doubt that Charles VI's accusations were not un-founded. There was no seneschal in Guyenne in September 1398. In a letter written in Bordeaux on 25 September of that years,[26] the Gascon council wrote to the then constable of France, Louis de Sancerre, expressing their desire to live in peace with their neighbours, and explaining how, to their surprise, they had not received any news of the twenty-eight-year truce from Richard, and how they had written to the lord of Pons, marshal Boucicaut, the seneschal of the Agenais, the lady of Albret, Gaillart de la Motte, and other French lords and captains, explaining that they had expressly required all those in English obedi-ence to respect the truce in all its details. They had also sent letters under the seneschal's seal to the constable of France, who had supreme command on the frontiers of Guyenne, requesting him to give a similar undertaking for those on the French side.

Some of the more elaborate arrangements for the enforcement of truces date from the earlier agreements prior to 1360, when many of the problems were being tackled for the first time. Inspection teams were set up to stop sieges in progress and to assess the strength of garrisons in order that the *status quo* could be restored if and when they ran out.[27] Places in dispute were handed over for the duration of a truce to the papal nuncios responsible for its mediation or to officers responsible to them.[28] The principal captains and other notable persons on either side were to swear in one another's presence to abide by its terms, and specific arrangements were made for captains of fortresses in the Pas-de-Calais to meet on the conference ground between Calais and Guines for that purpose; upon the request of either party they were to attend meetings there to settle disputes between them.[29]

Prior to 1360 most truces included provision for the appointment of wardens, whose business it was to see that their terms were adhered to, and judges who were to deal with matters which the wardens failed to attend to and to settle disputes between them.[30] The ineffectiveness of these arrangements is indicated by special provisions arrived at in 1353-4, when the ratification of peace preliminaries lay in the balance. For not only were the wardens and judges replaced by more responsible conservators, but in Artois, Picardy and Boulonnais these were high-ranking noblemen and king's councillors (the duke of Lancaster, the earl of Arundel and Bartholomew Burghersh for the English; the count of Montfort, the constable of France and Robert de Lorris for the French) who undertook to become hostages in Paris or London if infringements, which were to be reported to the captains of Calais and

Saint-Omer, were not corrected within forty days.[31] The latter arrangement, though risky, appears to have been reasonably effective. In the
spring of 1354, for instance, Lancaster, Arundel and the earl of Huntingdon wrote to Guy de Boulogne and the chancellor of France, Pierre
de la Forêt, complaining of infringements by the French, and both the
cardinal and the chancellor did their utmost to bring the malefactors
to account.[32] Then, in December, when Lancaster was on his way
south to the peace conference at Avignon, the mayor and *échevins* of
Amiens presented him with a petition for the redress of infringements
of clauses of the truce guaranteeing free passage for merchants, which
he immediately sent on to the king and council for their attention.[33]
But the most striking example of the effectiveness of the English war-
ranty occurred in July 1355 when, upon complaint by the warrantors,
a commission of inquiry was sent into the Pas-de-Calais to investigate
alleged infringements by the English captain of Guines, John Danseye,
who had had burnt a bastide which the French had erected before
Guines and was consequently removed from office and imprisoned by
the captain of Calais.[34]

The truce concluded at Bordeaux on 23 March 1357 differed from
other truces of the 1340s and 1350s in that it was negotiated as a preliminary to peace overtures with a captive king. For this reason, and also
because after the battle of Poitiers the war was spreading throughout
the whole of France, with the formation of the Free Companies, the
activities of Navarrese troops in Normandy, and growing anarchy
throughout the kingdom, more complex arrangements had to be made
for its enforcement.[35] Captains were made responsible for infringements
committed by soldiers of their garrisons or by any other person to whom
they gave shelter and protection. Disputes arising between troops in the
frontier districts were to be settled by the captains of the respective
parties, and all other malefactors were to be brought before the wardens
of the truce or other justices. The taking of prisoners, ransoms and
protection money or *pâtis* (also called *souffrances de guerre*) was forbidden, save that special arrangements were made to deal with prisoners who had broken their faith, with unpaid ransoms and arrears of
pâtis. Cases concerning the latter were to be brought before judges
appointed specifically for that purpose (one for either side in Guyenne
and Languedoc, Brittany, Normandy and Picardy) by the marshals,
and if the plaintiff was resident in England he was to present his case
before a joint commission to be set up on the conference ground, which
was now situated between Guines and Ardres. Although the employ of

wardens and judges was retained, the number of wardens and the regions in which they were to serve was greatly expanded. As we shall see, this in itself, and the fact that the arrangements for the enforcement of the truces were becoming increasingly complex and far-flung, was a mark of the fact that warfare had become endemic and that the central authorities were powerless to stop it.

This is well illustrated by the next truce, concluded at Chartres on 7 May 1360, and which was different from its predecessors in that its purpose was to regularise the situation in the period which was to elapse between the conclusion of peace preliminaries at Brétigny on the following day and their ratification at Calais on 24 October.[36] In July and August, both French and English commissioners were appointed to redress infractions of the truce by their side and the necessary safe-conducts were issued for their passage through France.[37] Then, on 30 September 1360, the earl of Kent was given a commission as the king's captain and lieutenant in France, with the express purpose of seeing that the truce was enforced by English captains in Normandy.[38] At Calais on 23 October, King John appointed five conservators-general of the truce, and on the twenty-eighth Edward III issued commissions for the delivery of fortresses taken by allied forces contrary to its terms.[39]

The problems which confronted these men are well illustrated by the experiences of one of the English commissioners, Amanieu d'Albret, lord of Langoiran. On 13 September 1360, John ordered 'all lieu-tenants, captains, seneschals, *baillis*, *prévôts*, mayors, *échevins*, guardians of bridges and gates, of bastides and good towns, and all other officers and subjects' to allow him to pass freely throughout the country with a retinue of twenty armed men to carry out the job.[40] Details of the difficulties which he encountered in Berry have been preserved in two notarial instruments drawn up by the chancellor of Bourbonnais, Pierre de Giac, on 4 and 5 December following.[41] They tell how Albret arrived in Berry to carry out the evacuation of fortresses taken by the English and Gascons since the conclusion of the truce and of how he fared at two places: Brouillamenon and Sainte-Thorette on the banks of the river Cher near Bourges. At Brouillamenon he addressed the captain, a Gascon called Morilhon, in the following words:

Morilhon, you are occupying the place of Brouillamenon, which you have taken and occupied during the truce, which is against the ordinance, wishes and oaths of my lords the king of England and the prince of Wales. I command you, on behalf of my said lords the king and the prince that, for fear of displeasing them and on pain of being banished from the kingdom of England and the duchy of Guyenne, and of all other perils of my said lords, that you immediately depart from the place of Brouillamenon, which you have taken and occupied during time of truce and peace, and that you surrender it to its rightful owner.

Morilhon replied that he would not, because he did not hold the fortress by virtue of the Anglo-French wars, but had received his captaincy by grant of a local seigneur called Hutin de Vermeilles and the lady of Sully, and he produced their letters of commission to substantiate his statement. This Albret clearly did not believe; but he was powerless to do anything more than to forbid the captain to take part in a private feud between Vermeilles and the lord of Sully, to reiterate his request that the fortress be evacuated, and to have the entire proceedings drawn up into a public instrument substantiated by both French and English witnesses.

That evening, he arrived at Sainte-Thorette, which was controlled by an English captain, William Bardolf, who was subsequently one of the captains of an English contingent of the Great Companies. On requesting to see the captain or his lieutenant, he was met by Bardolf's brother who said that William had gone to near-by Vierzon. In the presence of Bardolf's brother and six of his companions from the garrison, together with his own witnesses, Albret then forbade them to make war in France and instructed them to inform the captain to quit the fortress and to appear before him at Mehun-sur-Yèvre on the following morning. Bardolf duly showed up at Mehun with a bodyguard of his companions, and Albret addressed him as he had the captain of Brouillamenon. To this Bardolf replied that he had not seen anyone that year whom he would care to surrender the fortress to, since he had not taken it during the truce and it was part of his *pâtis*; he would therefore not give it up until the surrounding countryside had paid what was due to him. Albret then forbade him to take sides in the war between Vermeilles and Sully, and requested him to accompany him to Bourges to defend his case, since the *bailli* of Bourges, who was then with Albret, and who had undertaken that no harm would come to Bardolf, had several complaints to make against him. In an attempt to persuade the captain to accompany them, Albret pointed out that he had, in any case, a much surer safe-conduct from the Black Prince; but to this Bardolf replied with a stream of abuse, saying, among other things, that if the said *bailli* had a safe-conduct from God he would not take advantage of it unless he were escorted by a bodyguard of his companions. And with this entourage the three of them went off to Bourges, the captain and *bailli* fulminating against one another on the way, and where Albret finally heard their respective cases; but having insufficient time to reach a verdict, he instructed the captain to appear before the king's council in London on 2 February, to answer to all the charges which the *bailli* had against him in respect of his activities in Berry. Whether or not Bardolf did appear on that day is not clear; but from what is known of his subsequent career it is probable, to say the least, that he was contumacious. He told Albret to his face that he would not do so unless the *bailli* was also summoned to appear on the same day to make his accusations in person. There was nothing more that this representative of the royal authority could do but to forbid the captain to make war in France and have the entire proceedings once more drawn up into a public instrument.

In effect, the problem of enforcing the truce was merging into the much larger issue of executing the peace, of evacuating vast unmapped territories bound up in terms of feudal geography, in which captains and their troops put out of employ by the cessation of hostilities were forming independent Companies fighting for their own profit and living on the proceeds of *pâtis* and ransoms levied in the districts under their control. Morilhon and Bardolf were just two such persons in Berry; but throughout the whole of France there were many more like them.

It was for this reason, among others, that on 20 January 1361 Sir John Chandos was appointed 'lieutenant and captain-general . . . and special conservator' of the peace and truce throughout France, with extensive military as well as judicial powers to evacuate all allied towns and fortresses situated in regions which, under the terms of the treaty of Brétigny, were to be retained by the French, and, together with six other persons later associated with him, to receive all the lands, towns and castles ceded to the English.[42] The story of this episode in the life of the future constable of Aquitaine, a soldier respected in both English and French circles for his justice and impartiality, yet later to become the Black Prince's right-hand man, has never been properly told, although it deserves to be; for he kept a very full account of his journeys throughout France, going about the business of, first, handing over places in allied control to the French and, second, of securing the transfer of towns and castles in Aquitaine into English hands.[43] But, interesting as the details of Sir John's work undoubtedly are, it is not appropriate to say more about them here, for they are primarily concerned with the execution of the peace of Brétigny, and not with the truce.

When the next truce was concluded, on 27 June 1375, it was in very different circumstances; for Charles V and his generals had secured the reconquest of nearly all of the lands ceded to the English at Brétigny, and John of Gaunt, who headed the English embassy on this occasion, was negotiating from a very weak position. Nevertheless, this truce, and its extension to 1 April 1377, is important in the development of new ideas of truce and of the machinery for their enforcement. The notion of a long truce, which was to be taken up again in the 1380s and 1390s and finally agreed to in 1396, was first mooted, and provisions for a treaty of forty years were actually drafted, but rejected. However, agreement was reached, not only on a temporary cessation of hostilities and the handing over of the towns of Saint-Sauveur-le-Vicomte in Normandy and of Cognac in Saintonge to officers responsible to the papacy for the duration of the truce; provisions were also made for the withdrawal of allied forces which had recently disembarked in Brittany, save 200 men whom the duke could retain for the defence of such places as he then held in the duchy.[44] This idea of easing tension through a reduction of forces was taken up again in February 1382 when, although agreement could not be reached on a general truce, both sides agreed not to raise further forces for service in France or at sea before 1 June, not to increase the normal garrison forces, and to recall all captains and lieutenants employed in field forces in Guyenne over and above those necessary for garrison service. In particular, the English required that the marshal of France and the forces newly sent under his command into Aquitaine should be recalled, that no further French forces should be sent to the frontier districts, and that no military enterprises should be undertaken outside the normal garrison warefare.[45]

Equally interesting are the novel ideas for the enforcement of the extension of the truce of 27 June 1375. This was to be cried and published throughout England and France, and conservators were appointed for all the affected regions (Brittany, Languedoc, Guyenne, Auvergne) with full powers to deal with infringements committed by land and sea, and for the restoration of goods of prisoners; but additional arrangements were also made for the main trouble spots in Picardy, Brittany and Guyenne.

In Picardy, the truce was to be cried and published simultaneously by an officer of either side in all the Channel ports and the principal towns and fortresses, particularly in the Pas-de-Calais – two obvious danger zones. Four conservators appointed for this region were to repair all infringements, make good all damages which occurred by land or by sea, and have it cried that all goods taken from merchants and others since the truce began were to be restored forthwith and that all prisoners taken during the same period were to be released without ransom. For this purpose, at least two of the four conservators for the region (one for either side) were to assemble at some place between Calais and Saint-Omer, or between Calais and Boulogne, for 16 August, furnished with full powers to jointly hear complaints, repair infringements and generally see that justice was done. They were also to make arrangements for the setting up of a permanent resident commission; if this could not be agreed upon by 16 August, they were to inform the mediators at Bruges in order that the pursuivants might be informed and other arrangements made.

In Brittany, the French conservators were to assemble at Lesneven and their English counterparts at Saint-Mathieu in Finistère by 29 September, ready to deal with all complaints concerning infringements committed in all marches, save in such places as special conservators had been appointed. In Guyenne, the conservators were to be on duty by the same date, the French at Périgueux and the English at Bergerac; but complaints could be lodged, at the plaintiffs' convenience, in either Picardy, Brittany or Guyenne. Meanwhile, the ambassadors at Bruges agreed to send letters close direct to all judges, officers and other lords ordering them to restore goods and prisoners taken since the truce was concluded and to have all cases in dispute sent before the conservators.

Needless to say, this time-table was not adhered to; but although delays occurred, the programme was carried out. On 24 September Edward III wrote to the papal nuncios responsible for mediating the truce, requesting a month's delay for the arrival of the English conservators in Brittany, which he claimed had been made necessary by contrary winds and other causes, although Duke John IV protested that he had never been consulted about the entire arrangement in the first place.[46] For Gascony, the seneschal Sir Thomas Felton, Sir William Elmham, governor of Bayonne, and the Soudan de la Trau, seneschal of Landes, had been appointed conservators as early as 28 June 1376;[47] but it seems likely that the chief man in the south was the king's esquire, John Fastolf, who was sent 'overseas for the keeping of the truce . . . and to repair attempted infringements of it', and he only drew wages for the period from 5 November to 31 December 1376.[48] In Picardy, too, things moved rather slowly. Ralph Ferrers's account for a mission there to enforce the truce is for much the same period: 6 November to 17 December.[49]

However, rather more is known of the work of the conservators in Picardy. The two Englishmen involved were Ferrers and the captain of Guines, Sir John Harleston. They met their French counterparts, Jean de Longvillers, lord of Engoudsent and late captain of Boulogne, and Jean, lord of Sempy, captain-general in Picardy, at Marquise; on 12 December they reached an agreement on the manner in which they were to proceed, which was ratified by Edward III on 8 January following.[50] By its terms, they agreed to assemble at Marquise during the first fortnight in January and to oblige themselves under oath to have all goods known to have been seized restored to their owners by 2 February, without prorogation and without outrageous charges, especially such goods as were known to have been seized by Englishmen from Calais, London, the South Ports and the Channel Islands, and by Frenchmen from Amiens, Abbeville and other ports between Boulogne-sur-Mer and Royan. Unproven cases of infringement were to be heard by the conservators in the following manner: plaintiffs were to bring before them two of the most notable merchants, burgesses or other sufficient persons who were willing to give evidence for them, swear to its authenticity and append their seals to it in writing. The conservators were then to append their seals to such documents, have them displayed in a public place, instigate a thorough search for the goods in question, arrest those found culpable and restore the goods to their rightful owners within seven months of the receipt of information as to their whereabouts. Whenever such information could not be had, they were to inform their respective kings and councils within fifteen days of the conclusion of the investigation, so that such cases could be taken up by the central authorities. However, these investigations were not to be conducted by the English further than Boulogne-sur-Mer, and those of the French no further than Calais; in either case they were to be concluded within one month. Mutual security dictated these limitations, for by 1377 Franco-Castilian naval preparations for descents on the south coast of England, and English defence arrangements in the southern ports were well advanced. John of Gaunt had given his country a breathing-space in which to prepare for the inevitable attacks; but until 1387 England found herself under the perpetual menace of invasion.[51]

IV

With the failure of French preparations for the invasion and conquest of England in 1385-7, two factors of major political importance favoured the conclusion of a long truce, if not of peace. In the north, Philip the Bold of Burgundy, who had secured the county of Flanders on the death of his father-in-law, County Louis de Male, in 1384, was coming to realise that an aggressive policy towards England was incompatible with his economic interests in Flanders and the support of his Flemish subjects.[52] In the south, John of Gaunt, after the failure of his expedition to Galicia, concluded a treaty with John I of Trastamara in July 1388, whereby he renounced his claim to the Castilian throne, while providing for his daughter, Catalina, to be married to John's heir, at the same time abandoning the alliance with Portugal, where another daughter, Philippa, was married to the king.

Gaunt was now moving rapidly toward a wider international settlement, perhaps finally having settled for an enlarged duchy of Aquitaine to be held by him of the French Crown (thus getting round the problem of sovereignty), which had first been mooted at Bruges in 1375, was again raised at the truce conference in the summer of 1384, and which almost came about in 1393.[53] A settlement with France was now a preliminary to the ending of the Great Schism, and it was towards this goal that he was now moving. Already on 20 July 1388, John I issued a procuration for a Castilian embassy to attend the next truce conference at Leulinghen.[54] Six days later, in his capacity as lieutenant of Aquitaine, Gaunt appointed an embassy which, on 18 August, concluded a truce with the envoys of the duke of Berry for all the lands lying south of the river Loire and west of the Rhône, and which was to last until 16 March 1389.[55] On the 9 March this was extended until 31 July[56] and, meanwhile, arrangements were made for a major international truce conference to be held at Leulinghen before its expiry. Thus the long period of truce that saw out the century was ushered in.

But if the political obstacles to peace were now being eliminated one by one, with Gaunt's renunciation of the Castilian throne in 1388, Burgundian control of French royal policy (especially after 1392 when Charles VI had his first attack of madness), the surrender of Cherbourg to Charles of Navarre in 1394 and of Brest to the duke of Brittany in 1397, and Richard II's marriage to Charles's daughter Isabella in the previous year; nevertheless the military, economic and strategic obstacles remained insurmountable. The draft treaty of 1393 failed because of resistance to it in Bordeaux rather than in Paris or in Westminster; the surrender of Cherbourg and Brest, and suspicions that a like fate was planned for Calais, created a bellicose reaction in England that was taken up by the duke of Gloucester. But most important of all, the ambassadors responsible for negotiating the truces were unable, on either side, to dismantle the frontier garrisons in Picardy and Guyenne, or to eliminate the activities of royal and independent Companies within these areas. The real impediments to truce enforcement lay in the personnel of the conservators, the problem of military finance, and the private rights of soldiers under the contemporary Law of Arms. These three factors will now be examined.

V

There is every evidence that from the conclusion of the truce of Leulinghen in 1389, both Richard II and Charles VI meant business.[57] Between 1390 and 1394 commissioners were regularly appointed by either side to deal with infringements committed in Gascony: to stop raiding parties from the frontier garrisons from capturing towns and fortresses, pillaging the surrounding countryside, and levying new and unwarranted ransoms or *pâtis*.[58] They were to assemble together to hear all such cases and, where necessary, proceed against the contrariants by force of arms; but most significant of all, the conservators of the truces were themselves found to be culpable of all of these things, and between 1390 and 1396 repeated demands were therefore made for their reinforcement, dismissal and replacement by more substantial and impartial men, which the commissioners were empowered to carry out.[59]

On 28 February 1390 Richard appointed Sir John Trailly, newly appointed mayor of Bordeaux, his predecessor in that office, Sir David Cradock of Nantwich in Cheshire, and his son Sir Richard Cradock, to make sure that the conservators appointed in the previous August did their work properly.[60] There can be little doubt that Sir Richard Cradock, who may already have been and was certainly subsequently retained by the king,[61] was the main person in all this. His father had held office as mayor of Bordeaux since 1382[62] and Richard, who had probably spent most of those years in the duchy, was thus well versed in Gascon affairs. In November 1379 he had been sent out there, along with Trailly and others, to supply the then lieutenant of the duchy,

John Lord Neville, with much-needed reinforcements, and had been taken prisoner by the French when coming to England from Gascony in 1384.[63] In August 1389, by which time he was keeper of the strategically vital castle of Fronsac, he once again crossed to England, doubtless giving a very full report on the situation in the south.[64] In the spring and summer of 1390 he was the key figure in Richard's attempts to ensure that the truce was enforced; he was provided with privy seal letters to the principal English captains and lords of the duchy ordering them to see that it was respected, and was empowered to deal with all infringements of it.[65]

Meanwhile, Charles VI sent a delegation to England complaining bitterly about the capture of certain castles and fortresses by Richard II's lieges in Gascony. They arrived while Cradock was still on his fact-finding tour in the duchy, but on 23 July a council was summoned to meet at Windsor on 29 August, by which time he had returned. On the following day the French ambassadors were given a safe-conduct for themselves and fifty men-at-arms to go to Aquitaine, and on 31 August they were given letters of passage for their journey. By 26 September one of them, Master Nicole de Rancé, was back in England with a further report on the matter and, in consequence, on 30 September Cradock was appointed one of the English commissioners instructed to meet their French counterparts to see that it was enforced, and he again crossed to Gascony in the following month with Richard's instructions on the matter. On 6 October the port authorities at Dover were instructed to speedily provide shipping for him and Sir William Elmham (another of the English commissioners then in England) to sail for Aquitaine with a bodyguard of fifty mounted men to deal with 'certain misprisons committed by the king's subjects there contrary to the present truce'.[66]

For his part, on 16 October Charles VI appointed Renaud de Pons to treat with the newly appointed seneschal of Aquitaine, Sir Richard Scrope, complaining that a number of the English conservators of the truce were themselves responsible for some of the infringements, and that in spite of repeated instructions from Richard, they still refused to comply with its terms.[67] However, he added that he had been informed that Scrope, had recently arrived in Bordeaux with special powers from Richard and John of Gaunt to see that the fortresses in question were returned and that other infringements were put right. To this end Pons was to assemble with Scrope, to request the repair and return of the fortresses to their previous occupants, to give letters of discharge to those who handed them over, and to repair infringements by the French.

It is quite clear that breaches of the truce were occurring almost daily, and once again Cradock was called upon to go to Aquitaine to deal with them. On 11 December he appointed Thomas Maistresson of Nantwich his attorney in Cheshire, left for London, and from 5 March to 6 April 1392 was once again involved in Aquitaine with infringements of the truce.[68]

Meanwhile, on 8 April 1392, the truce of 18 June 1389 was prorogued until 29 September 1393 by the English and French ambassadors meeting at Amiens;[69] but before John of Gaunt returned to England the French ambassadors required him to request Richard to appoint additional conservators in the frontier regions of Guyenne, Normandy and Brittany who were to be 'notable men, with sufficient power and authority to keep the said truces . . . , and to see that the *pâtis* were reduced'.[70] This was seen as being particularly necessary if a long truce were to be concluded at the next meeting of ambassadors scheduled for 1 July, in which event Richard was to appoint as conservators 'men of great power and authority, notables who wished to see reason and justice . . . , and also that the *patis* which they levied would be reduced, and that payment of them would be demanded in a gracious manner, without rigorous constraint.'[71]

Richard speedily pursued the matter, and during the first fortnight in July, while he was residing in Nottingham castle, a whole series of commissions was issued. The local conservators named in the truce of 8 April were reinforced by a group of supposedly responsible citizens who were to operate in the trouble spots, Sir Richard Cradock, significantly, in all of them; they were to inquire into infringements speedily and without long process, repair the same and require their French counterparts to do likewise for breaches committed by their side.[72] On 20 July the latter (Hugues de Boulay, Charles VI's chamberlain Guillaume, alias Braquet de Braquemont, and Master Nicole de Rancé) secured letters of protection and safe-conduct from Richard II until the following Easter to go by land and sea to Aquitaine and elsewhere with a retinue of thirty men-at-arms and thirty archers to apply themselves to the matter of infringements.[73] Cradock had already received letters of protection for the same purpose on 4 July,[74] and on 14 July Richard addressed letters close to twenty-three of the principal captains in Aquitaine, giving strict instructions for them to see that the truce was observed by them and the men of their garrisons.[75]

Nevertheless, a year later matters still remained unsettled. The French complained that allied forces in Aquitaine had taken towns and fortresses and captured men and beasts contrary to the tenor of the truce. To deal with this, on 11 June 1393 Richard appointed yet another commission to meet their French opposite numbers, and which could employ armed force to carry out their work.[76] They were to present themselves before the captains of all frontier garrisons where infringements had been committed, and to see that mutual restitutions were made. Any allied captains or anyone associated with them who disobeyed their decisions were to be banished from England and Aquitaine; in that event the commissioners were to proceed against them 'by force of arms and by all manners which they could employ to do this'. Unsatisfactory conservators were to be removed from office and replaced by others, and all allied captains were to be obliged to swear to observe the truce and to do everything they could to see that it was kept.

The extent of the problem which faced the commissioners is well illustrated by a letter of John Trailly, interim governor of Aquitaine and conservator-general of the truce there, written to the lord of Mussidan from Bordeaux on 19 June 1389.[77] It appears from this that the mayor and consuls of Périgueux had complained to Trailly about a *pâtis* which, they claimed, Mussidan had been levying from them for about fourteen years. Despite the fact that John of Gaunt, as lieutenant in Aquitaine, had prohibited him from raising this, nevertheless on 23 April Mussidan had raided the town, taken a number of prisoners together with a sizeable number of livestock and other booty, and taken them off to his castle of Mussidan. As a result of requests from both the seneschal of Périgord, as local conservator, and the lord of Pons, as general conservator for the French, Trailly had repeatedly requested Mussidan to restore the prisoners and booty and to present himself before one of the French conservators along with the mayor and consuls; but since he had refused to do either, in accordance with the truce Trailly had granted the mayor and consuls a hearing and summoned Mussidan, or someone having full powers to represent him, to appear before him in order that the matter could be fully debated and justice done. What is significant about this story is that Mussidan was himself one of the English conservators of the truce in Périgord. Nor were his reported infringements of the truce unique, as appears from the records of a number of inquests which the commissioners of the truces ordered to be made into ravages committed by other conservators in Guyenne in the 1380s and 1390s.[78]

An investigation of the personnel employed as conservators at once reveals the magnitude of the problem, for the majority of them were the principal lords and captains of the areas in which they served. The English conservators in Picardy and Flanders, for example, were the captains of fortresses in the march of Calais; in Normandy and Brittany they were the captains of Cherbourg and Brest; but in Aquitaine, the Auvergne, Rouergue and elsewhere in the south they included some of the most famous *routier* captains of the period: men like Ramonnet du Sort and the bastard of Garlans in Auvergne and Rouergue, Nompar de Caumont in the Agenais and Quercy, Seguin de Badefol in Périgord and the Sarladais and Perrot le Béarnois in Limousin.[79] The fact that these men, whether royal or independent captains, held the effective power in the regions to which they were appointed, in no way assisted the observation of the truces, especially in a period of crisis in royal and seigniorial revenues which may well have obliged some of them to live off the countryside surrounding the castles they controlled. But who else could be appointed?

The truces were thus so frequently broken that most conservators and even some commissioners were more inclined to defend the interests of their party than to indemnify injured enemies or aliens. This is well illustrated by another letter from Trailly, written in reply to a letter delivered by the herald of the lord of Pons, and complaining of his judgement in a case concerning one Guiot Potart.[80] Trailly complained that Pons's method of proceeding in the case was contrary to the entire tenor of the truce: that the conclusions arrived at in the royal letters enclosing Potart's petition were as yet unproven; that the manner in which Pons had examined and secured his information on the case was irregular; that his judgement was not tenable; that his request that Trailly carry out Pons's judgement on the basis upon which it had been arrived at was out of the question. Trailly argued that according to written law a plaintiff must pursue his case in the court of his defendant's lord and judge, and that consequently Potart's case should have been brought before the court of the seneschal of Gascony as conservator-general of the truce, since the dispute was with the burgesses and inhabitants of Bordeaux, who were the defendants in this case. Even supposing Pons was the rightful judge, he could not give judgement on the evidence of the plaintiff and the information provided by him without hearing the defendant's case. Moreover, according to the terms of the truce a plaintiff's case must be heard by the conservators of the defendant's party and a commission directed to Pons by Charles VI had required that judgement should be given in accordance with the terms of the truce.

Pons had clearly acted in this irregular manner because Potart had on several previous occasions brought his case before the English conservators and judgement had been given against him. Nevertheless, Trailly agreed to allow the case to be brought before the seneschal of Aquitaine, providing that Pons was willing to hear the cases of twelve burgesses of Bordeaux who had seen their goods pillaged contrary to the tenor of the truce, and of others who were held prisoner by the French, one of whom had died, so Trailly claimed, through the harsh conditions of his imprisonment.

The tone of the letter is bitter enough: in spite of repeated requests to Pons for the French infringements to be amended, he had received no response, and for the burgess who had died in prison nothing could now be done. He was, moreover, amazed that Pons's herald had not awaited a reply, and was consequently suspicious that Pons was up to no good, since they had previously agreed to make no move against one another without due warning. He consequently requested a speedy answer as to whether it was safe for those in English obedience to enter Pons's circumscription as conservator without fear of marque or reprisals, and he concluded his letter by pointing out to Pons 'for we shall conduct our affairs in like manner as you conduct yours.'

More serious was the failure of the commissioners to carry out their duties properly. During the course of his interrogation at the Châtelet in 1391 the celebrated *routier* captain, Mérigot Marchès claimed that one of the English commissioners appointed to enforce the truce in Limousin in 1390, an esquire called Richard Scot, had come to speak to him at his stronghold of Vendais (le Roc de Vendas), had publicly requested him to depart therefrom in accordance with the terms of the truce, on pain of banishment and all other manner of penalties; but at the same time had privately informed him that he was not to quit the stronghold, but was to defend it as best he could.[81] As if that were not enough, he also claimed that the duke of Lancaster had sent Sir Richard Cradock (who, as we have seen, was a knight of the king's chamber and one of Richard II's most trusted commissioners for the truce) with letters instructing him to hold on to all the fortresses under his control since, as soon as the truce ran out (16 August 1392), he intended to conduct an expedition in France and would need his co-operation.[82] But great as the problem of finding an effective machinery of truce enforcement undoubtedly was, it was nothing by comparison with the obstacles created by the levying of protection money, upon which the entire structure of military finance had come to depend.

VI

The levying of protection money, of *pâtis*, *souffrances* or *sûretés de guerre*, *raencons du pays* and *billets*, had many sides to it.[83] Such payments could be regarded as ordinary profits of war by the Companies and other independent troops who raised them. They could also be regarded as purchasing immunity from war – sometimes for persons and property within extensive regions – by those who paid them, and they were often themselves not unlike truces.[84] Finally, they could be levied from individuals and communities as a kind of tax for the upkeep of royal garrisons in the frontier districts, and herein lay their greatest impediment to peace: they were indispensable to the protagonists in the conduct of the war.

As a method of financing royal garrison forces, the levying of protection money was already operative in Brittany and Guyenne in the 1340s and 1350s, and rapidly spread throughout France after the battle of Poitiers, when independent Anglo-Navarrese forces came to occupy towns and castles all over the country.[85] A varying number of parishes were tied to a fortress and were obliged to pay a fixed levy to the receiver of the garrison, who kept a schedule of ransoms due from each parish. Payments were usually made quarterly, partly in money and partly in kind, and a receipt or *billet* could also be issued, for a payment, testifying that the person who purchased it lived in an area paying *pâtis*. Many of the smaller garrisons only collected revenues from a few parishes, but the more important establishments often controlled an entire region. In Brittany in the 1350s as many as 220 parishes were ransomed to the garrisons of Bécherel and Ploërmel; Saint-Sauveur-le-Vicomte controlled 263 – almost the entire Cotentin Peninsula – in 1371, and Brest 160 in 1384 – almost the whole of Finistère together with the offshore islands. Some idea of the revenues derived from protection money may be had from the accounts of the receiver-general of Brittany which show that in 1359–60 this amounted to over £10,500 sterling for the three principal garrisons of Vannes, Bécherel and Ploërmel alone – a figure more than double the average annual revenues of Gascony in the years 1348–61. This was a substantial sum, considering that the ordinary revenues of the Crown in the same period were in the region of £35,000 a year. In 1377 the Commons estimated the cost to the Exchequer of maintaining garrisons in France at £46,000: £24,000 on the garrisons in the march of Calais and £4000 on Brest. In 1371–2, when there were no exceptional troop concentrations at Calais, the cost to the English Exchequer amounted to £19,284. In 1378 the pay of the captain of Brest stood at £3333, with munitions over and above that sum. In the period 1373–9 English subsidies to Guyenne amounted to more than £20,000 a year. All of this in a period when ordinary revenues, without parliamentary subsidies, only amounted to around £35,000 a year, was a very heavy burden on English resources. Inevitably, the government was obliged to let the frontier garrisons live off the country. In 1379 subsidies to Guyenne were terminated and in the succeeding years the pay of the captains of Brest was gradually reduced. The troops came increasingly to live off the countryside surrounding their fortresses, in much the same way and with much the same consequences as had occurred in Brittany and Normandy earlier in the century. Only at Calais and Cherbourg was any serious attempt made to finance the garrison forces from England. Bearing in mind that the French had often to rely on the same form of military finance in the frontier regions, nothing could have been more conducive to the violation of the truces.

There could thus be no solution to the problems created by the levying of protection money other than, on the one hand, the evacuation of all frontier garrisons, and, on the other hand, the elimination by force of arms of the *routier* captains, for the most part scions of noble families whose fortunes had gone down in the world and who had come to depend upon them for their livelihood. The only other alternative was to bring them under central control. It was in the interests of both the French and the English authorities to do this, whether to protect the civilian population in their obedience or to increase their own revenues. Already in the truce of 1357 and the draft treaty for a forty-year truce put forward during the negotiations at Bruges in 1376, it was proposed to abolish ransoms and *pâtis* altogether; but this was clearly so impracticable that it had to be rejected.[86] The first concerted attempts at control appear to have been made during the truces concluded between 1384 and 1396, and the abuses they sought to prevent make depressing reading.[87] The levying of ransoms and *patis* was so unremitting upon the country folk that they met demands for payment with armed resistance or fled the ransom districts taking what possessions they could with them. Villages, parishes, even entire ransom districts had become deserted. Captains met failure to pay within the required terms with reprisals of death and the confiscation or burning of the properties of the debtors. In these conditions the truces were constantly being violated, and their negotiators sought to prevent their infringement by:

(1) Prohibiting any increase in the ransom rates or the levying of new ransoms.

(2) Empowering the conservators of the truces to have excessive ransoms diminished and to fix the rates according to the number of hearths in each district and according to the wealth of the inhabitants.

(3) Prohibiting captains from taking undue reprisals and making the conservators of the truces and the civil authorities of the affected regions responsible for levying debts. Only if they failed to do this within given delays could the captains proceed to extract payment by force; but then only of the debt in question, together with a specified proportion of the debt (up to a quarter or a fifth) for damages and expenses.

To encourage the repopulation of deserted areas – which was becoming a major problem – those inhabitants who chose to return to the ransom districts from which they had fled would not be expected to pay any arrears, and if no ransoms had been levied for a year or more in the districts to which they returned, then they were only obliged to render such dues as were normally paid to the local *seigneur*. Even those not formerly inhabitants of the deserted districts were to pay only the normal dues. Nobody was to pay ransoms in more than one district; but the conservators of the truces were empowered to constrain inhabitants who fled the districts to pay their debts.

During the negotiations for the twenty-eight-year truce in 1396, the English were at first willing to consider the prohibition of all ransoms, save at Brest and in the Channel Islands, in return for an annuity from Charles VI to maintain the garrisons on the frontiers of Guyenne; but, in the end, this did not prove possible and it was agreed that the levying of ransoms should be allowed to continue everywhere.[88] All that the ambassadors could agree to was the appointment of high-ranking commissioners to see that the rates were moderated,[89] a step which seemed increasingly necessary to prevent the exodus of inhabitants from the affected regions, which was aggravating the economic problem in the duchy. They were to leave Paris for the frontiers of Guyenne on 1 May 1396 and, once there, to secure all the information they required from the affected parties, to inquire into the manner in which *pâtis* were being levied, and to compile a list of all the reductions that seemed appropriate before the end of August. Cases which remained in dispute, or which they could not settle by that date, were to be brought before an even more high-powered commission at Leulinghen by 29 September – John of Gaunt and the duke of York for the English and the dukes of Berry and Burgundy for the French. But although the commissioners met in divers places on the frontiers,[90] and some attempt was made to get the provincial Estates to vote the necessary subsidies for the upkeep of the garrisons,[91] in the end this did not prove possible and the commissioners meeting in Leulinghen had to content themselves with an agreement that all *pâtis* being levied in Guyenne were to be reduced by a quarter, until some other remedy could be found.[92] It was also agreed that all other new subsidies and maltotes being levied by the *seigneurs* and captains of castles and fortresses were to be raised immediately, save only, on the English side, the revenues customarily due to the duke of Aquitaine and other long-established *péages* and customs necessary to finance the government and administration of the duchy.[93] But when Nicolas Paynel was sent on his mission to Richard II in August 1398, Charles VI complained that, although the French had reduced the *pâtis* being raised by their side by a quarter, the English garrison forces had failed to follow suit.[94] When, at the beginning of the following year, some of them joined the Captal de Buch in a war with the French over the county of Foix and the *vicomté* of Nébouzan, which the constable of France, Louis de Sancerre, had been ordered to seize, the latter threatened to cut off all the *pâtis* which they received in the *sénéchaussées* of Toulouse, Quercy, Agenais, Landes, Bazadais and Bigorre.[95] Already before the deposition of Richard II, it was a most uneasy truce.

Not until the truce of Tours in May 1444 was a systematic effort made by both the English and the French to solve the problem by prohibiting the levying of all forms of protection money and replacing it by a direct tax, the *taille*, which was to be raised by the civil authorities of the affected regions and by the conservators of the truce. Already in the previous year, in an ordonnance published at Angers on 26 January 1443, Charles VI had attempted to regularise the situation in French-held territories in Anjou and Maine by reducing the number of garrison forces maintained there by levies on the local population, by bringing all such payments under central control, forbidding the local collectors from using brutal methods in their collection, and prohibiting French troops from demanding any other sums.[96] But the truce of Tours envisaged a regularisation of the situation on all frontiers, and arranged for a meeting to be held with the earl of Suffolk at Rouen during the following month, when the entire business was thrashed out.[97] It was then agreed that:[98]

In Normandy, Anjou, Maine and Perche, and at Mantes and Le Crotoy, all *pâtis, courses, sauvegardes, billets, congés,* and all other exactions and charges were to be brought to an end, and the *pâtis* being raised from the places in the obedience of either side were in future to be levied like the *taille* by a specially appointed treasurer and receiver-general and his deputies, or (in Anjou and Maine), by the conservators of the truce. No action was to be taken over arrears for the quarter down to March 1444 (except in cases where persons had been detained, imprisoned or otherwise obliged for non-payment prior to the conclusion of the truce) and payments for the quarter down to the end of June were to be organised by the conservators of the truce. Details were worked out for the different affected regions on the following basis:

(1) In Normandy and Perche, and at Mantes and Le Crotoy either side was to give a statement of the total *pâtis* received, with details of the parishes and villages from which they were collected. These declarations were to be certified by the captains or their lieutenants of the places in question under their seals and signs manual, and to be made available at Vernon on 1 August. The totals for either side were then to be added together and divided equally, and if one side were thereby to receive more than the other from places in their obedience, they were to pay the difference to the other side at the nearest and most convenient places. If they failed to do so, then the treasurer and receiver-general of the side getting more than its share was to issue a letter of obligation to the other wide, promising to pay the sum in question.

(2) In Anjou and Maine the same process was entrusted to the conservators of the truce for either side.

(3) In Picardy and the Burgundian lands, Philip the Good was to decide by 1 August whether or not he wanted a similar system enforced.

Since the English would have received 18,000 *livres tournois* a year more than the French by the arrangement, at a meeting in Nancy it was agreed that they should pay this sum to the French receiver-general together with a further 2156 *livres tournois* to the garrison of Bellême;[99] but there were a good many difficulties over this, as is evident from a *memoire* drawn up by Suffolk in Rouen on 3 April 1445, which records the points at issue with Jean Havart, esquire, and Master Jean Fromont, who were acting for the French general Dunois, in his capacity as conservator-general of the truce, which Havart was to deliver to Charles VII or his council.[100]

To begin with, the English disputed French claims to *pâtis* and other revenues, rights and jurisdiction in the lordship and *vicomté* of Beaumont-le-Roger, the castellanies of Pontorson, Saint-James-de-Beuvron and Saint-Suzanne, and in the parish of Granville. On the other hand, in drawing up the declaration of the total revenues received by them, at a meeting in Le Mans, they claimed to have included figures for *pâtis* in certain parishes in the county of Vendôme which they did not in fact enjoy, and they claimed that allowance should be made for this, if they could not be collected.

The conservators-general of the truce were so occupied with all this and other business that they had not had time to assemble together. People on either side were consequently complaining of the time and money they had to expend over disputes, since they were invariably referred to a joint commission of the conservators-general by the local conservators. Suffolk therefore suggested the setting up of a joint commission of two conservators from either side, who were to be notable men, but not in charge of any town or fortress in the frontier districts and not otherwise employed. They were to be continually on the move throughout the territories in either obedience, hearing cases and giving judgements from which there could be no appeal. They were to be accompanied by sufficiently strong bodyguards to protect their persons and to enforce their judgements, and be paid wages and expenses out of the revenues of either side equally.

Nothing had been done in the fourteenth century to compare with this; but despite the new and far-reaching measures now adopted, the problem of the independent Companies remained. While there is ample evidence that the English authorities in Rouen made every effort to eliminate all allied troops not resident in the royal garrisons, but who were operating on their own account by levying *pâtis* and other forms of protection money, it is clear that they were powerless to do much about it.[101] No solution was in fact found until the reconquest of all the territories controlled by the English, save Calais, had been accomplished. There was no diplomatic solution to a situation in which warfare had become endemic in society.

BIBLIOGRAPHICAL NOTES

There is as yet no over-all study of truces in the later Middle Ages, although many of the sources referred to in the Bibliographical Note to the second essay in this volume (see pp. 72–3 above) are also relevant to this study. Of necessity, much information must be sought in a large number and variety of sources. For the more important published documentation reference should be made to the *Foedera, Conventiones, Litterae, etc.*, or *Rymer's Foedera* (original edition, 20 vols, 1704–35; Record Commission edition, ed. A. Clarke, J. Bayley, F. Holbrooke and J. W. Clarke, 4 vols in 7 parts, 1816–69), which includes the texts of many of the truces, commissions to ambassadors, etc., and which may be supplemented for this purpose by the *Oeuvres de Froissart*, ed. Kervyn de Lettenhove (25 vols in 26, Brussels, 1867–77), xviii, and Adae Murimuth, *Continuatio Chronicarum*, and Robertus de Avesbury, *De Gestis Mirabilibus Regis Edwardi Tertii*, ed. E. M. Thompson (Rolls Series, 1889). Further documentation touching the truce negotiations of 1374–93 is to be found in E. Perroy, 'The Anglo-French Negotiations at Bruges, 1374–1377', *Camden Miscellany*, xix (1952); *Voyage littéraire de deux Bénédictins*, ed. E. Martène and U. Durand (2 vols, Paris, 1721–4), ii, 307–60; H. Moranvillé, 'Conferences entre la France et l'Angleterre, 1388–93', *BEC* l (1889), 367–80. Many of the expense accounts of ambassadors and others involved in the negotiation and the enforcement of the truces are analysed in L. Mirot and E. Déprez, 'Les ambassades anglaises pendant la guerre de Cent ans', *BEC* lix (1898), 550–77; ibid., lx (1899), 177–214.

Among the secondary literature, particular reference should be made to M. Keen, *The Laws of War in the Late Middle Ages* (1965), especially to ch. 11, and to lives of two men actively involved in the truce negotiations: J. Chavanon, *Renaud de Pons, Conservateur des trêves de Guyenne, vers 1348–1427* (La Rochelle, 1903), and K. A. Fowler, *The King's Lieutenant: Henry of Grosmont, First Duke of Lancaster, 1310–1361* (1969). The problem of military finance is dealt with in my 'Les finances et la discipline dans les armées anglaises en France au XIVe siècle', *Actes du Colloque International de Cocherel, Les Cahiers Vernonnais*, iv (1964), 55–84.

References to *Rymer's Foedera* cited in the notes to this essay are to vols iii and iv of the Record Commission edition, and to vols vii and subsequent volumes of the original edition.

NOTES

1. *The Tree of Battles of Honoré Bonet*, trans. and ed. G. W. Coopland (Liverpool, 1949), pp. 189–90.

2. J. G. Dickinson, *The Congress of Arras, 1435* (Oxford, 1955), p. 78.

3. *Foedera*, iv, 137–8; E. Martène and U. Durand (eds.), *Voyage littéraire de deux Bénédictins*, ii, 341, 346, 352, 355 and *passim*.

4. On this question see E. Perroy, *L'Angleterre et le Grand Schisme d'Occident*, ch. ix.

5. Arch. nat., J 636, no. 14 (Esplechin), J 637, no. 17 (Malestroit), *Foedera*, iii, 136–8 (Calais). The texts of these truces have been published, with translations, in Robertus de Avesbury, *De Gestis Mirabilibus Regis Edwardi Tertii*, ed. E. M. Thompson (Rolls Series, 1889), pp. 317–23, 344–51, 396–406.

6. *Foedera*, iii, 136–8, 166, 170–1, 177–8, 184–5, 197–8, 232, 254–5, 261–2, 276–7, etc.

7. Ibid., vii, 418–21, 438–43, 622–30, 714–18, 748, 769–76, 820–32.

8. General truces were concluded at Bordeaux on 23 March 1357 (ibid., iii, 348–51), at Chartres on 7 May 1360 (ibid., iii, 486), and at Bruges on 27 June 1375 (ibid., iii, 1031–4, 1048–9). A truce concluded on 18 August 1388 in all the lands south of the Loire and west of the Rhône (ibid., vii, 595–8) was extended to 31 July 1389 at Bergerac on 9 March 1389 (Arch. nat., K 53B, no. 80; Arch. comm., Périgueux, E 11, no. 3). Other local truces were concluded from time to time between the captain of Brest and the duke of Brittany (Arch. dép., Loire-Atlantique, E 120, nos. 13 and 14), and, during the course of peace and truce negotiations, in the Picardy region (e.g. Martène and Durand, op. cit., ii 347–9, 351 and *passim*). See n. 84 below.

9. Martène and Durand, op. cit., ii, 331, 334, 336–40 and *passim*.

10. See K. A. Fowler, *The King's Lieutenant* (1969), *passim*.

11. *Foedera*, iii, 136, 173, 177, 184, 197, 232, 253–4, 261, 268, 283; PRO, E.101/313/14, 18–19, 25; E.372/193 m. 34d, 197 m. 38d, 198 m. 38d–39d; cf. Fowler, op. cit., *passim*.

12. *Foedera*, loc. cit., and iii, 182, 227, 275–6; PRO, E.101/313/1, 15, 21, 24, 33; E.372/193 m. 34r, 194 m. 45d, 198 m. 38d; cf. Fowler, op. cit., *passim*.

13. *Foedera*, iii, 182, 184, etc. It was customary to depute the senior ecclesiastic of an embassy to be its spokesman (F. Funck-Brentano, 'Le caractère religeux de la diplomatie du moyen âge', *Revue d'histoire diplomatique*, i (1887), 117).

14. *Foedera*, vii, 413–14, 418–21, 429–31, 438–43, 710–11, 728–9, 769–76, 820–30; BM, Additional Charter 11310; H. Moranvillé, 'Conferences entre la France et l'Angleterre, 1388–93', *BEC* l (1889), 365 and 'Pièces Justificatives', no. iii. For the retinues, see *Foedera*, iv, 147–8; ibid., vii, 415, 431, 433–4, 467–8, 738, 741.

15. Martène and Durand, op. cit., ii, 329–37.

16. Ibid., pp. 331–42. The truce, concluded on 14 September 1384, was not issued from Leulinghen, but in the form of separate letters issued simultaneously by Berry and Burgundy from Boulogne (*Foedera*, vii, 438–43) and by Gaunt and Buckingham from Calais (Arch. nat. K 53A, no. 34).

17. Martène and Durand, op. cit., ii, 307–60.

18. E. Perroy, 'The Anglo-French Negotiations at Bruges, 1374–1377', *Camden Miscellany*, xix (1952).

19. e.g. in 1350 the bishop of Norwich sent Robert Tanny, sergeant-at-arms, and Richard Sadtok, esquire, 'pro medietate vadiorum suorum Vasconie et Britanie pro treugis deferendis ad partes predictas' (PRO, E.101/313/1); but, despite a safe-conduct from the French, Tanny was killed at Tours (*Calendar of Papal Letters*, iii, 48–9).

20. e.g. PRO, C.81/1332/46.

21. e.g. *Foedera*, iii, 170, 171, 276–7; ibid., vii, 421, 444, 633–4, 748–9; ibid., viii, 43.

22. e.g. Arch. nat., J 865, no. 6; J. Chavanon, *Renaud de Pons, Conservateur des trêves de Guyenne, vers 1348–1427* (La Rochelle, 1903), 'Pièces Justificatives', no. xlix.

23. e.g. the 'garde du seel establi sur le pont de Xauntes' (Arch. nat., K 53A,

no. 34; K 53B, no. 80). They were also issued by the lieutenants of the *baillis* and *sénéchaux* (e.g. Arch. comm., Périgueux, E 11, no. 3).

24. e.g. on 12 February 1384 Nicholas Dagworth and Robert Cholmesle were instructed to leave for Aquitaine to 'notificandum, publicandum et solempniter proclamari' the truce there (*Foedera*, vii, 423), and Dagworth drew wages for the period 20 February to 16 June 'pro treugis nuper captis inter deputatos domini regis et deputatos adversarii sui Francie proclamare faciendi et tenendi' (L. Mirot and E. Déprez, 'Les ambassades anglaises pendant la guerre de Cent ans', *BEC* lix (1898), 550–77, and ibid., lx (1899), 177–214, no. cdlxxi).

25. Arch. nat., J 644, no. 23.

26. Arch. dép., Hérault, A 1, fo. 241r–v.

27. Avesbury, op. cit., pp. 319, 347; Arch. nat., J 637, no. 17.

28. e.g. Vannes in 1343 (Avesbury, op. cit., p. 345; Arch. nat., J 637, no. 17), the town of Florence and the castle of Pauillac in Gascony in 1350 (*Foedera*, iii, 198), Saint-Sauveur-le-Vicomte in Normandy and Cognac in Saintonge in 1375 (ibid., pp. 1033–4; Perroy, 'The Anglo-French Negotiations at Bruges, 1374–1377', *Camden Miscellany*, xix, nos xxiv–xxvi).

29. *Foedera*, iii, 177, 184, 198, 232, etc.

30. Ibid., pp. 137–8, 178, 197–8, 232, etc.

31. Ibid., pp. 254, 277–8.

32. E. Perroy, 'Quatre lettres du Cardinal de Boulogne, 1352–1354', *Revue du Nord*, xxxvi (1954), 163–4; Edinburgh University Library, MS 183, fo. 53v. They were all warrantors of the truce (*Foedera*, iii, 276–7).

33. BM, Cotton MS, Caligula D III, fo. 32r.

34. *Foedera*, iii, 305, 308. The commissioners claimed expenses for the period from 18 July to 16 August (PRO, E.101/312/36).

35. *Foedera*, iii, 348–51.

36. Ibid., p. 486. The dauphin's instructions for its proclamation were issued on the same day, and those of Edward III to the sheriffs on 24 May (ibid., pp. 485, 495).

37. Ibid., pp. 504, 507.

38. Ibid., pp. 509–10. He concluded an indenture with the king on the same day, and orders were given for the arrest of shipping for his passage to France (ibid., p. 510).

39. Ibid., pp. 514, 546–7.

40. Arch. dép., Basses-Pyrénées, E 38.

41. Ibid.

42. *Foedera*, iii, 555; *Procès-verbal de délivrance à Jean Chandos, commissaire du roi d'Angleterre, des places françaises abandonnées par le traité de Brétigny*, ed. A. Bardonnet (Niort, 1867), pp. 124–5, 125 n. 1.

43. Ibid., pp. 124–5.

44. Perroy, 'The Anglo-French Negotiations at Bruges, 1374–1377', *Camden Miscellany*, xix, no. xlv.

45. *Foedera*, iv, 141, 143.

46. Perroy, 'The Anglo-French Negotiations at Bruges, 1374–1377', *Camden Miscellany*, xix, no. i and appendix ix.

47. *Foedera*, iii, p. 1059.

48. Mirot and Déprez, op. cit., no. ccclxxxi.

49. Ibid., no. ccclxxxii.

50. *Foedera*, iii, pp. 1068–9.

51. See pp. 105–7 above.

52. See *CPR 1385–1389*, 502–3.

53. Perroy, 'The Anglo-French Negotiations at Bruges, 1374–1377', *Camden Miscellany*, xix, 11 (1375); F. Lehoux, *Jean de France, duc de Berri, 1340–1416* (4 vols, Paris, 1966–8), ii, 113 n. 9 (1384); J. J. N. Palmer, 'The Anglo-French Peace Negotiations, 1390–1396', *TRHS* 5th ser., xvi, 81–94 (1393).

54. *Foedera*, vii, 624–6.

55. Ibid., vii, 595–8, 627. Gaunt was appointed lieutenant in Aquitaine on 26 May 1388 (T. Carte, *Catalogue des rolles gascons*, London and Paris, 1743, i, 175 nos. 12, 13) apparently by the duke of Gloucester and with the assent of Parliament (P. E. Russell, *The English Intervention in Spain and Portugal in the time of Edward III and Richard II*, Oxford, 1955, p. 504).

56. Arch. nat., K 53B, no. 80; Arch. comm., Périgueux, E 11, no. 3. Berry was empowered to extend the truce by letters of Charles VI dated Paris, 9 February 1389, and he appointed his envoys by letters dated Mehun-sur-Yèvre, 20 February 1389 (Arch. nat., K 53B, no. 80).

57. e.g. *CCR 1380–1392*, pp. 22, 34, 129, 210, 379, 410; *CCR 1392–1396*, pp. 32, 324; *CCR 1396–1398*, pp. 113, 347, 357, 367.

58. *Foedera*, vii, 656–8, 684, 724–5, 730, 747.

59. Moranvillé, op. cit., 'Pièces Justificatives', no. ii, p. 374; *Foedera*, vii, 724–5, 775; Arch. nat., J 644, nos. 16–18.

60. *Foedera*, vii, 656–8. Trailly was appointed mayor on 16 February 1390 (Carte, op. cit., p. 176, no. 11).

61. He was a 'king's knight' by 15 April 1398 (*CCR 1396–1399*, p. 258).

62. *Bordeaux sous les rois d'Angleterre*, ed. Y. Renouard (Bordeaux, 1965), p. 569.

63. He was employed in Gascony until 1 November 1380 (PRO, E.404/15 m. 40d). For his detailed account of expenses and those of John Sandes, see PRO, E.101/38/27. On 26 May 1384 the archbishop of Bordeaux confirmed a loan secured by the abbey of Sainte-Croix to pay his ransom (*Archives historiques du département de la Gironde*, xiii, no. xxxvii).

64. Letters of protection were issued to him as keeper of Fronsac on 26 August 1389 (Carte, loc. cit.).

65. He drew wages for the period 3 March to 3 August 1390 for a journey to France and Aquitaine 'cum certis litteris de privato sigillo directis diversis capitaneis in dominio Aquitainie pro conservacione treugarum inter regna Anglie et Francie, et reparacione attemptatorum contra easdem' (Mirot and Déprez, op. cit., no. dvii).

66. For the details set forth in this paragraph, see *The Diplomatic Correspondence of Richard II* (Camden Third Series, xlviii, 1933), no. 123 and notes; Carte, op. cit., p. 177; *Foedera*, vii, 684; *CCR 1389–1392*, p. 210.

67. Chavanon, op. cit., 'Pièces Justificatives', no. xliii.

68. *Calendar of Recognizance Rolls of Chester* (36th Report of the Deputy Keeper of the Public Records, 1875), Appendix ii, p. 129; Mirot and Déprez, op. cit., no. dxii.

69. BM, Additional Charter 11310; this was ratified by Richard II on 5 May 1392 (*Foedera*, vii, 717).

70. Moranvillé, op. cit., 'Pièces Justificatives', no. ii, p. 374.

71. Ibid.

72. *Foedera*, vii, 724–5 (commission of 1 July 1392). The trouble spots named were the Bordelais, Basse Gascogne and Les Landes; the *sénéchaussées* of Saintonge and Angoulême; of Poitou, Limousin and Auvergne; Périgord; Quercy and Rouergue; the Agenais; the *sénéchaussées* of Bigorre and Toulouse.

73. *Foedera*, vii, 730. They had been employed in Aquitaine on similar business in the previous year. In a letter written in Libourne in February 1391

they required Bérard d'Albret, lord of Sainte-Bazeille, to repair breaches which the English commissioners complained had been carried out by his men and those of the lord of Albret against the tenor of the truce, and they ordered all French officers to see that their judgements were respected (Arch. dép., Basses-Pyrénées, E 51).

74. Carte, op. cit., p. 178 no. 1. Two days previous Cradock had secured a protection for William de Scolehall to accompany him in his retinue (*Calendar of Recognizance Rolls*, loc. cit.).

75. Edinburgh University Library, MS 183, fo. 79r.

76. *Foedera*, vii, 747.

77. Arch. comm. Périgueux, EE 11, no. 2.

78. e.g. an inquest concerning ravages committed in the lands of the lord of Albret (notably in the castellany of Casteljaloux) on 9 January 1385 by the English conservator in Limousin, Pierre Arnaud de Béarn (Arch. dép. Basses-Pyrénées, E 49), and another which the French commissioners ordered to be made into ravages committed in the lands of the lord of Albret between April 1383 and March 1390 by the troops of Nompar de Caumont, who was one of the English conservators in Agenais and Quercy (Arch. dép. Basses-Pyrénées, E 51).

79. *Foedera*, vii, 446–7, 598, 629–30, 717, 775.

80. Arch. nat., K 54, no. 44.

81. *Registre criminel du Châtelet*, ed. H. Duplès-Agier (2 vols, Société des bibliophiles français, Paris, 1861–4), ii, 192–3.

82. Ibid., p. 196.

83. For a preliminary investigation of this question, see M. Keen, *The Laws of War in the Late Middle Ages* (1965), Appendix 1.

84. e.g. the *patiz*, *seurtes*, *suffrences* or *seguranssas* concluded between the English authorities in Gascony (lieutenant, royal council or seneschal) and the lords of Albret and Sainte-Bazeille, their subjects and allies, in 1380, 1382 and 1386 (Arch. dép., Basses-Pyrénées, E 48–9). These were framed in a similar manner to the truces of the period, involving the appointment of conservators, etc., and they do not appear to have involved any payments. A similar agreement was concluded with the lady of Albret in 1407 (Arch. comm., Saint-Macaire, EE 1, no. 1).

85. For what follows, see K. A. Fowler, 'Les finances et la discipline dans les armées anglaises en France au XIVᵉ siècle', *Actes du Colloque International de Cocherel, Les Cahiers Vernonnais*, iv (1964), 57–74, and *The Age of Plantagenet and Valois* (1967), pp. 165–72. The use made of *billets* is brought out in a letter of John of Gaunt as lieutenant in Aquitaine, dated Bordeaux, 23 July 1389, and bearing a note on the dorse: 'La declaracion des bilhetes faite par le duc de Lencastre' (Arch. nat. K 53B no. 83).

86. *Foedera*, iii, 349; E. Perroy, 'The Anglo-French Negotiations at Bruges, 1374–1377', in *Camden Miscellany*, xix (1952), nos. xxxi art. 7, and xxxviii art 7.

87. *Foedera*, vii, 420, 442–3, 597, 627, 771–2, 825–6; cf. Fowler, 'Les finances . . .', cit. supra., pp. 78–9.

88. *Foedera*, vii, 812–13, 825–6.

89. Ibid., pp. 825–6, 832–3, ibid., viii, 223–5. If possible, these were to be Sir Thomas Percy, Sir William Elmham and a clerk for the English, and the *vicomté* of Melun or Jean de Vienne, admiral of France, Guillaume Le Bouteiller and Master Nicole de Rancé for the French (Arch. nat., J 644, nos. 16–18). Bouteiller and Rancé were in fact accompanied by the count of Sancerre (ibid., no. 23).

90. Arch. nat., J 644, no. 23.

91. e.g. the lord of Pons assembled the Estates of Saintonge at Pons and Saintes for this purpose, but without success (D. d'Aussy, *La Saintonge pendant la guerre de Cent ans, 1372–1453*, Société des archives historiques de la Saintonge et de l'Aunis, La Rochelle, 1890, pp. 17–18).

92. Arch. nat., J 644, no. 23. John of Gaunt wrote to his seneschal of Guyenne, Jean de Grailly, to that effect from Calais on 9 November 1396 (Arch. dép Hérault, A 1, fo. 215r–v).

93. E. Perroy, *L'Angleterre et le Grand Schisme d'Occident* (Paris, 1933), p. 415, Pièces Justificatives, no. xiii. Arch. dép. Hérault, A 1, fo. 217r–v (Letter of John of Gaunt to his seneschal of Guyenne, Jean de Grailly, dated Calais, 10 November 1396).

94. Arch. nat., J 644, no. 23.

95. Arch. dép., Hérault, A 1, fo. 243r–v (letter of Sancerre to the seneschals in question, instructing them to inform the captains involved to that effect).

96. A. Joubert, *Les invasions anglaises en Anjou au XIVᵉ et XVᵉ siècle* (Angers, 1872), pp. 174–83.

97. *Foedera*, xi, 59–67. The French embassy at Rouen was led by Pierre de Brezé and Jean Havart (G. du Fresne de Beaucourt, *Histoire de Charles VII* (6 vols, Paris, 1881–91), iv, 18).

98. A. Huguet, *Aspects de la guerre de Cent ans en Picardie maritime, 1400–1450*, ii (Paris, 1944), Pièces Justificatives, no. xciii, pp. 495–6.

99. viz. 22,500 *livres tournois* for five quarters (Arch. nat., K 68/1, no. 2; K 68/12, no. 7).

100. Bibl. nat., Pièces originales, vol 1494, Havart 33850, no. 16.

101. *Chronique du Mont-Saint-Michel, 1343–1468*, ed. S. Luce (Société des anciens textes français, 2 vols, Paris, 1879), ii, Pièces diverses, nos. ccxlix, ccli, cclvi, cclxii, cclxviii, etc.

NOTES ON CONTRIBUTORS

C. T. ALLMAND, Lecturer in Medieval History, University of Liverpool; formerly Lecturer at the University College of North Wales, Bangor; graduate of Oxford; author of a doctoral thesis on 'The Relations between the English Government, the Higher Clergy and the Papacy in Normandy, 1417–1450' (Oxford, 1963), and of numerous articles on the English occupation of Normandy and Anglo-French relations in the fifteenth century.

PHILIPPE CONTAMINE, *maître de conférences*, University of Nancy; formerly *assistant* at the Sorbonne; graduate of Paris; author of *Azincourt* (Paris, 1964), *La guerre de Cent ans* (Paris, 1968), and of a doctoral thesis, which is shortly to be published, *Guerre, état et société à la fin du Moyen Age. Etudes sur les armées des rois de France, 1337–1494.* He is at present preparing a book for publication *La guerre au Moyen Age.*

KENNETH FOWLER, *see cover*; Reader in History, University of Edinburgh; graduate of Leeds; author of *The Age of Plantagenet and Valois* (1967) and *The King's Lieutenant; Henry of Grosmont, First Duke of Lancaster* (1969).

H. J. HEWITT, Headmaster of Saltash Grammar School, 1927–52; graduate of London; author of *Medieval Cheshire* (Manchester, 1929), *The Black Prince's Expedition of 1355–1357* (Manchester, 1958) and *The Organization of War Under Edward III, 1338–62* (Manchester, 1966).

JOHN LE PATOUREL, Research Professor in Medieval History, University of Leeds; graduate of Oxford; author of *The Medieval Administration of the Channel Islands, 1199–1399* (Oxford, 1937), *The Manor and Borough of Leeds* (1957), and of numerous articles on Anglo-French history in English and French periodicals. He is at present engaged on a study of the relationship between the kingdom of England and the various appendages that were the dominions of the men who were kings of England, but which were not included in the realm.

J. J. N. PALMER, Lecturer in History, University of Hull; graduate of Oxford; author of a number of articles on Anglo-French diplomatic relations in the fourteenth century; is preparing for publication a book *Charles VI and Richard II: The Hundred Years War from 1380–1399.*

MICHAEL POWICKE, Professor of History, University of Toronto; graduate of Oxford; author of *Military Obligation in Medieval England* (Oxford, 1962) and co-editor of *Essays in Medieval History Presented to Bertie Wilkinson* (Toronto, 1969). He is at present preparing for publication a *History of England, 1154–1485.*

C. F. RICHMOND, Lecturer in History, University of Keele; graduate of Leicester; author of a number of articles on the English navy in the fifteenth century and of a paper 'Fauconberg's Kentish Rising of May 1471'.

Index